CANTORS AT

Concordia Publishing Hous

THE CROSSROADS

Essays on Church Music
in honor of

WALTER E. BUSZIN

JOHANNES RIEDEL, EDITOR

St. Louis, Missouri

ML
3000.1
.C3

Concordia Publishing House, Saint Louis, Missouri
Concordia Publishing House Ltd., London, E. C. 1
© 1967 Concordia Publishing House

Library of Congress Catalog Card No. 67-13141

MANUFACTURED IN THE UNITED STATES OF AMERICA

CONTENTS

PREFACE

The contributors to this publication have presented the essays which follow as an appropriate tribute to the lifelong endeavors of Walter Edwin Buszin. By thus honoring this distinguished scholar, gifted teacher, and venerable leader in the field of church music, the collection of essays will not only pay much-deserved respect to Dr. Buszin himself, but they will also help perpetuate that high standard of exploration in the field of church music to which he has devoted his unflagging efforts.

Dr. Buszin received his basic musical and theological training at Concordia College, Fort Wayne, Indiana, and Concordia Seminary, St. Louis, Missouri. His further training at Northwestern University, Union Theological Seminary, and the University of Chicago prepared him for teaching at Concordia Theological Seminary, Springfield, Illinois; Bethany Lutheran College, Mankato, Minnesota; Concordia College, Fort Wayne; and Concordia Teachers College, River Forest, Illinois. In recognition of his achievements, Valparaiso University awarded Walter Buszin an honorary doctorate in music in 1954. Since 1947 Dr. Buszin has been professor of hymnology and liturgics at Concordia Seminary, St. Louis.

Ever since his youth the study of the heritage of church music has been Walter Buszin's constant preoccupation. Having become imbued with the great church music literature of the past, he has recorded his knowledge in many essays of varying depth and content. His writings are invariably marked by a combination of the general and the specific, the scholarly and the layman-like, for they are dedicated to the member of a congregation — be he musicologist or chemist, singer or banker.

At a time when indifference, misinformation, and lack of knowledge prevailed in the realm of church music history writing in America, Dr. Buszin began systematically to delineate his interpretations of the lives and works of great masters of the past. In this way he helped to set into motion a pendulum which began to swing rather strongly — and which has been swinging ever since — toward the revival of and the familiarization with the Renaissance and Baroque music of the church. Dr. Buszin does not, however, have a single-track mind; his interest is not limited to the music of the past. On the contrary, he sees merit in contemporary music; for instance, he sees in jazz at least a means by which the schmaltz of the gospel hymn may be overcome.

One of the main pillars of his heritage-conscious writings is his revelatory approach to organ music and its composers. In composer-oriented essays the great "pedal points" of German organ music from the 16th-century colorists through J. S. Bach are presented in accurately detailed fashion. A comprehensive essay on "Organ Music for the Liturgical Service" demonstrates Dr. Buszin's insistence on practical implications of his scholarly work in that he includes sections on "how to accompany the congregation in hymn singing and how to accompany liturgical chant."

His large output of practical editions of choral and organ music is proof of Dr. Buszin's devotion to putting into practice what he spells out in his essays or reviews. He himself worked with choral groups, such as the Bethany College Choir, the Lutheran Choral Society in Mankato, Minnesota, and the Concordia College Choir in Fort Wayne. His presentation of editions also evidences Dr. Buszin's ever-present concern for the role of the layman in the liturgy of the church, for he selected for editorialized publications only those compositions which have a specific and historical meaning for those worshipers who are not mere onlookers but *dramatis personae,* that is, performers of the liturgy (to use Dr. Buszin's own words). Although his output seems to favor the Baroque elements in church music, some of his publications broadened to include significant compositions of the Renaissance and Reformation eras. This widened scope appears, for instance, in the publication of Sixt Dietrich's antiphons.

Dr. Buszin has consistently been concerned with enlarging the musico-aesthetic liturgical experience and understanding of the church service on the part of the average parishioner. A great many of his essays belong to the storehouse of general hymnological and liturgical information. The latter is a felicitous revelation to the layman rather than to the professional, to the searcher rather than to the researcher.

His concern for the layman does not, however, cause Dr. Buszin to write down to anyone's pop level. The contrary is true, for when he feels the urge to teach the deficiently informed parishioner, he selects specific topics (such as wedding music) or he gives detailed and appropriate hints on performance of certain parts of the propers of the service. The teacher in him realizes the necessity of congregational education in the preservation of the church's musical heritage; therefore he sees the need for establishing a sense of values in connection with the preservation of this heritage.

Another area in which Dr. Buszin has rendered outstanding service to the ideals of Christian worship is his considerable part in the production of a number of Lutheran hymnals and service books. As consultant of the Intersynodical Committee on Hymnology and Liturgics of the Synodical Conference, which produced *The Lutheran Hymnal* in 1941; as co-worker and editor of various shorter hymnals for conventions, armed-services personnel, and other special purposes; as musical consultant for *Culto Christiano*, 1964, the hymnal for Spanish-speaking Lutherans; and as the chairman since 1951 of the Commission on Worship, Liturgics, and Hymnology of The Lutheran Church — Missouri Synod, Dr. Buszin has provided a leadership for which generations of worshipers will be grateful.

There is one aspect of this man's career which is almost unknown except to church musicians and church music historians, namely, his editorship of *Response,* the official journal of the Lutheran Society for Worship, Music, and the Arts. The editorship of a journal which is new and which has as its purpose the study and promotion of Christian worship, music, ecclesiastical art, literature, and drama constitutes a manifold challenge. First, the editor must guard his journal against contributions that would detract from worship. Dr. Buszin's theological grooming assured that the worship-linked goals of *Response* would be stressed.

Second, the editor must establish through his selection of essays a clearly observable balance between the various fields of the arts and music. Dr. Buszin's deep knowledge of the boundaries as well as the intercommunication of the arts in relationship to worship and to faith, coupled with his love for the various art forms and institutions and with his belief in the cultural values inherent in liturgical worship and the ecclesiastical arts, combined to undergird his wisdom in finding an appropriate balance between the various articles of each individual issue. Another criterion for the selection of articles for the journal has been the widely varied nature of the readership of *Response*. Writings for and by the enlightened layman had to coexist with writings for and by professional theologicans, scholars, and artists. Because of his realistic awareness of his readers, Dr. Buszin has met this requirement by maintaining a happy medium in his selection of materials.

The *cognoscenti* in matters of church music have long recognized Dr. Buszin as one of the pioneers in rendering reliable accounts of the great masters of church music in good, readable English prose. His essays also display his earnestness as a teacher of people — whether they are seated in a classroom, gathered in a lecture hall, or assembled in a committee room — and his sincere, kindly admonition that they give every part of their service to the church, rather than to dissipate their efforts in the pursuit of self-glorification or professionalism.

The essays in this book are by American, German, and Swiss specialists: leaders of the church, theologians, and musicologists, directors of church music schools and university professors, composers and editors of church music magazines and other periodicals, specialists in the field of hymnology and liturgy; students, friends, and colleagues have also made their unique contributions.

Part I is dedicated to tradition, Part II to contemporary music. The articles on tradition testify to Dr. Buszin's primary ambition, namely, to be a musicological herald of the musical inheritance, strength, and richness of the church. The flashes of opinions, the interpretations, and the accumulations of research data in the contemporary section are a testimony to the great breadth of Dr. Buszin's interests and activities and to his disdain for musical and other "clodhoppers" (to use the good words of Georg Rhau).

In his essay on tradition, F. Joseph Smith delivers several thrusts against traditional musicology and traditional quasi-rationalistic theology when he argues for a new *Kirchenlied* which is to be written in free form and time. In spite of the insistence of the rabid adherents to a certain type of chanted singing, Smith feels that the "freed" rhythm of the *new* church hymn should pattern itself on the hyperrhythmic writings of men like Stravinsky.

The late Miss Ruth Ellis Messenger, former editor of *The Hymn*, quarterly publication of the Hymn Society of America, submits a brief study of the 11th-century sequence *De Nominibus Domini* and a commentary given on this text by the noted Renaissance humanist Judocus Clichtoveus.

The record of chanting psalm tunes in parts of England is illustrated by Leonard Ellinwood through examples taken from Tallis (1567/1568), Morley (1597), Clifford (1664), and Boyce (1760).

In his contribution Lincoln B. Spiess discusses at great length the variability of meanings of such terms as sonata, fugue, discant, descant, diaphony, organum, and *canto de órgano* from the 9th century to the 17th. The discussion of the term *canto de órgano* helps to throw new light on the practice of polyphonic music in 17th-century New Mexico.

Louise Cuyler gives us not only an account of the musical activity in Augsburg and its *Annakirche*, ca. 1470–1630, but also a short history of the city of Augsburg and of her most prominent patrons, Maximilian I and the Fuggers. Miss Cuyler's work also distinguishes musicians such as Hofhaimer and Gumpelzhaimer.

In his essay, "The Hymns of Zwingli and Luther: A Comparison," Markus Jenny contends that the psalm settings and freely created songs of Luther and Zwingli revolve around themes of consolation and trust and not so much about themes of struggle and victory. They emphasize the "old loyalty," the trust and love of one another, that "sense of oneness" which only God can give to His people on earth.

The ingenious work of Pierre Pidoux on the question whether the polyphonic settings of the Genevan Psalter by L. Bourgeois, Arcadelt, Certon, Jannequin, Jambe de Fer, and Goudimel were intended to be church music asserts strongly basic musical differences between the Reformed Church and the Lutheran Church. The incompatibility of congregational psalm singing and choral performance is stressed.

Konrad Ameln's masterful essay helps to set off Leonhard Lechner from his illustrious teachers and contemporaries as a great master in his own right. This essay, together with Dr. Ameln's Lechner article in *Die Musik in Geschichte und Gegenwart*, Vol. VIII, provides a spirited, poignant, and scholarly biography of this great composer of the latter half of the 16th century.

J. Murray Barbour sounds a fanfare for the longevity and endurance of certain texts and tunes in the various editions of the *Unpartheyisches Gesang-Buch* ("Unpartisan Hymnbook") of the Mennonite Church in America of the past and present.

In his "Michael Praetorius on Concertato Style" Harold E. Samuel makes a great deal of the first species of the concertato style, of the theory and practice of the *concerto per choros* style. The short discussion on the second species, the *solo concertato* style, presents the idea that German composers of the 17th century found it unattractive as such and rather merged it with the *concerto per choros* style of writing.

The Bach specialist, Alfred Dürr, in addition to listing Bach's 53 chorale cantatas, shows the growth and development of certain texts and chorale tunes as used by Bach in his chorale cantatas.

Dr. Buszin's successor as editor of *Response*, Gerhard M. Cartford, has contributed an essay on the general problem of musical expression. His "Kierkegaard and Mozart" presents Kierkegaard's view of music as a purely aesthetic expression into which the question of ethicality does not enter. The essay is a lucid exposition of the *Don Juan* topic in general and of the specific treatment in Mozart's opera *Don Giovanni.* Kierkegaard's interpretation of *Don Juan* is in sharp contrast with contentions of other authorities in the field; English and French scholars treat *Don Giovanni* as a farce, but the Germans treat it as a tragedy, Cartford concludes.

Some of the essays in the contemporary section cut through to the very heart of the problems of contemporary music in the church of today: its direction, its performance possibilities, its struggles, and its representatives. An appropriate introduction to this section is the contribution of Jan Bender, a 4-part canon on the Benediction of Philippians 4:7.

The question "Whither Church Music?" Edgar S. Brown answers with an assessment of two perplexing counterquestions: What kind of music should be permitted and encouraged in the church? What training must be given to those performing the music so that their efforts do not attract attention to the performer but rather to that which he or she proclaims? Dr. Brown welds these two questions into one answer by requesting that "music serve the words."

Other contributions to this section of the volume, without predetermined planning, revolve around issues in one or the other of Dr. Brown's questions. Miss Pfatteicher and Armin Haeussler contribute liberally to the treatment of the problems clustering about the dilemma of church music and hymnody, the way they emerge, accrete, and become a serious deterrent to those who want to improve the musical and hymnological situation in the church. Some aspects of Dr. Brown's first question may have been answered in Earle Copes's important survey of Protestant church music in 19th-century America by referring first to an evenly aligned first generation of American church musicians such as Clarence Dickinson, John Finley Williamson, F. Melius Christiansen, and Leo Sowerby. Söhngen's concluding essay reemphasizes the principle that only an artistically valid expression of the music of its own time can be church music in the ultimate and profoundest sense, but Söhngen excludes 12-tone music from the church, since no lay church choir or *Kantorei* would be able to sing it.

Brown's second question is partly answered by Karl Ferdinand Müller's essay on "Church Music Instruction in the Church Music Schools of Germany." Müller brings into focus a short history of a church music educational process which led to the establishment of church music schools in Germany. Wilhelm Ehmann's "Changes in Choral Singing in Europe Today" deals with several types of choral organizations. Ehmann has a perceptive ear for distinctions between these groups and the new and different roles these groups have assumed in Europe since World War II.

This volume came into being in this manner: the editor approached church music experts both here and abroad, asking their cooperation in the preparation of a book which would serve as an appropriate tribute to the efforts of Dr. Buszin. It was decided that the format of such a book could best be that of a series of essays by these authorities, each of whom would write concerning his own special area of interest and investigation. The essays were then sent to the editor, who emendated and translated them when necessary. The result is a collection of authoritative materials, diverse, though interrelated, presented to the reader in English.

JOHANNES RIEDEL

THE CONTRIBUTORS

Konrad Ameln is known through his outstanding work as coeditor of the *Handbuch der deutschen evangelischen Kirchenmusik* and as the hymnology editor of the *Jahrbuch für Liturgik und Hymnologie.*

J. Murray Barbour, professor of musicology at Michigan State University at East Lansing, has published *Tuning and Temperament, The Church Music of William Billings,* and *Trumpets, Horns, and Music,* in addition to important essays on a variety of topics.

Jan Bender, at present on the faculty of Wittenberg College, Springfield, Ohio, has composed many choral and organ works in a style which forms a bridge between traditional and modern music. Through his compositions Bender wants to educate lay people to become acquainted with today's church music.

Edgar S. Brown, Jr., executive director of the Commission on Worship of the Lutheran Church in America, is known for his writings concerning worship and the contemporary church. This special interest also prompted his book entitled *Living the Liturgy.*

Gerhard M. Cartford, who succeeded Walter E. Buszin as editor of *Response,* specializes in the heritage of Scandinavian Lutheran music in America.

V. Earle Copes is the editor of *Music Ministry,* a monthly publication of the Methodist Church.

Louise E. Cuyler, head of the musicology section at the University of Michigan, Ann Arbor, is known for her writings on Isaac's *Choralis Constantinus* and for her editing of the third volume of that work.

Alfred Dürr is the editor of the new edition of Bach's works and the coeditor of the *Bach Jahrbuch,* both of which are sponsored by the Neue Bach Gesellschaft. He is also author of *Studien über die frühen Kantaten J. S. Bachs.*

Wilhelm Ehmann, director of the Westfälische Landeskirchen-musikschule in Herford, Germany, is known for his work concerning certain aspects of performance practices of Evangelical church music. In connection with this work he has recorded much music and published *Das Schicksal der deutschen Reformationsmusik, Die Chor-führung,* and *Tibilustrium, das geistliche Blasen.* To *Leiturgia, Hand-buch des evangelischen Gottesdienstes,* he contributed the essay "Das Bläserspiel."

Armin Haeussler is the author of the widely acclaimed *The Story of Our Hymns: the Handbook to the Hymnal of the Evangelical and Reformed Church.*

Markus Jenny, a Swiss authority on Reformed hymnody, has published *Geschichte des deutschschweizerischen evangelischen Gesang-buches im 16. Jahrhundert.*

Ruth Ellis Messenger, the late editor of *The Hymn,* is the author of *Christian Hymns of the First Three Centuries, Ethical Teachings in the Latin Hymns of Medieval England,* and *The Medieval Latin Hymn.*

Karl Ferdinand Müller, director of the Kirchenmusikschule der Evangelisch-Lutherischen Landeskirche, Hanover, is the coeditor of *Leiturgia, Handbuch des evangelischen Gottesdienstes,* and of the *Jahrbuch für Liturgik und Hymnologie.*

Helen E. Pfatteicher is the editor of the monthly *Journal of Church Music.*

Pierre Pidoux wrote the two-volume work on *Le Psautier Hugue-not du XVIe siècle.*

Harold E. Samuel is music librarian at Cornell University.

F. Joseph Smith, a faculty member at Emory University in Atlanta, Ga., was formerly the abstracts editor of the *Journal of Ecumenical Studies* and is now a contributor to *Musica Disciplina,* a yearbook of the history of music published by the American In-stitute of Musicology.

Oscar Söhngen, chairman of various hymnological and liturgical commissions of the Evangelical Church in Germany, has written nu-merous works promoting "new music" in the church; these include *Die neue Kirchenmusik, Kämpfende Kirchenmusik,* and *Die Wiedergeburt der Kirchenmusik. Gestalt und Glaube,* a collection of essays written by students, friends, and colleagues of Söhngen, pays homage to this outstanding scholar for his pioneer work in musical and theological matters pertaining to the church music renewal in 20th-century Germany.

Lincoln Bunce Spiess, a member of the faculty of Washington University, St. Louis, has published a work entitled *Historical Musicology: A Reference Manual for Research in Music.*

I

CHURCH MUSIC
AND TRADITION

1

CHURCH MUSIC AND TRADITION

F. Joseph Smith

Musicians of all periods have made use of older idioms in their compositions.[1] Examples abound throughout the history of music but particularly since we have the beginning of a polarity of styles in the 17th century. The most evident case is, as we have learned *ad nauseam*, Monteverdi's use of the *stile antico*.[2] Mozart learned to trim his style to fit church law in some of his later Masses, thus consciously attempting a more archaic and reserved approach.[3] We see such composers as Michael Haydn almost completely influenced by this trend. We reach an aesthetic low point in the Regensburg school of the 18th century, at the very time when the Romance movement was engulfing the musical world. Without any such ecclesiastical inhibitions and minus any particular polarity of styles contemporary composers unabashedly employ forms, styles, and motifs of older music, approaching them in a new way as an integral part of their modern idiom. Thus the old and the new are transcended in a living composition. Whether we look at Hindemith, Stravinsky or Carl Orff, and a representative assortment of composers in all media, examples abound. Fugue, sonata, and concerto form and procedure are used; old texts and motifs are employed. Thus Orff uses medieval texts for his *Carmina Burana;* Hindemith employs the medieval *Es sungen drei Engel* in the opening pages of *Mathis der Maler;* Stravinsky makes use of Latin in his *Oedipus Rex* and *Symphony of Psalms.* Traditional materials, both musical and textual, far from being ignored in modern music, are actively utilized, but in a new way. Stravinsky philosophizes on this when in his *Poetics of Music* he states that every genuinely new music takes off from the ground of tradition. Tradition must be a living force that animates the present. It is not something inert, merely to be repeated all over again; rather it is a heritage received on condition that we make it bear fruit, before handing it on to our posterity.[4] Surely this holds true also for church music.

Walter Buszin speaks of theology and church music as *bearers* of the *Verbum Dei*.[5] Perhaps tradition in church music can be seen best from this perspective. Tradition is not just a passing on of inert materials; it is rather the live bearer of the musico-theological Word. Tradition bears the Word by helping it give rebirth to those who hear it. The Word comes by hearing. And hearing is primarily a musical phenomenon. A word, in general, is not both speech and music. Rather spoken word and sung word are identical. The difference is one drawn only by rationalistic western civilization, which defines music in a restricted, formalistic manner and then states that words can be set to music. Word, as spoken, is primarily musical, secondarily literary. Word, as literary, presupposes the *littera*, as written down and preserved apart from the original existential experience. But literary tradition, whether in music or literature, must always seek to get back to the lived experience and the living word. And thus if we were forced to say which was primary, the theological or the musical meaning of Word, we would have to say the musical; for theology, at least as we know it from recent tradition, has been heavily rationalistic, even as it hoped to be only Biblical. Biblical scholars still employ what a phenomenologist would consider a rationalistic language, even as they expound the existentiality of the Scriptures.

Surely the musico-Biblical Word was of the essence of Luther's protest, which was not just a negative thing but rather a positive attestation, i. e., a *bearing* witness, to the living Biblical tradition that was being all but smothered under the weight of a less than Christian cult and practice. Neither Luther nor modern Protestant and Catholic Biblical scholars call for a regression to primitive Christianity for its own sake; but it was especially Luther who pleaded passionately for a rebirth of a genuinely Biblical tradition. And this meant a reappraisal on a grand scale — something that was beyond the powers of most people of that era. Perhaps it is only today that the insights of Luther are being fully appreciated, not only by Lutherans, but by many non-Lutherans as well. The time is at hand when the Catholic scholar can and does make use of the prophetic message of Luther in Christianity, as the musician has made use of the Lutheran music of Bach. Christendom is now ready to make a reappraisal of its various traditions, to discover what is indeed a bearer of evangelical truth and what is the result of man's unfaithfulness and fallenness. We must be courageous enough to face the unfree element in Christian existence, which originally meant the fullness of responsible freedom. This unfreedom, this closing-off, is what Kierkegaard called the demonic in Christian man.[6] And surely these considerations are equally valid for a reappraisal of the tradition of sacred music. As we restore the ancient words of the Bible in modern times and make them stand for the existentiality of our own age, perhaps we can bring back the living tradition of music of all ages. If we speak once more of *kerygma* and *kairos,* perhaps we can begin to envision the new *hymnos,* the *Kirchenlied* of our own era. And if the kerygmatic approach in theology means announcing the good tidings of the Gospel in a new manner, and if *kairos* means a new depth of the fullness of Christian living in Christ, perhaps the new *hymnos* can aid us in comprehending Clement of Alexandria, when he called Christ the New Hymn.[7]

Before we can broach the difficult topic of tradition and church music, we have to examine the meaning of tradition as philosophical, musicological, and theological. It is hard to pretend that these are actually three entirely separate kinds of tradition. What is tradition as such? We know that the word means a handing down or a handing over. Merleau-Ponty writes that every translation is a kind of betrayal: every *traducteur* is a *traduceur.*[8] Indeed, a handing over can become a betrayal, whether it be a translation or a tradition; and translation is a kind of tradition, since it means literally a carrying over, a bearing of truth from one idiom to another. It is interesting that the Latin *traditio* means both tradition and betrayal. We come close to this meaning in the word extradition. Tradition is a betrayal when it means that truth is handed over to us inert, as a museum piece we are not allowed to touch, as a musical form which we must follow rigidly, as a straightjacket into which our existence must be forced. Yet tradition is not a betrayal in itself; rather truth is betrayed by people who do have the courage to use it fruitfully but out of fear and anxiety bury the talent. And thus Stravinsky tells us that only those are worthy of it who can animate it, make it come alive before passing it on to posterity. And surely to make tradition come alive means to infuse *new* life into it. A mere restatement of traditional positions, whether musical or philosophical, is inadequate. An overcoming of tradition is necessary.

What do we mean by an overcoming of tradition? In this we follow the thinking of Martin Heidegger, who calls for a "destruction" of traditional metaphysical thought.[9] He makes it plain here and in such later writings as *Überwindung der Metaphysik* that a destruction of the metaphysical tradition means a creative reconstruction of it.[10] It means putting into proper perspective that traditional ontologic which is the basis of theology and, at least indirectly, of what we call musicology. Putting in perspective means being loyal to all that is valid in tradition. It means overcoming a fixation on essence and an opening up of the existential horizon. It means putting less emphasis on philosophical and theological (we add, musicological) conceptuality, and letting things be as they are, rather than as they fit into our preconceived notions of what they ought to be. Thus the way is left open for a whole new perspective of being. Paul Tillich has made use of this insight in speaking of the God above traditional theism and atheism. Similarly an overcoming of musical tradition does not mean, as we see from music history, a denial of what has gone before, but a creative reconstruction and an openness for wholly different approaches to musical reality. Surely Stravinsky is a prime example of that, from the *Rite of Spring* through *Agon* and *Canticum Sacrum*. And especially in the *Pulcinella* he conducts what we might call an existential dialog with Pergolesi, making use of direct quotations and stylistic peculiarities of that Italian master. Especially in the field of music do we see the continual turnover of styles, the exploration of new horizons. We see also the resistance that such pioneers as Stravinsky met. Resistance is the lot of anyone with vision, and it has been meted out to musicians, philosophers, and theologians, who have, as Kierkegaard writes, shown people that you can say not only ABC but DEF also.[11] What people resist is a shift of modality. But it is precisely the ability to modulate that has characterized so much musical vitality in Western music and thinking. Modulation need not be only within a given tonal system; it means more than a simple transition from one key to another. It may connote a changeover to a completely new musical or philosophical perspective. And this is what we mean by an overcoming of tradition, whether musical or philosophical.

What is *musical* tradition? As we know, a musical tradition cannot be treated apart from its historical situation; and for church music this means that particularly the theological tradition is essential to it. Here again there is a question of putting things into their full historical context, in order that an overcoming of tradition may be authentic. In order to understand the written history of music, whether such writing be in words or notes, let us examine a few things about Christianity, which was of the essence of Western music history. Christianity became a book religion, Ernst Curtius tells us, but unlike Islam it did not begin thus. The living tradition of the early faith was only gradually concretized in the occasional writings that go to make up the Bible. Then the gradual establishment of a canon of authentic books guaranteed a solid Biblical tradition.[12] Similarly in music, the early tradition is for the most part an unwritten one, and only gradually did ear-music become eye-music, as we know from a detailed study of musical notation.[13]

The fact that an audial phenomenon becomes also visual is of utmost importance for the whole history and development of Western music, as distinguished from many non-Western musics. Music as visual is really eye-music, making possible the little manneristic tricks of medieval composers that we now call *Augenmusik*.[14] It makes possible an overemphasis on "form" — which is really a visual word. But most important of all, the preeminence of the visual in Western music makes it possible for us to visualize musical time as extended in space; and of course we even write it that way, from one side of the page to the other. This heavy use of the visual and spatial accounts for many of our problems with musical time, tempo, and interpretation. Musical time is not spatial and visual; it is an audial, existential phenomenon. And precisely here is where a new philosophy can come to the aid of contemporary composition. We have to overcome our fixation on written music, so that neither form nor musical aesthetics is a predominantly visual thing and therefore spatial and measurable. A break with tradition connotes more than tone-row, which is so much in debt to visual form. Form is not something to see on paper; it must become something we can hear. Certainly this is not absent from traditional musical forms; but it almost seems secondary at times.

Music, as written, is characteristic of Western civilization, and it goes hand in hand with a written theological tradition. And yet the Word comes by hearing, the New Testament tells us. Surely we see here the importance of looking on the *Verbum Dei* as a "musical" thing, rather than a "theological" one. It is for this reason that such reformers as Martin Luther put such emphasis on the *Kirchenlied* and good preaching. But again, it must be stated, it is not our intention to throw written music or theology overboard. We simply want to counteract any fixation on the *Verbum Dei* as written, rather than as lived, spoken, and sung. There are many civilizations that do not depend so heavily on what is written, if anything be written down at all. For us tradition, as a handing down, is too dependent on what has been written down. For others unwritten life, music, and ceremonial is handed down, and tradition is wholly or largely an unwritten one. Thus melodic types are handed down in a kind of practical pedagogy. Perhaps only in our civilization, beginning in the Middle Ages, was there such an attempt made to write down pedagogical methods for preserving musical traditions and for performance technique. Our civilization tries to write itself into history and bemoans the fact that countless centuries have gone unrecorded before the Sumerians invented writing (on account of commercial transactions) and passed it to Egypt and the Mediterranean, as a common patrimony.[15] But unrecorded history is still history. Our ancestors may not be known to us rationally in literature; but they are our hereditary progenitors, and all that they did is still somehow recorded in every movement we make. And perhaps it is only an existential-musical understanding that can profit us in attempting to reach back beyond written history to a comprehension of the life-movement of our forebears, as bearers not of a rational but of an existential truth. The history of Western tradition is to a greater extent than we imagine a literary one, a written one. We are dissatisfied with the unwritten. Music, thinking, and living has to be written down before it matters. We make a fetish of the written word. But a book is not as important as the least life. We cannot overlook the great contributions made to civilization by people who never wrote, or whose writings perished. Neither Thales nor Socrates seem to have written anything. And yet their importance in Western civilization is assured. Jesus never wrote anything that we know of, except in the sands, when defending the woman caught in adultery. Like the Egyptians, who felt that the written word preserved truth and who had an almost superstitious veneration for it as the receptacle of eternal verities, the Roman Church has insisted on the Latin language, for example. And even Biblical churches sometimes have what amounts to an undue emphasis on the Word as Writ. Surely such traditions must be overcome if truth is to live beyond the mere written word.

Whether a life or a musical composition is written down or not is a secondary thing, however important this may be for the present and for posterity. To be sure, secondary things cannot be ignored; on the contrary, they must be duly appreciated and cherished. But they cannot be allowed to displace what is primary. They must "second" the primary motion and movement. "Secondary" means what favors; in this case, what favors the primary thing — life. And surely the written word has been of great advantage to musical and theological life. Its worth can hardly be overestimated. And yet, there must be no idolatry of the word. The great teacher, the great musician and composer, is great even if he never writes a book or a note. If we examine the work of some of our greatest composers, we see that they have often been primarily great keyboard "improvisers" first and what we would now call composers secondarily. Handel's organ concerti come to us mostly as rough sketches. But today no one may dare to improvise with him in a musical-existential dialog. His organ works must be played note for note. Is this not fetishism? The same holds for Bach, who would not have played the same composition the same way twice. Yet today we memorize him according to the letter and forget his truly great spirit. Is this not a "tradition" that ought to be overcome? When it comes to the word, as musical or as spoken, certainly the living tradition is more important than the written, if we were forced to choose specious and captious arguments used by some unbiblical theologians to prove the authenticity of bogus religious practices before the Reformation. What Luther sought to restore was not just the letter of Holy Writ but a Biblical faith and a more authentic Christian life.[16] We can no longer go along with the Council of Trent in making Scripture and tradition two substantially different sources of Christian truth. With Max Heinz we are tempted to say, "Whoever says Scripture, says also tradition." [17] Thus also with the musical *Verbum Dei*. We cannot postulate a two-source theory here either. Nor can we ignore the living tradition and musical practice in favor of the purely theoretical works of the Middle Ages and Renaissance. One of the most common mistakes among scholars of medieval music is to believe that the entire solution to a given problem can be gotten only by a study of theoretical texts and written music. Granted that musicology gives us the music and the texts of much of musical tradition, we cannot ignore the fuller context of medieval culture and a largely unrecorded musical thinking and practice if we hope to gain full insight into musical tradition as a living rather than as a wholly literary or musicological thing.

Music history as we know it is largely the history of church music. This is so until the rise of "secular" forms and a gradual polarity between church style and that of the theater or court. In a real sense there is no distinction between the sacred and profane until the beginnings of the Baroque era. The polytextual motets of the Middle Ages display a rich interplay of what we now call religious and secular themes. But to the child of those times all things were sacred. It is only in modern times that we drive the distinction between secular and profane music to extremes, and this is done mostly by religious people, who are generally short on both music and theology. In the last century secular music was at least great art, if it was not fit for use in church. So much of the church music of those times, for example, that of Aiblinger and Ett, like much of the popular church music of our times, is hackwork. Perhaps this goes hand in hand with the low position of theology among many in the church, to say nothing of aesthetics. We know that even Biblical theology was dealt an almost fatal blow by the Enlightenment and by the hypercriticism of the last century.[18] Perhaps the rise of a truly meaningful music and theology, together with a new aesthetics of church music as the bearer of the Word, is just beginning in our times. It is ours to prepare the ground. So many thinkers and artists now look on Christianity as generally irrelevant to the times, despite the good will of many and attempts at *aggiornamento*. A man like Sartre has been called an atheist. But this may be rather unfair. He merely considers the God of many Christians as somewhat irrelevant. Compared with the brilliance of such a literateur and philosopher, the words and works of the general theologian pale. But surely the Word does not depend entirely on man. And can we be simply indifferent to the theological dimension, as Sartre seems to be? Is that an authentic position or is it but a pose? But even if it is a philosophical pose, and a brilliant one at that, it is at least not a philosophical imposture. So much of scholasticism seems to be a pose and an imposture, especially when it serves up a latter-day metaphysics of God and man, despite the telling critiques of Kant, Nietzsche, Kierkegaard, and Heidegger.

It is true that Nietzsche said God is dead.[19] But what did he mean if not the God of a dead theological tradition? Nietzsche wrote further that we need the arts, particularly music, to keep us from perishing by the truth. By this he meant that we need the living, bodily art of music to keep us from being stifled by a theological truth that had developed a Platonic-Aristotelian spirituality of the soul at the expense of the whole man. The traditional God of rationalistic theologies was a metaphysical god. Such a god lives apart from the colorful, warm life on the earth. Surely the Biblical scholar is particularly well equipped to see that Nietzsche was making room for the living God, and we might add, for a living music that will enable us to worship the living God of the Scriptures. A revival of a solidly Christian church music will have to bring with it an overcoming of traditional theologico-musical concepts based on a metaphysical God — before whom, as Heidegger writes, it is possible to sing and dance.[20]

Music is not just a rational thing, as man is not just a rational animal. Neither rationality nor animality are adequate to define *who* man is. Man is rather what Merleau-Ponty calls the body-subject (or more precisely the *corps propre*).[21] This is strikingly parallel to what Scripture scholars call the "living flesh," undivided into body and soul. (The latter is a Platonic-Aristotelianism.) And yet so much of our musical tradition is based on rationalism of one kind or another. Medieval music theory is based on a metaphysical *ens numeratum*, Jacques de Liège tells us.[22] Modern musicology depends on scientific rationalism. The *Speculum musicae* subsumes and presents in encyclopedic form the whole rationalistic approach of the Middle Ages. Modern musicology has often come to mean a preoccupation with manuscripts and scientific methodology rather than with living music, though this tendency is being corrected. Music in these cases appears to be a thing of the head rather than of the whole bodily man. Biblical theology does not exaggerate the laudable efforts of reason at the expense of the whole man's experience. We are familiar with Luther's critique of reason and of scholasticism. His was not a scurrilous attack on reason, but a Biblical-existential critique of rationalism in theology. The whole man is far deeper than merely rational man. As a result, a theology and a church music must be not just for rational man but for the whole man in the whole church. Rationalistic theologies and music theories are a product-construct of Western civilization. But the "universal" European church is not necessarily the same as a world church. And a rationalistic theology and music is not necessarily a world theology and music. Music must not become the bearer only of a quasi-rational tradition. The *Kirchenlied* must not therefore be the bearer of a rationalistic dogma that appeals to the head only, and mostly to the head of a trained theologian. Thus the texts of our hymns and antiphons should be Biblical, for they then appeal to the whole man. This appeal is not so much an aesthetico-theological appeal set to music, as it is a call *(ap-pellare)*, the voice of the encounter between man and his covenantal God.

However, it is not only the texts of the *Kirchenlied* that have to show an overcoming of rational-theological tradition. Also the whole idea of form and time must be of a new age and understanding. Traditional concepts of form depend heavily on the visual and spatial, and both metrics and form are the stepchildren of a rationalistic mode of thinking and composing. We see what a tremendous influence the *trias harmonica* had with reference to Baroque thinking. We know how important rational proportions were for the Middle Ages. We see how crucial spatial form is to the music of the tone-row. Such music is indeed quite "cerebral" and makes more sense on paper or in the "mind's eye" than it does to the ear. But it is not just a harmonic question or one of musical styles. Even the triadism of the 3-part song form was construed rationally, as a musical form conforming to right reason. It was again a thing of the head rather than of the whole man. And the *Verbum Dei* was often brought to man in a rational-theological manner and clothed in a form that, even if it did not originate rationalistically, was later forced into musico-rational patterns. This is especially evident in the development of the whole metric system, which would never have come about without the philosophical orientation of Boethius and the music theorists of the Middle Ages. Both a new musical form, as audial rather than as visual-spatial, and a new musical metrics are called for to meet the needs of a new age. This does not mean to deny the valid insights of reason and rational theory but merely puts it all in badly needed perspective. And thus the stage is set for new creations, which are not just deviations from the rational norm — and therefore could not in fairness be called "irrational."

The new Christian *Kirchenlied* would be one that has learned from, but is not wholly dependent on, traditional hymn forms. The new hymn would be in free form and free time. Freedom does not mean disorder but openness for a new kind of order and structuring. The closed form, like the closed system, should be difficult for the Christian to bear, since he is, as Luther states, a free man. It is freedom to be his genuine and responsible self in encounter with others. Christian encounter ought to be a free one. Koinonia can hardly be commanded or enforced. The music of free Christians should not only reflect but be the true expression of their basic Biblical freedom and encounter. To be "practical," perhaps we could take some hints from Stravinsky or Hindemith, or any contemporary worth his salt. We would not need to merely imitate Stravinsky's nonsequential metrics, as for example in parts of the *Rite of Spring* and elsewhere, but with his help we could certainly learn to sing a hymn in something more than the monotonous traditional meters. And if the new hymn is one in which "free rhythm" is employed, we do not thereby mean the flat, lifeless rhythm of a certain kind of chant singing, which through equalization of all values claims to liberate music from the restrictions of exact meter. To call equalization of all notes freedom is, to say the least, facetious. But it is typical of a theological system that has tried to equalize everything. There is hardly anything conceivably more restrictive than such "free" rhythm. The "beauty" which results from an artificial maneuvering of both voice and rhythmic lines in this kind of singing is pretty well the musical equivalent of a theological leveling-out process that reaches a climax in a spirituality as inauthentically Christian as it is Plantonic.

If we speak of a renewal of the church today, then when we speak of church music and tradition, we speak also of an overcoming of it. We overcome church music, as contemporary music has overcome traditional musical idiom, by taking off from the ground of tradition. Perhaps a Hindemith or a Stravinsky can show us the way. And we can assuredly take the sacred works of Stravinsky seriously. It is unfair to call them concert pieces. In the rising church, church music must also rise, and it can do this only by a creative overcoming of tradition, both musical and theological. The musical and literary work of such men as Walter Buszin have brought nearer the day when the singing church and the rising church will be one again. This does not mean they will be singing only one tune! But it will mean that they will have transcended, each his own, tradition and musical idiom: not to form some sort of supermusic for a superchurch, but to live anew in an authentic Christian existence that unites all the profound riches of all traditions in a new form and in a new song.

NOTES FOR CHAPTER 1

1. W. Austin, "Traditional Forms in New Musical Idioms," *Report of the Eighth Congress, New York, 1961*, International Musicological Society, Vol. I, Papers, p. 100.

2. Leo Schrade, *Monteverdi, Creator of Modern Music* (New York, 1950). Manfred F. Bukofzer, *The Baroque Era* (New York, 1947), p. 64.

3. *Die Musik in Geschichte und Gegenwart* (MGG), IX (Kassel, 1961), pp. 739, 202.
   Alfred Einstein, *Mozart, His Character, His Work* (Oxford, 1961), trans. Mendel-Broder, p. 319, chapter 18, "Church Music." The author speaks of the old style as *stile osservato*. If there is any criticism of Mozart's Masses, it is not that they are not fit for church. Rather their dualism is aesthetically objectionable, the unresolved dialog between old and new styles. Certain portions of the Mass, as the *Cum sancto* and *Et vitam venturi* had to be treated in archaic fugal and polyphonic manner. Thus the dualism of a mixed style.

4. Igor Stravinsky, *Poetics of Music* (New York, 1956), pp. 58—59.
5. "Theology and Church Music as Bearers and Interpreters of the *Verbum Dei*," *Concordia Theological Monthly*, XXXII, No. 1 (January 1961), 15 f.
6. Søren Kierkegaard, *The Concept of Dread*, trans. W. Lowrie (Princeton, 1957), p. 106.
7. Oliver Strunk, *Source Readings in Music History* (New York, 1950), p. 63.
8. Maurice Merleau-Ponty, *Sens et Non-Sens* (1948).
9. Martin Heidegger, *Sein und Zeit*, 9th ed. (Tübingen, 1960), p. 19.
10. Martin Heidegger, *Vorträge und Aufsätze*, 2d ed. (Pfullingen, 1959), p. 71.
11. Kierkegaard, p. 124. Here he takes after the theology of good works, and rigid orthodoxy, which he calls demoniacal.
12. E. R. Curtius, *Europäische Literatur und Lateinisches Mittelalter*, 3d ed. (Bern, Munich, 1961), pp. 261 f.
13. Willi Apel, *The Notation of Polyphonic Music 900—1600*, 4th ed. (Cambridge, 1953).
14. Gustave Reese, *Music in the Renaissance* (New York, 1954), pp. 43, 311, etc.
15. Fr. Cornelius, *Geistesgeschichte der Frühzeit* (Leiden and Cologne, 1962), II, passim.
16. Cf. his "Von den guten Werken" in *Luthers Werke in Auswahl*, ed. O. Clemen (Berlin, 1950), I, p. 227 f.
17. M. Heinz, "Neuere Forschungen über das Traditionsprinzip," *Internationale kirchliche Zeitschrift*, Jan.—March, 1963, I, p. 51.
18. D. H. Wallace, "Biblical Theology: Past and Future," *Theologische Zeitschrift* (Basel), March—April 1963, pp. 88 f.
19. Martin Heidegger, "Nietzsches Wort 'Gott ist tot,'" *Holzwege* (Frankfurt am M., 1957³), pp. 193 f.
20. Martin Heidegger, *Einführung in die Metaphysik* (Tübingen, 1953). The French commentary on this work, *Vers la fin de l'ontologie* is difficult to take seriously; it was written by Jean Wahl, who had done the service of showing the connection between Kierkegaard and Heidegger.
21. Maurice Merleau-Ponty, *La structure du comportement*, pp. 231, 239, etc.
22. Jacques de Liège, *Speculum musicae, I, corpus scriptorum de musica* (CSM), 3 (Rome, 1955).

2

DE NOMINIBUS DOMINI

Ruth Ellis Messenger

With cheerful voice I sing
The titles of my Lord,
And borrow all the names
Of honor from His Word.

Hymns and Spiritual Songs

Centuries before Isaac Watts responded to the impulse to praise God in a series of hymns devoted to the Biblical names of deity, an anonymous author produced the Latin hymn before us. Extremely popular in the 11th century, it is remarkable for including within its 12 hexameter lines 50 names applied to deity in the Scriptures in the Hebrew, Greek, and Latin tongues.

ALMA CHORUS DOMINI

1 *Alma chorus Domini nunc pangat nomina summi:*
  Now let the choir sound forth the names of the Lord most high.

2 *Messias, soter, emanuel, sabaoth, adonai*
  Messiah, Savior, Emanuel, Sabaoth, Universal Lord,

3 *Est unigenitus, via, vita, manus, homousion*
  He is the Only-Begotten, Way, Life, Hand, Consubstantial (with the Father),

4 *Principium, primogenitus, sapientia, virtus,*
  Beginning, Firstborn, Wisdom, Virtue;

5 *Alpha, caput finisque simul vocitatur et est Ω,*
  Alpha, Beginning, He is called, and at the same time End, and He is Omega,

6 *Fons et origo boni, paraclitus ac mediator,*
  Fountain and Source of good, Paraclete and Mediator,

7 *Agnus, ovis, vitulus, serpens, aries, leo, vermis,*
  Lamb, Sheep, Calf, Serpent, Ram, Lion, Worm,

8 *Os, verbum, splendor, sol, gloria, lux et imago,*
  Mouth, Word, Splendor, Sun, Glory, Light and Image,

9 *Panis, flos, vitis, mons, ianua, petra, lapisque,*
  Bread, Flower, Vine, Mountain, Door, Rock, and Stone,

10 *Angelus et sponsus pastorque, propheta, sacerdos,*
   Messenger, Bridegroom, Shepherd, Prophet, Priest,

11 *Athanatos, kyrios, theos pantocrator, Iesus,*
   Immortal, Lord, God Omnipotent, Jesus,

12 *Salvificet nos, sit cui saecla per omnia doxa.*
   May He save us, to whom be glory forever and ever.

Analecta hymnica medii aevi, 53, 152

The editors of Volume 53 of the *Analecta hymnica,* Clemens Blume and Henry Bannister, find this hymn in manuscripts from all parts of Europe. More than 60 sources are cited from France (the earliest being a tropary of St. Martial of the 10th century), England, especially the great cathedral centers, the Low Countries, Germany, and Italy. In the editors' opinion the country of origin is probably France or England. So remarkable a diffusion testifies to a truly international character.

The commentary which accompanies the text below, is that of the noted Renaissance Humanist, Judocus Clichtoveus or Josse Clichtove, 1472–1543. It is reproduced here not only to illustrate the quality which hymnological studies had attained as early as 1500 but to introduce a scholar now all too little known.

Clichtoveus was born in Nieuport, Flanders, of a noble and wealthy family. He lived a student's life, attaining a master of arts degree at Paris in 1492 and later a doctorate in theology. A distinguished career followed as Clichtoveus became professor of the liberal arts, theology, and the Scriptures. Himself a disciple of Jacques Le Fèvre D'Etaples, a leading Humanist of France, with whom he collaborated in editing texts of classical authors, he attracted in his turn a group of pupils from all parts of Europe, among them distinguished scholars in their own right. In a period of religious conflict, Clichtoveus elected to remain faithful to the Church of Rome and may be said to have shared in the earlier aspects of the Counter-Reformation. His published works, comprising some 71 titles, cover the fields of the liberal arts, especially the Greek and Latin classics, as well as theology, philosophy, history, liturgy, and the Scriptures. Erasmus, his contemporary, appraises his scholarship in these terms: *Uberrimum rerum fontem, saecularibus disciplinis et christiana disciplina instructissimum.* (Quoted in A. Renaudet, *Préréforme et Humanisme* [Paris, 1953], p. 242.)

In 1516 Clichtoveus published the *Elucidatorium ecclesiasticum,* a Latin work as a guide to liturgical canticles, antiphons, sequences, hymns, and the canon of the Mass. This work achieved 11 editions and continued to be issued after the death of the author up to 1558. Written by a hymnologist of the first rank, his work superseded that of earlier commentators and set an example for future critics in this area of study. For four centuries and well into the period of Daniel and Neale, his word was authoritative and his statements quoted by all students of Latin hymns, including the masters of the subject. As a matter of fact, the commentary of Clichtoveus is valid under modern scrutiny, except in matters where modern scholarship has brought to hymnological studies facts or data not available in his time. A microfilm of the 2d ed., 1520, of the *Elucidatorium ecclesiasticum,* Columbia University, has been used for this study. The Commentary begins p. 43 r.

The sequence *Alma chorus domini,* Clichtoveus says, is sung in the churches of Paris at Vespers on the Feast of Pentecost. It is sometimes considered a prose because of its music, but he prefers to call it a hymn. His annotations, some 2,000 words in length, give the Scriptural references where the name in question may be found. Following the interlinear translation, the names are listed with Clichtoveus' Biblical citations. No comments have been added by the present writer. In attempting to identify the citations, one should recall that Clichtoveus was using the Vulgate, in which chapters only are indicated. Consequently, except in obvious cases, a verse citation must be tentative. English translations are from the King James Version.

1 *Messias or Christ,* anointed by the outpouring of the Holy Spirit, "We have found the Messias" (John 1:41).

2 *Soter* or *salvator,* "For unto you is born this day . . . a Savior" (Luke 2:11), "The Savior of the world" (John 4:42).

3 *Emanuel,* ". . . and shall call His name Immanuel" (Is. 7:14; Matt. 1:23).

4 *Sabaoth* or *militia coelestis* (Lord of hosts), the equivalent of the Hebrew Sabaoth. "Holy, holy, holy is the Lord of hosts" (Is. 6:3), "O Lord of hosts" (Jer. 11:20).

5 *Adonai* (Hebrew) or Universal Lord (Dominus), "Then the Lord said unto Moses . . . I am the Lord" (Ex. 6:1, 2), "O Lord, Thou art great and glorious" (Judith 16:13).

6 *Unigenitus,* "The only-begotten Son of the Father" (John 1:14).

7 *Via,* "I am the way" (John 14:6).

8 *Vita,* "I am . . . the life" (John 14:6), "I am the resurrection and the life" (John 11:25).

9 *Manus,* "Send Thy hand from above" (Ps. 144:7), "Mine hand also hath laid the foundation of the earth" (Is. 48:13).

10 *Homousion* or *consubstantialis* (of one substance), used in the Nicene Creed; "I and My Father are one" (John 10:30).

11 *Principium,* "The same that I said unto you from the beginning" (John 8:25), "In the beginning God created the heaven and the earth" (Gen. 1:1). (Some authors refer this term to Gen. 1:1.)

12 *Primogenitus,* "He created Me from the beginning before the world" (Ecclesiasticus 24:9), "The Firstborn of every creature" (Col. 1:15).

13 *Sapientia,* "In wisdom Thou hast made them all" (Ps. 104:24), "Christ Jesus, who is made unto us wisdom" (1 Cor. 1:30).

14 *Virtus,* "The power of the Highest shall overshadow thee" (Luke 1:35).

15–16 *Alpha* and *Omega,* "I am Alpha and Omega, the beginning and the ending" (Rev. 1:8; 21:6; 22:13).

17 *Caput,* "Precious ointment upon the head" (Ps. 133:2), "To be the head over all things to the church" (Eph. 1:22), "He is head of the body, the church" (Col. 1:18).

18 *Fons et origo boni,* "Every good gift and every perfect gift is from above and cometh down from the Father of lights" (James 1:17, Jer. 1 [unidentified]).

19 *Paraclitus* or *consolator,* "The God of all comfort" (2 Cor. 1:3, 4), "He shall give you another Comforter" (John 14:16).

20 *Mediator,* "One Mediator between God and men, the man Christ Jesus" (1 Tim. 2:5).

21 *Agnus* — Here follow seven names for the Son of God in the flesh. "Send ye the lamb" (Is. 16:1), "Behold the Lamb of God" (John 1:36).

22 *Ovis,* "As a sheep before her shearers" (Is. 53:7).

23 *Vitulus,* "And bring hither the fatted calf" (Luke 15:23).

24 *Serpens,* "Make thee a fiery serpent" (Num. 21:8), "As Moses lifted up the serpent in the wilderness, even so must the Son of Man be lifted up" (John 3:14).

25 *Aries,* "A ram caught in the thicket . . . and Abraham took the ram and offered him . . . in the stead of his son" (Gen. 22:13).

26 *Leo,* "The Lion of the tribe of Judah" (Rev. 5:5). Leo means *fortitudo* as in Prov. 30:30.

27 *Vermis,* "But I am a worm and no man, a reproach of men, and despised of the people" (Ps. 22:6).

28 *Os* — Here follow seven more names for the Son of God. "The voice said 'Cry'" (Is. 40:3-6). The Son speaks the will of the Father.

29 *Verbum,* "By the Word of the Lord were the heavens made" (Ps. 33:6), "In the beginning was the Word" (John 1:1).

30 *Splendor,* "Who being the brightness of His glory" (Heb. 1:3; Wisdom 7:25-6).

31 *Sol,* "Shall the Sun of righteousness arise" (Mal. 4:2).

32 *Gloria,* "The glory of the Lord is risen upon thee" (Is. 60:1); "Thy God thy glory," (Is. 60:19).

33 *Lux,* "The life was the light of men" (John 1:4); "I am the light of the world" (John 8:12).

34 *Imago,* "Who is the image of the invisible God" (Col. 1:15).

35 *Panis* — Here follow a third series of seven names. "I am the bread of life" (John 6:35).

36 *Flos,* "I am the rose of Sharon and the lily of the valleys" (Song of Sol. 2:1).

37 *Vitis,* "I am the true vine" (John 15:1).

38 *Mons,* "The stone was cut out of the mountain without hands" (Dan. 2:45; Ps. 66, 67 [unidentified]).

39 *Ianua,* "I am the door of the sheep" (John 10:7).

40 *Petra,* "And that rock was Christ" (1 Cor. 10:4).

41 *Lapis,* "The stone . . . is become the head stone of the corner"

(Ps. 118:22); "Behold I lay in Zion for a foundation, a stone" (Is. 28:16).

42 *Angelus,* one who announces; Because He announced the Father's will and good pleasure. "The Lord sent a word unto Jacob" (Is. 9:8); "I will send My messenger" (Mal. 3:1).

43 *Sponsus,* "Which is as a bridgegroom" (Ps. 19:5); "The Bridegroom shall be taken from them" (Matt. 9:15).

44 *Pastor,* "I am the good shepherd" (John 10:11); "That great shepherd of the sheep" (Heb. 13:20).

45 *Propheta,* "No prophet is accepted in his own country" (Luke 4:24); "It cannot be that a prophet perish out of Jerusalem" (Luke 13:33).

46 *Sacerdos,* "Thou art a priest forever after the order of Melchizedek" (Ps. 110:4; Heb. 7: passim).

47 *Athanatos* — Here follows a Greek series of three names. "Who only hath immortality" (1 Tim. 6:16); "Now unto the King eternal, immortal, invisible" (1 Tim. 1:17).

48 *Kyrios* or *Dominus,* "Lord of lords" (Rev. 19:16); "Thou, Lord, art exalted far above all gods" (Ps. 97:9; Heb. 1).

49 *Theos pantocrator* or *omnipotent,* "Thou hast created all things" (Rev. 4:11).

50 *Iesus,* "Thou shalt call His name Jesus" (Luke 1:31; Matt. 1:25).

One leaves the commentary of Clichtoveus with regret that he was not a musician. True, he referred to the tune associated with the hymn. The editors tell us that the melody, *Tuba,* is designated in two troparies from Winchester, 10th and 11th centuries, but rarely elsewhere. The sequence in hexameters is so uncommon that the appropriate melody may also have been rare. At all events there is an hiatus here in our knowledge to be filled in by some student of the liturgical music of this period. Then we might more fully appreciate the beauty of the vesper hymn as it actually sounded forth the praise of the Lord within the walls of the sanctuary.

3

FROM PLAINSONG TO ANGLICAN CHANT

Leonard Ellinwood

Thomas Tallis was one of the better-known, but by no means the only, English musician whose career in the monastery was brought to an abrupt end by the Reformation. It is difficult to realize, after the passage of 400 years, just how sweeping a musical revolution took place when the monasteries were suppressed by Henry VIII. Tallis was at Waltham Abbey, one of the last to be closed down in 1540; there, 5 boy choristers and at least 12 singing men were suddenly deprived of their livelihood. In many of the monasteries, as at Waltham, the daily services had been sung by choirs of men and boys supported by endowments that had grown during the five previous centuries. (A somewhat similar social change took place here in America a generation ago when the development of sound tracks rendered the old "silent movies" obsolete and threw several thousand theater musicians out of work.)

Chanting of the Psalms to various modal formulae in the daily Offices had been cultivated in England as well as on the continent ever since the codification of the daily Office in the Rule of St. Benedict, about A. D. 530. The actual psalm tones used, the melodic formulae sung, varied considerably all through the Middle Ages. There were many endings for each of the basic eight modes or tones. The Sarum forms, used widely in England until the eve of the Reformation, have been studied in detail (cf. W. H. Frere, "Psalmody," *Grove's Dictionary of Music and Musicians*). The following is the formula for Tone VIII₁:

By 1540, English musicians were aware of the problem they would soon face, that of adapting the traditional music to English texts in place of the customary Latin. Throughout the decade, composers also began to set anthems and canticles polyphonically in the vernacular. Manuscripts of their chants are almost nonexistent because so much of it was simply improvised out of their experience with the Psalms in Latin. In 1544 Cranmer published his English Litany with a simple form of chant which is still used today in Anglican services. Immediately upon publication of the first *Book of Common Prayer* on Whitsunday 1549, John Merbecke undertook the task of setting the entire work to a modified form of plainsong. His *Booke of Common Praier Noted* was published the following year. This is the adaptation of the above psalm tone which he printed for use with the Psalms at daily Evensong:

Over several centuries, professional choirs in the larger monasteries and cathedrals had cultivated the arts of descant and fauxbourdon, to provide polyphonic versions of these chants for festival occasions. It was but natural, then, for Tallis and others to set the Psalms in English in a similar manner. The following in five parts was composed by Tallis for use with Psalm 119 [2] at Evensong on Christmas Eve. It was written out in full to be sung antiphonally, verse by verse, between the two sides of the choir. The plainsong Tone I4 is in the tenor part:

Thomas Morley described the technique of descanting with a plainsong in his *Plaine and Easie Introduction to Practicall Musicke*, 1597. The following is his example for the "eighth tune," the same Sarum Tone VIII1 quoted above; it was printed without text, with the plainsong still in the tenor part:

Chanting the Psalms at daily Matins and Evensong continued in this manner, plainsong for weekday use and partsong for festival occasions, until the 1640s, when the Puritan Revolution and Commonwealth in England put an end to all choral services and destroyed most of the music books and organs.

With the Restoration in 1660, interest in the choral service returned, but two generations of potential choir boys had passed, and many traditions were lost. James Clifford's *Divine Services* (2d ed., 1664) prints the texts of nearly 400 anthems which remained in the cathedral repertories. It also contains 12 "common tunes" which in a general way follow the pattern of the plainsong tones, but in major and minor tonalities. With these are four chant tunes, set in four parts each, with the tenor part still carrying the plainsong. *Christ Church Tune* uses the same Tone I4 which Tallis did above:

Compare the following *Imperial Tune* from this same collection with Tone VIII1 as set by Morley above:

There is one final step. One hundred years later all memory of plainsong singing had passed, and melodies were shifted from the tenor to the treble part. Thus in William Boyce's *Cathedral Music*, 1760, the *Christ Church Tune* was printed as follows:

Chanting in parts has continued to the present time, with this particular chant often attributed to Tallis quite erroneously. Since the time of Boyce there has been a considerable evolution in the pointing of the prose texts of the Psalms for chanting. To adequately trace this history, one would have to begin again in the 1540s and follow the evolution of English pronunciation, for pointing and pronunciation are inseparable. Discussion of this phase of the history of chanting had perhaps best be left for another occasion.

4

INCONSTANCY OF MEANING IN CERTAIN MEDIEVAL AND RENAISSANCE MUSICAL TERMS [1]

Lincoln Bunce Spiess

The meanings of musical terms often vary widely from century to century. One of Viadana's vocal *Cento concerti ecclesiastici* (1602) is far removed from an instrumental concerto of Vivaldi; a sonata of Beethoven is a very distant relative of Kuhnau's *Biblical Sonatas* (1700). This metamorphosis of meaning is particularly the case with medieval and Renaissance music. A madrigal of Orlando di Lasso in the 16th century may be distantly related to a madrigal of Francesco Landini in the 14th century, but there is little physical resemblance in structure — though perhaps some resemblance in spirit. A Perotinus motet of the early 13th century seems to have no apparent relationship to one of Josquin des Prez, or of Palestrina, or of Praetorius. Yet the growth of the motet with its cantus firmus structure is only the first step in a long development, while Des Prez and Palestrina are the apex of the Renaissance motet. Praetorius' motets are a bridge between Renaissance style, which changes dramatically in the *Urania* of 1613 to motets in the Venetian style. (These 1613 works are influenced, as the composer himself says in his preface to *Urania*, by the "splendid composer and organist, Giovanni Gabrieli.") Again in 1619 Praetorius' motet structure changes to that of cantata-like compositions, still further removed from the ancestral Perotinus motet of the 13th century.

Fuga, or fugue, is another term whose meaning varies widely. In the 15th and 16th centuries *fuga* is a canon. It is used in that sense by Ockeghem, for example, and is defined in that way by Tinctoris in his dictionary of about 1475 *(Diffinitorium musicae):*[2] "*Fuga* is the identity of melody of the parts as regards the locations of notes and their rests."[3] About 1600 the meaning of *fuga* changes: on the Continent it develops to the fugue; but in England it develops in a different direction. Thomas Morley in his *Plaine and Easie Introduction to Practicall Musicke* (1597) uses the term meaning a "point of imitation," spelling it *f-u-g-e*. At one point Philomathes, the student, says: "I pray you take the fuge of my lesson and shew me how it might have been followed better." The Master replies, "Manie waies, and thus for one." A 5-part point of imitation follows.[4] At another place in the Morley work we find Philomathes asking, "What is a Fuge?" with the Master replying, "We call that a Fuge, when one part beginneth and another part singeth the same, for some number of notes (which the first did sing). . . ."[5] Morley's spelling — fuge — is interesting in the light of the American colonial "fuging tune" or "fuging psalm tune," the meaning of which goes back via England to Morley's time.[6] A fuging tune is a piece containing fuges, that is, a piece containing points of imitation, and has nothing to do with the Continental fugue except that both have common ancestors, the imitative motet for structure and *fuga* for their names.[7]

Now let us turn to five terms that require more detailed discussion, discant, descant, diaphony, organum, and *canto de órgano*. We must discuss them as a group because they are very much interrelated historically; they must be studied together in order to understand them individually.

First let us look at the spelling of discant and descant. Should one discant or should one descant? Dictionaries tend to ignore *either* discant *or* descant; the more liberal-minded dictionaries give you a "see discant" if you look for descant, or "see descant" if you look for discant. The spelling *discant* obviously is from the Latin *discantus,* whereas *descant* comes from the Old French *deschanter.* The earliest vernacular treatise on music uses the latter spelling: *Quiconque veut deschanter* — which occurs in the margins of the so-called "St. Victor" manuscript of the early 13th century.[8] The English took the French word and anglicized it literally to *descant,* just as *hautbois* became hautboys around 1600 and oboë later became oboe. The English have preferred the descant spelling ever since, though in Elizabethan times it still shifts back and forth, even in the same work.[9] Germany has always preferred the more recondite, Latin-related *Diskant.* We might make a nice distinction in English: when speaking of the Middle Ages *discant* is perhaps best because of its Latin origin; and with the Renaissance *descant* seems more natural because of its actual use in the English Renaissance and since.

Now let us consider the meaning of discant, descant, diaphony, organum, and *canto de órgano*. Organum and diaphony are the earliest of these terms, whereas discant, descant, and *canto de órgano* refer to later practices. Organum and diaphony (or *diaphonia*) begin to appear in the ninth century in the sense of primitive, note-against-note polyphony in either a rigid parallel motion or a slightly modified parallelism. These two terms, organum and diaphony, are synonymous at first and remain so even after the shift away from parallelism to contrary motion which comes with the 11th century.[10]

With the 12th century the meanings of diaphony and organum diverge just as two distinct polyphonic styles begin to appear. At the Abbey of Saint Martial in southern France and at Santiago de Compostela in northwestern Spain a new florid polyphony with a multiplicity of notes in the upper part is now "organum" exclusively, and the older note-against-note style is now diaphony (i. e., *diaphonia*).[11]

Organum continues to refer to the florid polyphonic style through the Notre Dame school (late 12th to early 13th centuries) and continues to be found in theoretical works to the turn of the 14th century.[12] In actual music manuscripts examples of florid organum disappear rapidly in the 13th century, the last examples of this style being in the *Còdex musical de las Huelgas* of Burgos, Spain, about 1300.[13]

Diaphony, or *diaphonia*, is the older, simpler style in the earlier 12th century, but by the mid-12th century it is replaced by a new term, *discantus*. At first *discantus* seems to be just a translation of *diaphonia*. It applies to the same older, simple style, and continues to refer to this simpler polyphony through the 13th century. It also begins to take on other meanings. *Discantus,* or discant, even comes to have the generic meaning of "polyphony" and is used in that sense as late as Thomas Morley in 1597.[14] In the 12th century, though, it was at first just a synonym for diaphony; as an anonymous writer of the 12th century wrote, "Diaphony is the congruous dissonance of tones; therefore we call this dissonance discant, or organum." [15] In another 12th-century anonymous treatise we have the earliest clear separation of organum and discant as two separate concepts:

> But this is definitely the difference between discant and organum, that discant always replies to its own cantus firmus by means of some consonance, with an equal number of notes . . . organum, however,

does not harmonize with its cantus firmus by an equality of notes but by an infinite multiplicity and by a certain remarkable flexibility.[16]

About the beginning of the 13th century a complication arises: *discantus* begins to refer to a voice part as well as a polyphonic style. It is the part just above the plainsong cantus firmus, which is the lowest part at this period.[17] Characteristic passages in theoretical works of the time will read, "if the *cantus* descends such and such tones, the *discantus* will rise such and such tones." [18]

In the 14th and 15th centuries a second tenor, or contratenor, becomes a standard part and is located below the tenor (cantus firmus). Reading from the bottom up, we would then have contratenor (or countertenor), tenor (or cantus firmus), and discant (or *discantus*). A fourth voice would be considered as the third voice up from the tenor and hence called the *triplum*.

With the later 15th century and the 16th century the *discantus* is moved upwards once more to become the topmost (i. e., "soprano") voice; it is often called "cantus" for short![19] Its vacated position becomes the *altus*,[20] and the contratenor is displaced by a true bass. The dispossessed contratenor often turns up as an alto part, now above the tenor.[21] So now, in the 16th century, we have the following parts, reading down: *discantus,* or *cantus* (also discant or descant); *altus,* or *contratenor* (also countertenor); tenor; bass. When a fifth part occurs, it is simply *quintus*.

Now to return to the narrative of discant and organum. In the 13th century discant takes on the generic meaning of "polyphony." In an anonymous treatise of about 1225 on "How to Make Ordinary Discant" *(Discantus positio vulgaris)*[22] we find the following passage:

> Of the types of discant, one is just discant, the other being organum — which, in turn, is itself dually subdivided into double organum and just organum. Again, returning to discant, one type is *conductus,* another type is the motet, and another is hocket. Discant, properly speaking, is the same in rests but different in notes, in other words, a consonant melody, as when some ecclesiastical melody is discanted at the fifth, octave, and twelfth.[23]

The famous Anonymous IV says about the same thing though in greater detail, devoting an extensive section to organum (Chapter IV, Part 2) and another to discant (Chapter IV, Part 3); then follows another full chapter called "About the Volumes and Diversities of Discants," with a description of the Notre Dame repertory (Chapter VI).[24]

In the 16th century *discantus,* discant, or descant can still mean polyphony in the generic sense as well as a vocal part of some sort; but it takes on *still another* meaning in Elizabethan literature, "to improvise." In Shakespeare's Richard III, when Gloucester reflects on his lonely misfit life, he says he has naught to do but

To spy my shadow in the sun and descant on mine own deformity.[25]

Later, when Buckingham is trying to make Gloucester seem the right man for the throne, he tells Richard to appear contritely between two bishops when the Lord Mayor arrives and

On that ground I'll build a holy descant.[26]

The best summation of the Elizabethan meaning of descant is that in Thomas Morley's *Plaine and Easie Introduction to Practicall Musicke* of 1597:

> The name of Descant is vsurped of the musitions in diuers significations: some time they take it for the whole harmony of many voyces; others sometime for one of the voyces or partes; & that is, when the whole song is not passing three voyces. Last of all, they take it for singing a part extempore vpon a playnesong, in which sence we commonly vse it: so that when a man talketh of a Descanter, it must be vnderstood of one that can extempore sing a part vpon a playnesong.[27]

Now a word about the Spanish term *canto de órgano:* This means simply "polyphony," or perhaps more precisely, "mensural music." It occurs in Spanish sources at least into the 17th century. We have already seen that discant became a generic term for polyphony; in Spain, something similar seems to have happened to the term organum, taking on a generic sense as *canto de órgano.* Examples of florid organum persisted in the Spanish *Còdex musical de las Huelgas* (ca. 1300)[28] after disappearing elsewhere; the term apparently continued on in Spain, changing in meaning to the broader sense of "polyphony" as well as acquiring a minor spelling variation.

There is ample evidence for this meaning of *canto de órgano,* of which we need only mention Bermudo's definition in 1555 in his *Declaración de instrumentos musicales.*[29] In Book III, Chapter 30 is entitled "De la diffinicion de canto de órgano" and in it we find, "Properly speaking, this is the definition of *canto de órgano,* that it makes harmony or melody which can be measured." [30] This is followed by several chapters on mensural music under the general heading of "Canto de órgano." [31]

In English translations of some major source works relating to New Spain — made by general historians, not by musicologists — *canto de órgano* has commonly been mistranslated as "chant accompanied by the organ," "organ chant," and similar readings. One example will suffice to demonstrate how misleading such a reading can be. A major source for our little knowledge of the state of music in New Mexico before 1680 is Fray Alonso de Benavides' *Memorial* of 1630,[32] and one significant passage relating to music is the following:

> . . . assi mesmo a leer, y escrivir a los muchachos, y a cantar, que es para alabar al Señor ver en tan poco tiempo tantas Capillas de canto de organo . . .[33]

> . . . likewise (the friars teach) the boys to read and to write, and to sing, which is something for which the Lord is to be praised to see in such a short time so many chapels with polyphonic music . . .

If "Capillas de canto de organo" is read as "chapels with chant accompanied by the organ," or "chapels with organ chant" one can see what a misleading picture of the state of music in New Mexico in the early 17th century results: availability of an organ is assumed (whether or not there were organs) and we are completely unaware of the existence of polyphonic music.[34] *Canto* does mean chant, and *órgano* does mean organ; but the phrase *canto de órgano* has a totally different meaning from its separate parts.

We have perhaps descanted on discant and *canto de órgano* all too long and with all too much obscurity, and it were best now to follow Thomas Morley's precept: ". . . if any man shall think me prolix and tedious in this place, I must for that point craue pardon, & wil here make an end, wishing vnto all men that discretion as to measure so to other men as they would bee measured themselves . . . (and so,) . . . seeing therefore further discourse wil be superfluous, I wil here make an ende."[35]

NOTES FOR CHAPTER 4

1. An abstract of an earlier version of this paper was printed in the *Journal of the American Musicological Society*, Vol. VIII (1955), pp. 144—147, as "Discant, Descant, Diaphony and Organum: A Problem in Definitions." Parts of that abstract are used with permission.

2. E. de Coussemaker, *Scriptorum de musica medii aevi nova series* (Paris, 1864—1876), IV, 177 ff.

3. Ibid., p. 76.

4. Facsimile edition, Shakespeare Association (London, 1937), p. 165.

5. Ibid., p. 76.

6. Irving Lowens clearly demonstrated this relationship in a paper for the American Musicological Society in 1952 and in an article in the Society's *Journal*, VI (1953), 43 ff. ("The Origins of the American Fuging Tune").

7. Morley uses the term "canon" in its modern sense; cf. facsimile edition, pp. 97—105.

8. Paris, Bibliothèque Nationale, ms. lat. 15139, *olim* St. Victor 813, f. 269ro— 270ro. In a recent modern reprint, *The Music in the St. Victor Manuscript* (Toronto, 1959), much of this marginal treatise was unfortunately masked out. The treatise is also reprinted in E. de Coussemaker's *Histoire de l'harmonie au moyen âge* (Paris, 1852), pp. 245—246.

9. Morley uses the terms "descant" and "discant" in the *Plaine and Easie Introduction* . . . ; cf. facsimile edition, p. 117 (". . . let me hear you sing a lesson of discant.") and p. 118 (". . . this kind of discanting was by my maister allowed, and esteemed as the best of all descant"). A generally available modern reprint of Morley's book (London, 1952) modernizes spellings so that one must use the facsimile for such matters.

10. The term *organum* has two additional meanings: in classical Latin it means "instrument," and in medieval Latin it may mean either "instrument" or "organ."

11. Usually these terms are not found in music manuscripts but in theoretical works on music.

12. Walter Odington, writing about 1300, still refers to organum but in only a few lines (cf. Coussemaker, *Scriptorum*, I, pp. 245—246. Anonymous IV, writing about this same time but as part of a description of an earlier period, refers to organum in considerable detail (cf. Coussemaker, ibid., I, 354—356).

13. Modern edition, edited by H. Anglès: *El Còdex musical de las Huelgas*, 3 vols., Barcelona, 1931.

14. Morley, facsimile edition, p. 70 (passage is quoted below).

15. ". . . Dyaphonia est congrua vocum dissonantia. Hanc ergo dissonantiam discantum sive organum appellamus" (from *De Traktatu tenorum*, reprinted in M. Schneider, *Geschichte der Mehrstimmigkeit*, II, 116).

16. "Inter discantum vero et organum hoc interesse probatur quod discantus equali punctorum numero cantui suo per aliquam semper consonantiam respondet aut positionem facit unisonam; organum autem non equalitate punctorum, sed infinita multiplicitate, ac mira quadam flexibilitate cantui suo concordat." The treatise, usually referred to as "Tractatus La Fage," is printed in the *Essais de dipththérographie musicale* (Paris, 1864) by Juste-Adrien-Lenoir de La Fage (p. 355 ff.); the quotation occurs on p. 360.

17. Cantus firmus, in its turn, may be called just "cantus" or "tenor." "Tenor" in this case means "leading part" and not a type of voice.

18. The *discantus* is also referred to as the *motetus*. Third and fourth voices are the *triplum* and *quadruplum*, above the *discantus*.

19. One need hardly be reminded of the potential confusion between *discantus* and *cantus firmus* when one speaks of *cantus* or finds the term in a theoretical source.

20. Or even "alto" — cf. Morley, facsimile ed., p. 129.

21. Hence the English use of "countertenor" as a male alto part (falsetto).

22. Coussemaker, *Scriptorum*, I, 94—97.

23. "Discantuum vero alius pure discantus, alius organum, quod est duplex scilicet organum duplex, et quod pure organum dicitur. (par.) Item alius conductus, alius mothetus, et alius est ochetus. Discantus ipse est idem in pausis, sed diversus in notis, consonus cantus sicut cum aliquis cantus ecclesiasticus in

quinta, octava et duodecima discantatur." (Coussemaker *Scriptorum,* I, 96.)

24. Ibid., I, 354—356 (Chapter IV, Part 2); 356—358 (Chapter IV, Part 3); 360—361 (Chapter VI).

25. Act I, Sc. 1, l. 27.

26. Act III, Sc. 7, l. 49.

27. Facsimile edition, p. 70.

28. Cf. n. 13 above. Cf. Nos. 7, 8, 37, 41, 42, 47.

29. Facsimile reprint by Bärenreiter, 1958.

30. "Propriamente habla esta diffinicion del canto de órgano, que haze harmonia, o melodia: el qual se puede medir . . ." (Ibid., f. 48vo).

31. In Book II of the *Declaración* chapters 16—19 also discuss *canto de órgano* in the same general way. Incidentally, the *Declaración,* in spite of its title, is a general theoretical work, discussing plainsong, polyphony, notation, and composition; only Book IV is devoted exclusively to playing the *vihuela* and the *órgano.* In Book V (devoted to composition), after a discussion of *contrapunto* (f. 132ro—134ro) — in the sense of "strict" counterpoint — there follows a discussion of *canto de órgano* in the sense of free, polyphonic composition (f. 134ro—135ro).

32. The original edition was published in Madrid in 1630 and is now one of the rarest of printed books (eight known copies in the United States and one in the British Museum). The principal modern edition for research purposes is the following: *The Memorial of Fray Alonso de Benavides, 1630,* Mrs. E. E. Ayer, translator; annotated by F. W. Hodge and C. F. Lummis; Chicago, Privately printed, 1916. This edition contains a complete facsimile as well as voluminous notes, in addition to the English translation. For further detail see the present writer's article, "Benavides and the State of Church Music in New Mexico, *circa* 1630," (in preparation) in the *Journal of the American Musicological Society.*

33. Ayer edition (cf. above), p. 170 (p. 96 of the facsimile section).

34. There have been five English translations made of the *Memorial,* including the Ayer edition above. These translations are compared as to musical references in the writer's article mentioned above. The most recent translation (still in print at this writing) is that by Peter P. Forrestal, *Benavides' Memorial of 1630,* published by The Academy of American Franciscan History (Washington, D. C., 1954). Forrestal translates "Capillas de canto de organo" as "choirs singing with organ accompaniment," p. 66.

35. Morley, (facsimile), p. 184 and unnumbered page at the end of "The Annotations."

5

MUSICAL ACTIVITY IN AUGSBURG AND ITS *ANNAKIRCHE*, CA. 1470–1630

Louise E. Cuyler

Augsburg is a very old city, one marked by the burden and the scars of momentous events. Many historic buildings and a tragically large portion of her art treasures were destroyed in the bombing of World War II. Faithful, tasteful restoration is taking place, however, and today's visitor will find many of the monuments, churches, storied sites looking much as they did a quarter of a century ago.

The citizens of Augsburg are proud of their city's heritage and like to recall that Munich, their burgeoning, prosperous neighbor, was founded as the result of a decision made in the Augsburg *Rathaus*.

Küchlin, a 15th-century poet and historian, held that a settlement on the River Lech existed by 1184 B. C. Generally, however, Augsburg's founding is placed much later, during the reign of Augustus Caesar. This tradition is borne out by the town's name: *Augusta Vindelicorum*, that is "Augusta of the South Germans," which later was shortened and Germanicized to simply Augsburg.

Augustus Caesar's fondness for his city on the Lech was to be inherited by several of his imperial successors, notably Kaiser Friedrich I in the 12th century and Kaiser Maximilian I at the beginning of the 16th. *Bürgermeister von Augsburg* was, in fact, a favorite nickname for Kaiser Max, and one which he appeared to relish.

Imperial favor led, naturally, to the erection of fine churches and other public buildings; it led also to development of Augsburg as a center of artistic, musical, and literary activity. Stirrings of a Renaissance spirit were evident in Augsburg, Innsbruck, and a few other Bavarian and Tyrolian towns when most of Germany and Austria was still a rough, crude, cultureless wasteland. Aeneas Silvius Piccolomini, inveterate traveler, diplomat, diarist, and the future Pius II (1458 to 1464), paints a vivid and somewhat depressing picture of Vienna in 1458, but one which could probably have applied with equal accuracy to many other Austrian and German towns of the day.

> . . . The wine cellars are so deep and spacious that it is said that Vienna has as many buildings under the earth as above it. . . . This city is in the diocese of Padua, but the daughter is in this case greater than the mother. . . .
>
> There is also a university here, with faculties of liberal arts, canon law, and theology; it is new, however, and established by papal charter. A great crowd of students flocks to it from Hungary and the upper regions of Germany. . . . There is also in Vienna today a fairly well-known theologian, who, they say, has written some histories that are not unprofitable. I would praise his teaching, if he had not lectured for two and twenty years on the first chapter of Isaiah and never yet come to the end. But the greatest flaw . . . is that they give too much attention to dialectic. . . . Those who are honored with the title of master of arts are examined especially in this one art. For the rest, they have no concern for music or rhetoric or the metrical art, although they require that certain verses and letters unskillfully edited by others should be taught. Oratory and poetry are almost unknown among them; for them, all study in logic is futile disputation, with hardly a solid foundation anywhere. You rarely find anyone who owns the works of Aristotle and other philosophers, but they use commentaries for the most part. The students largely devote themselves to pleasure, and are avid for food and wine; few come out with any learning, nor are they restrained by any discipline. Day and night they roam about, inflicting grave injuries on citizens, and their wits are completely addled by the shamelessness of the women.
>
> . . . .
>
> On the other hand, in so large and noble a city, there are many irregularities. Night and day, brawls are fought like military engagements: now the craftsmen against the students, then the citizens against the workers, and again some workers take up arms against others. Hardly a celebration goes by without a manslaughter; numerous murders are committed. When there is a brawl, there is no one to separate the contending parties; neither the magistrates nor the princes try, as they should, to prevent such great evils.
>
> . . . .
>
> The Viennese live, moreover, without any written law, they say that they live according to ancient customs, which they often distort or interpret as they wish. Justice is wholly venal. Those who have the means sin without punishment; the poor and unprotected are punished with the full rigor of the law. Oaths which have been sworn publicly are observed to the letter, because an oath which can be de-

nied has no force. Those who lend money for a certain period, if they should suffer any loss after the term of the agreement has expired, extort whatever sum they wish, and impose the highest penalty on the debtors. Pledges which are given for loans, if they are accepted, are not considered usurious. The Viennese fear excommunication only insofar as it is harmful to the reputation or may bring material disadvantages. Stolen goods which are discovered in the possession of the thief are surrendered to the judge. The Viennese do not, moreover, observe the ecclesiastical holidays strictly; meat is sold in the city on every fast day. The draymen never take a holiday.[1]

In Augsburg, however, at about this same time, the Meistersinger were already a thriving group, and had built there the first real civic *Meistersingerschule*. Proud, opinionated, clannish, these guildsmen probably prepared the way for widespread, quick acceptance of Reformation ideas by their anticlerical spirit and bold self-assurance.

Augsburg's period of greatest flourishing is often called *Die Fuggerzeit*. The wealthy bankers and merchants of the Fugger line, who made the city on the Lech their home, were wonderful patrons of all the arts and learning. For more than a century, after the time of the first Jakob Fugger (1459–1525), these men lavished wealth, enthusiasm, discernment on developing their native town as a cultural center. Churches were built or enlarged and refurbished; organs were commissioned and built for them; the finest singers, composers, and organists were brought and maintained in their service. The leading painters and architects of the day — men like Jörg Breu the Elder, Hans Burgkmair, Lucas Cranach, even Albrecht Dürer — were called into Fugger service, with the result that many of Augsburg's Renaissance buildings, including the Fugger palace itself with the superb "Ladies' Court" decorated by Burgkmair, are among Germany's great art treasures.

For the Fuggers, love of the arts was, however, no detriment to the development of financial acumen. These men held the Holy Roman Empire in pawn during much of the 16th century, when, eventually, their estimated capital reached the incredible sum of some 70 million marks. Emperor Maximilian I offered the imperial crown jewels in security for the loans he sought repeatedly; later he was forced to pawn, as well, many of the art objects he had commissioned. The right to develop silver mines in the Tyrol and copper mines in Bohemia were other concessions exchanged for Fugger cash by both Maximilian and his successors.

In one of history's curious coincidences, three men whose lives were to be closely intertwined were born in 1459: Archduke Maximilian of Habsburg, who became Emperor Maximilian I; Jakob Fugger, *der Reiche*, founder of the vast Fugger fortune, whose financial aid was to help Max weather many a crisis; and Paul Hofhaimer, greatest organist of his day, who brought great glory to the kaiser's *Hofkapelle*.

During the closing years of the 15th century the paths of these three men began to cross. Maximilian was crowned King of the Romans at Aix la Chapelle (Aachen) in 1486; this title was a kind of preliminary one to that of Holy Roman Emperor, which Max aspired to assume after the death of his father, Friedrich III. History is full of consequences of the fact that the post of emperor was not hereditary. Theoretically this provision discouraged dynastic monopoly, and assured the free election of worthy monarchs. Actually, the house of Habsburg retained the title for over six centuries, from the accession of Rudolf I in 1273; and the imperial electors were generally so susceptible to bribes that the chosen monarch often proved to be the candidate with recourse to the most money. An especially notorious case was the 1519 election of Maximilian's grandson and successor, Charles I of Spain, who ruled the empire as Charles V. On this occasion, Fugger money, supporting Charles, prevailed against a combination of Medici and other funds, offered in support of Francis I of France. Fascinating to speculate upon are the consequences in history, had the election gone the other way.

Seven years after the Aachen coronation, Maximilian became emperor elect; in 1508 he was given formal permission by the pope to assume the title of emperor, although his coronation never took place. This date becomes a useful tool for scholars attempting to date Maximiliana (manuscripts, books, engravings, and the like), since use of the double eagle of the Holy Roman Empire as a hallmark dates from 1508; before this, the single eagle, crest of the King of the Romans, was used.

Maximilian commenced to assemble his musical household in time for his 1486 coronation, drawing upon prominent former members of the glittering Burgundian *chapelle* which had been dispersed after the death in 1482 of Mary of Burgundy, Max's first wife. Jean Molinet relates this in fascinating detail.[2] The reactivated Burgundian group was combined later with the more modest Austrian *Kapelle*, and an early evidence of Jakob Fugger's interest in music comes in 1492, when Nicolas Mayoul, leader of the kaiser's singers, received a stipend which was "durch die Fugger ausgerichtet." [3]

Maximilian disliked Vienna for a variety of reasons, legitimate and merely personal, and spent as much time as possible in other parts of the empire. Favorite towns were Innsbruck in the Tyrol, a region ceded to Max in 1490, and Augsburg, which had been a *Reichstadt*, or free imperial city, for some 200 years. A significant result of the Tyrol annexation was that Paul Hofhaimer, already regarded as a great organist, came into Maximilian's service by reason of his attachment to the *Kapelle* of Archduke Sigismund of the Tyrol. He served the emperor until Max's death in 1519.

As for Augsburg, the imperial choir was officially transferred there from Innsbruck in 1492, with Hans Kerner as leader. Hofhaimer remained for a time in Innsbruck; the organist at Augsburg at this time is thought to have been Jakob Kellergraf. That Heinrich Isaac joined the *Kapelle* around 1496 is indicated by a letter of the kaiser's from Pisa, where he had been embattled for some time. This states in part: "Wir haben Hannsen Kerner, unsern obristen Caplan und Cantor, mitsambt 12 Knaben und Gesellen, darzue den Ysaac und sein Hausfrau gen Wien verordnet. . . ." [4] This entry also carries the information that the singers moved to Vienna later in 1496, which was the year of the establishment of the *Hofkapelle* there and the founding of the *Sängerknaben* group. Ludwig Senfl, then about six years old, who was the third of the great musicians to grace Maximilian's *Hofmusik*, appears on the first roster of singing boys.

According to the list of his journeys as compiled by Ulmann, [5] Kaiser Max visited Augsburg in 1489, 1490, 1492, 1496 (twice), 1500 (Reichstag), 1504, 1510 (Reichstag), 1515, 1516 (twice), 1517, 1518 (Reichstag). Since traveling monarchs carried their musical households with them, the assumption that the imperial *Hofkapelle* visited Augsburg in each of these years is reasonable. Of the three famous musicians who served the kaiser, Hofhaimer is known to have lived in Augsburg from 1507 until 1520, a year after Max's death, when the great organist returned to his native Salzburg to serve Cardinal Mathäus Lang, prince archbishop of this powerful see. Isaac, whose appointment as court composer was a flexible one that permitted him to travel freely, is known to have been present in Augsburg on many occasions, but probably never actually dwelt there. Young Ludwig Senfl, who inherited Isaac's post at his resignation in 1514, lived in Augsburg from 1516 until 1523. In 1520, the year after Maximilian's death, he published there the *Liber selectarum cantionum,* honoring the dead monarch who was so great a patron of music but dedicated to the powerful Cardinal Lang of Salzburg, who was an equally devoted music lover.

Maximilian's *Hofkapelle* is known to have performed at various times at the Augsburg Cathedral, which was the seat of Bishop Lang before he received the coveted Salzburg post; at St. Ulrich and Afra, then a Benedictine cloister possessing great art treasures and illumined manuscripts; and at St. Moritz, where, during the Reichstag of 1500, the choristers had "ain Spil gemacht" for the kaiser, for which service they received six gulden. Specially favored by Kaiser Max and his *Hofmusik,* however, was the *Annakirche* — the *Karmelitenkloster bei St. Anna,* as it was known before the Reformation. The remainder of this article will concern this historic church with its magnificent Fugger Chapel, scene of so many stirring events, and hallowed for music lovers by the procession of great composers and performers who flourished within these walls.

Today's visitor to Augsburg will find the *Annakirche* in the midst of downtown congestion that all but conceals the storied district, housing the Goldschmied fountain, the *Maximiliansmuseum,* and the house out of whose windows Philippine Welser surveyed the town. From the outside, this ancient structure presents a curiously mixed, multi-turreted aspect which is not inconsistent with its rich and varied history. The original foundation was through the prior and a group of brothers of the Carmelite Order *(Heilige Maria vom Berge Karmel),* who came to Augsburg in 1275, the year before it became a free imperial city. The earliest *Annakirche* was commenced in 1321. Much of the earlier compound was destroyed during the middle years of the 15th century; the nucleus of the restored structure, which still remains, was built in 1470. Surviving from the earlier time is the *Goldschmiedskapelle* in the southeast corner, a thank offering for Augsburg's delivery from the plague in 1419. The frescoes of this chapel, faded by time though they are, comprise, along with the Fugger Chapel, a precious segment of Germany's art history.

For musicians, the west end of the church, which encompasses the Fugger Chapel, holds prime interest. This chapel was endowed in 1509 through an agreement between Jakob and Ulrich Fugger and the prior of the Carmelite cloister, Johannes Fortis. The foundation deed pledged to enlarge the church by adding a chapel equipped with altar and choir stalls that would serve also as a Fugger tomb.

The chapel with its furnishings cost 23,000 gulden; it was consecrated in 1518.[6]

Emperor Maximilian attended his last Reichstag in Augsburg that same year. During this conclave, Albrecht Dürer made the sketch for his famous portrait of the kaiser, a likeness which shows the monarch to be aging and weary. Very likely he was grieved and apprehensive also over the gathering religious storm, rumblings of which were audible all through the Swabian district. He left Augsburg in September 1518, going first to Innsbruck, where his cruel rejection by the Tyrolian burghers shocked and saddened him. He then went on, through the winter mountains, to Wels, where he died the next January 12.

That the emperor's *Hofkapelle* performed often in the *Annakirche* may be assumed because of the location there of the Fugger Chapel, with its beautiful decorations and, eventually, its fine organ. The Fugger organ, built by Jehan Behaim of Dubrau, dates from 1512. A well-known woodcut by Hans Weiditz, dated 1519, shows Emperor Maximilian hearing Mass in Augsburg with his musicians present in impressive array. That the setting of this Mass is the *Annakirche* before the addition of the Fugger Chapel is almost certain; this I have proved to my own satisfaction by sitting in the venerable church with the woodcut in hand in order to study details like arches, pillars, and the balcony location. As Moser [7] has pointed out, however, the woodcut must have been prepared from sketches made before 1512, because the mighty Fugger cabinet organ with its wing paintings by Jörg Breu the Elder, dedicated that year, is absent. Instead, Paul Hofhaimer, easily recognizable from his distinctive profile, is playing an instrument known as the *Apfelregal*, so called because of the cylindrical shape of the tops of the pipes. Opposite him are the imperial singers. Their position, facing the organist, suggests *alternatim* performance, and this speculation is made plausible by the *alternatim* structure of all the propers in Isaac's *Choralis Constantinus* and of much of the ordinary as well. Fragments of description in writings concerning certain religious ceremonies at this time also mention how Master Paul "responded" to the singers.

A careful examination of the famous Weiditz woodcut reveals a wealth of information concerning performance of liturgical music in the early 16th century.

KAISER MAX AND HIS *HOFMUSIK* IN AUGSBURG

Moser [8] has pointed out the error in the portrayal of the organ: the longer, lower-pitched pipes appear above Hofhaimer's right hand,

EMPEROR MAXIMILIAN HEARING MASS IN AUGSBURG

Reprinted from Will Winkler, *Kaiser Maximilian I. zwischen Wirklichkeit und Traum,* 1950, Plate 20, between pp. 288 and 289, by permission of R. Oldenbourg Verlag, Munich, Germany in the conventional place for treble pipes. He suggests that the artist who cut the block neglected to make the necessary "mirror" transposition. My own observations prove, however, that all the architectural features of the church are correct, the placing of the balcony at the left being especially convincing. My conclusion is that the woodcutter reversed everything except the organ, which, since he was presumably no musician, he thought could remain as in Breu's sketch.

Hans Rem was the first official organist for the newly completed Fugger organ. Why Hofhaimer, who had resided in Augsburg since 1507, did not take the post immediately is not clear, but he did become Fugger organist in 1518.

By this time Augsburg, indeed the entire Swabian district, was on fire over the new ideas being preached so eloquently by Martin Luther and his followers. The *Annakirche* and the whole town of Augsburg were to become centers second only to Wittenberg in embracing and spreading the new doctrines. This must have been a time comparable only to a period of civil war, when brother opposed brother, old loyalties were shattered, and no one was certain of the future or where the truth lay. The completion and dedication of the Fugger Chapel as well as the installation of "Master Paul" as organist must have passed almost unnoticed in the turmoil of events during the summer of 1518. The Reichstag convened during the summer and continued well into the fall. The avowed purpose was to effect an alliance between the Holy See, Emperor Max, and King Christian of Norway, which coalition would, hopefully, wage a "Christian" war against the Turks. Another issue probably overshadowed this, however: Martin Luther, whose fiery sermons and fierce indictments of abuses in the church had raised a storm in Germany, was called before the diet to defend himself before Cajetan,[9] the newly appointed papal legate to Germany. Emperor Max left Augsburg on his long, sad journey in September, and most minds turned, in all likelihood, to this second, intensely local affair.

From this time (September 1518), the *Annakirche* became a principal bastion of Lutheran activity and, only a little later, a fountain of musical and scholastic development for the new faith. In 1517 Johann Frosch, a friend and admirer of Luther, had become prior of the Carmelite cloister there. Frosch was apparently a brilliant man — a composer and musical theorist, as well as a theologian. When Luther came to Augsburg for his ordeal before Cajetan, Frosch and some of the brother monks were his hosts. They helped Luther escape from Augsburg when he, having refused to recant before Cajetan, became a marked man.

The events of the next five or six years were chaotic and distressing. The *Annakirche*, clearly a focal point of Lutheran activity, finally went over to the new faith in 1525, when many of the Carmelite monks renounced their vows and Frosch first celebrated "das Abendmal nach Wittenberger Art."

Uncertainty exists even today about the Fugger Chapel and its donors during this tempestuous period. The patriarch of the line, old Jakob der Reiche, died the very year of the establishment of the new religion in the *Annakirche*. Jakob (also most of his heirs) remained loyal to the Catholic faith and instructed his nephews that he wished to be buried in a Catholic church. Whether they complied with his request is not known.

> Documentary proof is lacking whether the nephews really buried him in St. Anna or, in conformity to his dying word, in a Catholic church. . . . Of the crude wooden coffins in the vault at St. Anna, which, in moving humbleness, contain only skeletons resting in lime, none bears his name.[10]

Whatever the fate of its founder's bones, the Fugger Chapel, indeed the whole *Annakirche* compound, became a flourishing center of musical activity, once the violence of the religious upheaval had subsided. In 1531 a Lutheran *Gymnasium* was founded there; music was a principal subject of its curriculum, and by 1535 *Prediger* Hausmann could present a procession of poor *Sängerknaben* in public concert.

During the next 30 years, the names of Sixt Birck, Leonhard Baider, Georg Sturm, and Peter Paix appear prominently in the archives of the *Annakirche*. The religious peace ensuing after the Reichstag of 1555 brought relative tranquility back to this troubled district, and an atmosphere more conducive to pursuit of the arts.

Adam Gumpelzhaimer, who assumed the post of cantor and preceptor in the newly founded Lutheran *Kollegium* of St. Anna in 1581, was the major composer and musical scholar to be associated with the *Annakirche* during the remaining years of her heyday. His *Compendium Musicae* of 1591 had 13 editions, plus two reprints, as follows: 1591, 1595, 1600, 1605, 1611, 1616, 1618, 1625, 1632, 1636 (reprint of 1616 ed.), 1646, 1655, 1665 (reprint of 1618 ed.), 1675, 1681.

The *Neue Teutsche Geistliche Lieder*, 3-voice sacred songs brought out also in 1591, was reissued in 1602, 1611, and 1619. Rearrangements for four voices of these songs appeared in 1594 and 1602.

Since Gumpelzhaimer died in 1625 and his *Compendium* had seven editions after that date, one may infer that he was a man of considerable prestige.

As a result of the *Restitutionsedikt* of 1630, the choristers of the *Annakirche* were abolished and the organ taken over to St. Moritz, with Fugger permission. The choristers were reassembled two years later, but the great day of the venerable church was past. Along with the rest of Germany, Augsburg suffered deeply in the Thirty Years' War, and the once great city dwindled in prestige until, relinquishing its "free" status, it was taken over into Bavaria early in the 19th century.

For the 1818 anniversary of the Reformation, considerable restoration of the then decrepit structure was undertaken. The less-than-ideal consequences make assessment of the true artistic and historic significance of the *Annakirche* difficult.

During the World War II bombings of 1944, the mechanism, cabinet, and facade of the organ were totally destroyed. It is now fully reconstructed, earlier photographs and drawings having served as models. Fortunately several of the organ "wings" with Jörg Breu's paintings were rescued. Those of special musical interest — the scenes which Moser [11] has suggested may have representations of several musicians of Kaiser Max's *Hofkapelle* — were, lamentably, not back in place in the summer of 1963, nor was I able to learn their fate.

NOTES FOR CHAPTER 5

1. From *Historia Frederici III imperatoris*, trans. Mary Martin McLaughlin, in *The Portable Renaissance Reader*, pp. 208—213.
2. Jean Molinet, *Chroniques*, Vol. III.
3. Walter Senn, *Musik und Theater am Hof zu Innsbruck* (1954), p. 34.
4. Senn, p. 28.
5. Heinrich Ulmann, *Kaiser Maximilian I*, 2 vols. (Stuttgart: J. C. Cotta, 1884 to 1891).
6. Philipp Maria Halm, "Adolf Daucher und die Fuggerkapelle bei St. Anna in Augsburg," *Studien zur Fugger-Geschichte*, VI (Munich: Duncker & Humblot, 1921).
7. H. J. Moser, *Paul Hofhaimer*, 1929.
8. Ibid.
9. Not to be confused with St. Cajetan, a contemporary. The pope's new ambassador was born Gaetano Da Tiena, from which name the sobriquet "Cajetan" was naturally evolved. This Cajetan was founder of the Theatines and became, eventually, both a cardinal and archbishop of Palermo.
10. Götz Freiherr von Pölnitz, *Jakob Fugger* (1949), p. 660.
11. H. J. Moser, *Paul Hofhaimer*, 1929.

6

THE HYMNS OF ZWINGLI AND LUTHER: A COMPARISON

Markus Jenny

In any genuine Protestant hymnbook the first of the three great European reformers, Luther, is sure to be represented. No hymn by Calvin is found in any hymnbook,[1] while Zwingli holds a middle position. One or the other of the more recent hymnbooks puts his name into the index of the hymn writers, for occasionally one or two of his hymns can be found — most frequently the so-called Kappel Song, *Herr, nun heb den Wagen selb* ("Guide, O Lord, Thy Chariot Now"); less often the Pestilence Song, *Hilf, Herr Gott, hilf in dieser Not* ("Help, Lord God, Help in This Distress").[2] Zwingli's third hymn, a rhymed version of Psalm 69, *Hilf Gott, das Wasser geht mir bis an d'Seel* ("Help, God, the Floods Assail My Very Soul"), can be found only in Swiss hymnbooks and only up to the end of the 17th century. More hymns from Zwingli's pen have not survived, nor have any other hymns become known under his name. The present discussion will also refrain from a consideration of melodies which on the basis of a stylistic analysis and evolution would be identified as melodies written by Zwingli. We would like emphatically to refer to the fact that Zwingli's three preserved hymns, which will serve us as the only material for the comparison of this essay, represent only a section of his output of hymns. They have to be evaluated as types — each hymn must be seen as characteristic for a greater number of similar hymn creations.[3]

Thus the *scope* of the two hymn repertories which we want to compare is very unequal. Although Luther left us only 36 hymns, he fills almost all sections of a hymnbook. Zwingli comes to our attention only at one or two places in the hymnbook. Zwingli of course had no motivation to serve a singing, worshiping congregation with his creative talent. Therefore it does not make any sense to establish in detail the topics Zwingli does not mention in his hymns, in contrast to Luther; they would be almost as numerous as Luther's hymns.

Zwingli knows neither the liturgical hymn (hymns of praise, *Leisen* and hymns derived from them, hymns which originated in the sequence and antiphon with their corresponding function) nor the catechism hymn. Zwingli uses only one of the forms bound to a model, the psalm hymn. Here one Zwingli hymn stands opposite six written by Luther. In comparing the remainder of Luther's hymns with Zwingli's hymn output, neither the instructional nor the liturgical Luther hymns should be discussed, but only those created for use in the home or for private devotion and those created from personal motives. There are eight or nine such pieces by Luther; only two by Zwingli. The following is a list of Luther's hymns according to their usage for the catechism (C), the liturgy (L), or private devotion (P). The classification of some of the songs under these three headings perhaps needs still closer investigation. What I indicate in the following is to be understood only from the hypothetical viewpoint. One should observe that I think only of the original intention of the creator of the song and not of a later usage which might please everyone.

I	II	III	IV	V
		Year of publication	*Use of hymn*	*No. of stanzas*
Name of hymn	*First line*			
Ten Commandments (long version)	That man a godly life might live	1524	C	12 (10+2)
Ten Commandments (short version)	Wilt thou, O man, live happily	1524	C	5
Credo (Trinity)	We all believe in one true God	1524	C(L?)	3
Lord's Prayer	Our Father, Thou in heav'n above	1539	C	9(7+2)
Baptism	To Jordan came our Lord the Christ	1541	C	7
Communion (before)	Jesus Christ, our blessed Savior	1524	C/L	10
Communion (after)	O Lord, we praise Thee, bless Thee	1524	C/L	3
Veni, Redemptor	Savior of the nations, come	1524	L	8(7+1)
A solis ortus	Now praise we Christ, the Holy One	1524	L	8(7+1)
Christmas *Leise*	All praise to Thee, eternal God	1524	L	7
Hostis Herodes	Why, Herod, unrelenting foe	1541/3	L	5
Easter sequence	Christ Jesus lay in death's strong bands	1524	L	7
Easter *Leise*	Jesus Christ today is risen	1524	L	3

Pentecost *Leise*	We now implore God the Holy Ghost	1524	L	4(1+3)
Veni, Creator Spiritus	Come, Holy Ghost, Creator blest	1524	L	7
Veni, Sancte Spiritus	Come, Holy Ghost, God and Lord	1524	L	3
Sanctus	Isaiah, mighty seer, in days of old	1526	L	(1)
Litany/Trinity	God the Father, be our stay	1524	L	3
Media vita	In the midst of earthly life	1524	L	3
Nunc dimittis	In peace and joy I now depart	1524	L	4
Te Deum	Lord God, we praise Thee	1528/9	L	(1)
Psalm 12	O Lord, look down from heaven, behold	1523/4	L	6
Psalm 14	The mouth of fools doth God confess	1523/4	L	6
Psalm 67	May God bestow on us His grace	1523/4	L	3
Psalm 124	If God had not been on our side	1524	L	3
Psalm 128	Happy the man who feareth God	1524	L	5
Psalm 130	From depths of woe I cry to Thee	1523/4	L	5
Da pacem	Peace in our time, Lord God, bestow	1529	(L?) P?	(1)
O lux beata	Thou who art Three in Unity	1543	P	3
(Christmas)	From heaven above to earth I come	1534/5	P	5+10
(Christmas)	To shepherds as they watched by night	1543	P(L?)	6
(Church)	A mighty Fortress is our God	1528	P	4(3+1)
(Church)	I love her dearly, precious maid	1535	P	3
(Church)	Lord, keep us steadfast in Thy Word	1542	P	3
(Reformation)	By help of God I fain would tell	1523/4	P	12
(Reformation)	Dear Christians, one and all, rejoice	1523/4	P	10

We observe that the hymns which are intended for the liturgy are created, without exception,[4] according to some preexisting model. They fall, except some of them, into the years from 1523 to 1526, while the hymns that were originally probably not allotted to the liturgy are not directly or not at all related to a preexisting model and originated, with two exceptions, at a later time. The exceptions in the first group are the didactic hymns on the Lord's Prayer and Baptism, which completed the catechism cycle, and the Epiphany hymn, which rounded off the festival cycle. The *Sanctus* hymn is the only piece from 1526. Of the liturgical hymns of 1524 not a single one was written for the *ordinarium missae;* the *Credo* hymn was not originally intended for the Mass but for the instruction (and perhaps the worship service) of the catechism. At any rate, it was sung on Trinity Sunday at the main service (according to Walther!). Neither is the *Sanctus* (1526) of this cycle a transformation of the Mass *Sanctus* to a hymn, but rather a narrative leading *toward* the *Sanctus*. In contrast to Zwingli, Luther made liturgical use of the hymn. However, he resisted the danger, which people unfortunately fell into later (and still do today!), of making a hymn out of every major part of the liturgy. He is in agreement with the ancient church when he does not tamper with the text particularly of the ordinary of the Mass.[5] In this he agrees entirely with Zwingli, who, although he undoubtedly could have done so, did not transform the *Gloria* of his Communion liturgy (1525) into a congregational hymn. Rather, he wanted the congregation to recite a literal German translation antiphonally.[6] The *Te Deum* hymn, which again could not have been intended for regular liturgical use, represents another exception.

Beyond the comparison of the psalm hymns, there is essentially only one other comparison left — that of Luther's freely created hymns (the last seven of the above compilation) with those of Zwingli's that were likewise created without any liturgical or catechetical foundation. We deal on both sides with only a few pieces. Indeed, it is even conceivable that Zwingli composed more such freely created hymns than Luther. It is known, as we said before, that a number of Zwingli's hymns are lost, whereas a loss of hymns is not known, nor can it be assumed, in Luther's case.

When we speak of "freely created" hymns, we do not intend to say that they lack any relation to the hymn tradition. On the contrary, our two hymn creators of the Reformation era do not differ at this point. In both a vital relationship also to the extraliturgical hymn tradition of the late Middle Ages can be recognized. Text and music of "From Heaven Above" go back to an old dance and serenade song (Böhme 271 and 281); the first stanza of the hymn represents a sacred parody of the serenade stanza with the tune of the garland song used since 1569 for "From Heaven Came the Angel Host." It is the very first tune of "From Heaven Above" (as in Kluge, 1535, where the song appears for the first time). An older song tradition stands behind the beginning of *Nun freut euch, lieben Christen g'mein.* The melody of a 15th-century Easter hymn, *Nun freut euch, Frauen unde Mann, dass Christ ist auferstanden,* is used in the first printed version (it is used today for *Es ist das Heil uns kommen her;* consult the *Erfurt Enchiridion,* 1524). We can assume that Luther started with this hymn; its meter is not encountered before. But even the tune which is used today for this hymn and which had appeared already in the *Achtliederbuch* is related to a folk tune (Böhme, 635). It is also obvious that the beginning of Luther's first song, *Ein neues Lied wir heben an* ("By Help of God I Fain Would Tell"), agrees entirely with popular song creation. Luther intentionally chose this minstrel-song beginning without having a specific song of this category in mind. In *Sie ist mir lieb, die werte Magd* we may assume that Luther wrote a parody to a specific song of praise dedicated to a woman. At least, Luther consciously and cleverly imitated the style of such love songs in the first stanza.

We notice similar facts in Zwingli's case. It is true, we do not find in his three hymns any proven *textual* connection with any older German song. To find such a connection we would have to consider the songs of his friend and colleague from Zurich, Leo Jud, who chose a late medieval song of St. Beat as a model for a Protestant song (*Gott's Gnad' und sein Barmherzigkeit;* cf. Jenny, No. 183). Or we would have to refer to the funeral song of his son-in-law Rudolf Gwalter (*Nie noch nimmer so rught mein G'müt;* cf. Jenny, No. 185), which represents a classic contrafactum of a love song in Arnt von Aich's song book (ca. 1510). It is not impossible that such contrafacta may have been among Zwingli's lost songs. Unfortunately nothing has survived. But H. J. Moser [7] has shown that the *tune* of Zwingli's Kappel Song is connected with a folk tune which has come to us in two different versions: in Heinrich Isaac's *Missa carminum* (as the tenor of the Kyrie II) [8] and in a setting by Caspar Othmayr printed in 1549 *(Ich weiss mir ein Maidlein hübsch und fein).* [9] We have reason to assume that Zwingli, in August 1529, while stationed with the Zurich army before Kappel during the first Kappel war, gave to this short song of supplication originally sung to a completely different tune a new popular tune to make it more singable for his soldiers. This use of a known folk tune fits neatly into his philosophy whereby singing and making music do not represent an activity that displeases God; Dominik Zili, a preacher at St. Gall, in a discussion with Zwingli in 1529/30 had proposed quite the opposite. [10]

We have already approached the problem of *style* in these songs. Let us anticipate the result of the comparison: Zwingli's and Luther's songs are equally characterized by the juxtaposition and simultaneous appearance of genuine popularity and genuine art. This is not something one expects to find. Is this not the defect of our music today that artistic music and popular music break away from each other?

This becomes particularly evident in the field of song composition; the most popular song, the hit song, usually is devoid of any artistic pretension. Here we must make two specific statements:

First, we find that Luther and Zwingli employ the style of the society song of their time (the so-called court-tune style), Zwingli in a more pronounced way, although Luther uses it also. We deal with a consciously soloistic style. The songs that represent it were performed as solo songs to lute accompaniment or in the guise of a tenor tune around which gravitates a setting of string or wind parts. The classic examples of this style are represented in the song book of Arnt of Aich (Cologne, ca. 1510), known to Zwingli's close and distant associates. The strophic structure and melody outline of the Pestilence Song and Zwingli's Psalm 69 make them perfect examples of this style, also inasmuch as Zwingli provided them with four-part settings. Unfortunately only a fragment of one of these settings survived.[11] The Kappel Song has also come to us in a court-tune version. The manuscript F X 21 of the Basel University library includes an isolated tenor partbook from a collection of 4-part song settings that contains not only the known tune of this song but also a tune which is kept in the soloistic style of the Lutheran tunes mentioned above. It is impossible to imagine that this tune could have been written once the other, more convincing tune in the folk-song style had been composed; it must be considered the earlier and original tune.

Luther does not seem to have been a composer of polyphonic settings. In the last decades the people doing the research are more and more convinced that Luther himself created some of his song tunes. Yet no polyphonic settings of these tunes from his own pen are known. He liked to leave the task of the *Symphonetes* to Johann Walter and others. Among the tunes of his songs that of *Sie ist mir lieb, die werte Magd* ("I Love Her Dearly, Precious Maid") shows exactly the same characteristics as Zwingli's tunes: (a) rather long strophes with short rimed lines, (b) cadence melismas on one syllable, (c) abundant usage of the eighth note, (d) often rhythmically complex formations. None of his other songs is precisely in this style. But at least three tunes, all very likely written by Luther himself, belong to this style. This is most evident in "In Peace and Joy I Now Depart." Probably one of the most difficult in the entire hymnbook, this tune, with the exception of *Sie ist mir lieb*, is the most difficult Luther melody. Even the new *Evangelisches Kirchengesangbuch* (EKG) does not present its original version. And yet this version, simplified for practical use, is more difficult than the original form of "A Mighty Fortress Is Our God." I doubt that the hymn with this tune has ever been a part of the active repertoire of any singing congregation. Valuable as this song may be, I do not think it could be appropriated by any congregation today. Even "A Mighty Fortress Is Our God" has not remained untouched by this style; only here its elements are melted down into a tune which is more completely adjusted to congregational style. These elements (of the court style) prevent this tune from becoming full of pathos, keep it in balanced control. They are placed so carefully, however, that they do not pull the tune away from the congregation. In my opinion, a congregation that usually sings the original version of the Reformation chorales, can sing the original version of "A Mighty Fortress" without any, or with only a little, effort; it will profit thereby considerably. Because of its court-tune style this tune is one of our most lively ones; its well-balanced vivacity makes it simply a supratemporal creation.

In Protestant church music of the Reformation period the court-tune style is joined by quite a different style, one that is not much younger but much more "modern." Although the society songs still have a Gothic quality particularly in their polyphonic settings, the tunes and settings of the other group have a Renaissance-like plainness and simplicity. As a part of its revival of antiquity, the Renaissance intended to renew music according to the ancient artistic sources. Thus the composition of odes originated; in shaping these melodies, metrically long and short syllable values of the Latin texts were reproduced by corresponding note values; ode composition helped to originate the cantional style. For in liturgical music these endeavors resulted in a disuse of the ornate *concentus* and an increased use of the simple *accentus*. Thus in his proposal for a temporary change of the Mass according to a Protestant point of view (*De canone missae epichiresis* of Aug. 29, 1523), the Christian humanist Zwingli retained for the present certain choral songs which did not contradict the Word of God. He asked of the Gradual only that it *ad breviorem mensuram notarum stringatur*, while he rejected Sequences completely as *aniles fabulae et rhythmi inurbanissimi*.[12] The plain syllabic medieval *cantio* and the syllabic *hymnus* came to comply with these efforts. The simplest folk tunes pointed in the same direction. Thus Luther stripped hymn tunes of their traditional melismas and adjusted the number of their notes to the number of syllables ("Now Praise We Christ, the Holy One"; "Come Holy Ghost, Creator Blest"). With the help of hymn tunes he created simple and new tunes ("Savior of the Nations, Come"; "Peace in Our Time, Lord God, Bestow"; "Lord Keep Us Steadfast in Thy Word"). Zwingli proceeded similarly when he gave his short song of supplication ("Guide, O Lord, Thy Chariot Now") a simpler tune adequate for group singing among the soldiers. The tune is syllabic with exception of the melisma that extends the 2-syllable fourth line and a passing tone in the fifth line. At two places in one stanza a short syllable is represented by a corresponding note value in a striking fashion, a typically humanistic trait not found in Luther. The changes in the succession of long-short values at the end of the first and last lines can be understood only in this way and not as hemiolas (the first syllable of *Wagen, Namen,* and *freventlich* is short in the East Swiss dialect!). In neither Luther nor Zwingli does the simple ever show a trend toward the trivial, as it does whenever rationalism tries to be simple and folklike. Here, too, it is true that limitations reveal true masters. Even these simple song formations are artfully constructed. For Luther one need only think of the agreement between the first and the last line of the melody in "Savior of the Nations, Come," something of which the ordinary singer is hardly aware, or of the rich word-tone relationship in "From Heaven Above" (second melody, 1539); as for Zwingli, one need only think of the extremely artistic yet unaffected rhyme structure of the Kappel Song, or of the brilliant rounding off of the entire song by contrasting the first line of the melody with the last.

One could forget all these accordances between Luther and Zwingli and only point to the fact that we are dealing with obvious things: both hymn writers are contemporaries who come from two corners of the same cultural area.

Less obvious are the accordances that result from an investigation of the *origin* of the comparable hymns of the two reformers. In both cases we meet with the same juxtaposition of striking biographical background and practical motivation, where the latter seems to be subordinate to the former.

Luther's freely composed hymns owe their origin to certain historical events that can be very distinctly defined; since this is all well known, no detailed discussion seems to be called for. Not only do Luther's hymns fill an entire hymnbook, but his life can be described very clearly by means of his hymns.[13] A striking parallel to this is seen in the fact that Zwingli's first two biographers, the parson and chronicler Johannes Stumpf and Zwingli's successor in Zurich, Heinrich Bullinger, used the Pestilence Song and the Kappel Song to illustrate their biographical descriptions.[14] It is true, just in this matter the statements of the oldest biographers require careful examination. But from it we learn that Zwingli could not possibly have written the Pestilence Song during or right after his illness in the pest of 1519. Arthur Rich has proved [15] — what hymnology since then has constantly overlooked — that the Pestilence Song could not have originated before the middle of 1520, for only then did a change in Zwingli's thinking occur. This song is one of many evidences of this change from an Erasmus-like Christian humanism to a reformed faith. This change in his thinking does not stand in any proven casual connection with his illness in the plague. On the contrary, it is Zwingli's poetic freedom that makes him represent this inner event under the image of that external occurrence. Nothing forces us to date the poem for those days when the new knowledge first dawned on Zwingli. Indeed, we think it even completely impossible that this kind of mature knowledge could have come to him by then. It is much more likely that a certain time interval between the events of 1519/20 and a new situation of suffering were needed to bring forth the merging of the sickness experience in the plague and the new knowledge that arose half a year later. This new situation of suffering which wrested from the reformer the impassioned plea that he represents as the prayer of the sick may have been the 1525/6 struggle over the reorganization of the church. We would like to date the origin of the song at this time. We should note, too, that the hymn based on Psalm 69 is so close to the Pestilence Song in form and content that we have to assign it to the same time. Since its form shows a little less skill, we feel urged to assume that it may have originated shortly before the Pestilence Song. In his seminar for the clergy (*Prophezei*) Zwingli was at this very time expounding the Psalms. There is such a close relationship between the notes for his lectures on the Psalms in the *Prophezei* and his work of psalm rhyming that we must assign them to the same time. It seems that during his preoccupation with the Psalms Zwingli discovered that Psalm 69 was of great importance as the expression of his own faith. This prompted him to recreate this psalm in rhymed verse. A further attempt in the same direction produced the freely created Pestilence Song.

The parallel that we find in the origins of Luther's first hymns can only support these assumptions. When two Flemish monks were burned at the stake in Brussels, Luther's singer's tongue was loosed

in "By Help of God I Fain Would Tell." Thereupon he composed
a second hymn that presents his reformatory insight in the form of
autobiographical poetry. Here, too, the biographical element is only
a pretext as it were. (The important thing is to give expression to the
relationship between Christ and his servant.) A significant difference
between "Dear Christians, One and All, Rejoice" and Zwingli's Pestilence Song is that in Luther's hymn Christ addresses despairing man;
Zwingli, on the contrary, expresses his thoughts in the form of a prayer
that despairing man addresses to Christ.

Zwingli's Kappel Song must also have originated around that
time. Internal evidence shows that it cannot possibly have been conceived, as the biographers maintain, in the camp near Kappel in 1529.
Zwingli would not have said in those days *Herr, nun heb den Wagen
selb! Schelb wird suscht all unser Fahrt* ("Guide, O Lord, Thy chariot
now, Or our cause will surely fail"). But if the song was already in
existence at this time, the second and third stanzas lent themselves
very conveniently to being sung by the soldiers from Zurich encamped
before the city of Kappel. In form and content, though with an older
tune, this third song stands so close to the other two songs that we are
almost forced to date it at the same time — around 1525/6. We need
only compare — this one example might suffice — the beginning of the
hymn based on Psalm 69 *(Hilf, Gott, das Wasser geht mir bis an
d'Seel)* with the beginning of the Pestilence Song *(Hilf, Herr Gott,
hilf in dieser Not)* and with the acrostic of the Kappel Song *(Herr
Gott, hilf.)* The growing antagonism of some of his friends, who were
turning more and more toward the radicalism of the Anabaptists, gave
Zwingli a great deal of trouble from 1523 to 1526. The return to the
old loyalty for which he pleads in the third stanza of the song that
was later sung near the city of Kappel may refer to the state of unity
with these friends and fellow combatants of former times. Only later
was it used to refer to the old Helvetic loyalty that was so much endangered in the struggles for the new faith.

In a surprisingly similar fashion Luther's "A Mighty Fortress Is
Our God" leaves the matter open as to who the "enemy" is. An un-
told amount of material has been written around the riddle of this
question. Naturally the first application was to the pope and the entire Roman Church, particularly when the song was dated around
1521 and connected with Worms. In more recent times G. Wolfram [16]
has opposed this conception. He connects the hymn with the Turk-
ish menace of 1529 and adduces parallels from two pertinent works

of Luther. But here, too, the solution does not nearly come out as even as the author imagines. As far as I know, the most recent suggestion in this matter is that of W. Stapel.[17] His statements in connection with this discussion are not without irony. In the introduction to Luther's pamphlet against Carlstadt, Zwingli, Oecolampadius, etc. ("That These Words of Christ, 'This Is My Body, etc.,' Still Stand Firm Against the Enthusiasts," January to March 1527) Stapel finds a quotation similar to the first stanza of this hymn, and he immediately concludes: "Thus it appears certain to me that the hymn originated in Luther's fight with the *Schwarmgeister,* whom he always described as possessed and driven by the devil. . . . It is therefore not directed against the Roman Church but against the rationalists." If this is correct, all those who had the hymn sung on the occasion of Zwingli's anniversaries and festivals would have to blush! In reality we do not know and we will never know exactly when (it must have been in 1527 or 1528) Luther wrote the hymn down in its present form and released it to be printed. Therefore we do not know which of the dangers threatening him and the church at that time was in the foreground of his thinking. I do not think it necessary to know this either. In spite of all sturdy concreteness the words of the hymn are kept in such general terms that they admit different interpretations. Luther himself may not have interpreted them always in exactly the same fashion. We discover quite often that a sentence usually applied to a specific situation can be declared valid in another, completely different context. It is not completely impossible that when Luther wrote this hymn or one of its stanzas, he was on occasion thinking also of Zwingli. This would have a noteworthy parallel in that Zwingli, while writing *his* Reformation song, would have thought of those people who meant for him — *mutatis mutandis* — what he meant for Luther, that is, left-wingers or extremists.

Another conjecture may be added in this connection. Various reasons have led us to the conclusion that Zwingli's Kapell Song originated in 1525/6, that it was taken up again with some changed meaning in 1529, and that its melody was also altered on this occasion. Should we not reckon with a similar procedure for Luther's Reformation hymn? On the basis of Spitta's and Stuhlfauth's observations, I once asked [18] whether one ought not to assume that this hymn was composed by stages during the time of the plague of 1527. I have sung and thought through the hymn repeatedly since then and have again and again become aware of a certain lack of unity. In disagreement with the two authors mentioned above, I would today prefer no longer to speak of three stages in the composition of this hymn by Luther, but of only two. The first three stanzas form a unit, after all. These stanzas talk about the devil, the Christians attacked by him, and about the consolation for them. The first and the third stanza correspond exactly: the *Stollen* speaks of our Shield and of the confidence which we have in it, while the *Abgesang* describes the enemy ("The old evil foe" and "This world's prince" occur at exactly the same place in the stanza!). The first stanza concludes by pointing to the fact that one has to take this enemy seriously; the third stanza insists that it is easy to fell him if one provides himself with the right kind of help. The middle stanza forms a contrast to the contents of the external stanzas in an extraordinarily artful fashion: while the first half of each of the external stanzas talks always of our strength (which we have, thanks to Christ), the first half of the contrasting stanzas refers to our lack of power (without Him); while the second half of each of the external stanzas describes the devil and his power, the corresponding half of the contrasting stanza refers to Christ and His sovereignty. It is hard to imagine anything more perfect than this tripartite composition. Around the turn of the 16th century, the preferred number of stanzas was three. (The number of polyphonic settings in three parts of the late Middle Ages agrees with this; only with the Renaissance did 4-part writing gain that canonic standing still characteristic of it today.) One needs to take a good look at the number of stanzas in Luther's hymns (in the last column of the chart above). Of the 33 hymns with more than one stanza, exactly one third have three stanzas. This is no more a coincidence than the fact that of the three preserved hymns of Zwingli two have three stanzas. Luther has no hymns at all with two stanzas. There are three Luther hymns which have four stanzas; however, the Pentecost *Leise* likewise shows a ternary structure in that Luther interprets the traditional first stanzas as an introduction followed by the prayer in three new stanzas. These three stanzas are connected with one another by means of an analogous design *(Du wertes Licht, Du süsse Lieb, Du höchster Tröster;* in addition, the third line always begins with *dass).* Of all the remaining hymns by Luther, only seven indicate an even number of stanzas. For the longer hymn on the Ten Commandments the even number consists of the number of the commandments, plus two frame stanzas. The number of stanzas in the two Christmas hymns was based on the Latin model, from which one could separate the doxology

(7+1). Only hymns with an odd number of stanzas have a middle stanza. It becomes conspicuous that in Luther's hymns the middle stanza quite often contains the main message, even in hymns not organized on a Trinitarian basis, where the middle stanza is automatically the Christological one. Take, for instance, the baptismal hymn. Here the middle stanza contains the main message to such an extent that we might take it for the entire hymn. It speaks of Christ in an accentuated way: "Also God's Son Himself here stands." The same can be said of the middle stanza in the first part of "From Heaven Above": "This is the Christ, our God and Lord." In the Christmas *Leise* the entire structure is symmetrical. The first and last, second and sixth, third and fifth stanzas correspond to one another; but the middle stanza contains the real message:

> Thou comest in the darksome night
> To make us children of the light,
> To make us in the realms divine,
> Like Thine own angels, round Thee shine.

Even in the hymn based on Psalm 130, the contents and form of which were taken from the psalm model, Luther arranged to have the middle stanza be the pivot point of the entire hymn. In this stanza the tone changes from distress to joyfulness. Such, we assume, is the case also with the original 3-stanza form of "A Mighty Fortress Is Our God." The middle stanza brings the main message and the name of Jesus Christ. A comparison with the psalm on which the hymn is based leads to the same result; the first three stanzas agree with the first three verses of the Biblical model, while the fourth stanza extracts hardly anything from the Biblical text. The fourth stanza must have been added later. Here "the old evil foe," "this world's prince," no longer occurs in the singular, so that we are uncertain as to which secular power is meant. But there is a group ("they") about which the poet makes very concrete statements. These enemies will not let God's Word stand, and on top of it all they want to be thanked for their efforts. They do everything possible to take the life, the possessions, the honor, and the family of their adversaries. Here the Schwärmer have to be eliminated. Although, according to Luther's opinion, they did not let the Word stand as it was written, they did not proceed with brutal force. On the contrary, the Romans or the Turks are very much in question. Indeed, this stanza — in contrast to the first three stanzas — can be understood only against the contemporary background of this double menace which threatened the

Christians of Germany. An application of this stanza to modern times does not come off well. Only with some effort can it be applied to the menace of Communism that threatens Christianity. Add to this that the pathos of this stanza ("And take they our life . . . Let these all be gone") gives rise to not unjustified scruples in the minds of the congregations that sing it. (With good reason Switzerland discarded a national anthem that contained similar exaggerations.) It is worth noting that in the fourth stanza of the original text the word-tone relationship at the beginning of the *Abgesang* is not as felicitous as in the corresponding places of the first three stanzas (the second syllable of *nehmen* being stressed by the melisma). In view of these considerations, would it be a sacrilege to suggest the elimination of this stanza in our hymnals and the restoration of the text in its conjectural original form? Of course, one can only conjecture why Luther added this fourth stanza. It is possible that originally he did not intend this personal song to be released for congregational singing, but when it was released, he added this stanza as Zwingli must have given another tune to his song under the same circumstances. Perhaps with this in mind, the title can also be explained. The song is not, of course, a rhymed version of Psalm 46. But perhaps the title was to show that the song, like others based on the Bible or the church's traditional, was useful liturgically.

 Thus we have arrived at the question that cannot be answered easily: What purpose did both our reformers have in mind when they wrote their hymns? It cannot be overlooked that Luther is a creator not only of strictly liturgical hymns. If the customary chronological order of his hymns is correct, his first creations ("By Help of God I Fain Would Tell" and "Dear Christians, One and All, Rejoice") were not originally liturgical hymns; neither were his later hymns. "Lord, Keep Us Steadfast" is a children's song; "From Heaven Above" is intended for Christmas celebrations in the home; "I Love Her Dearly" is a solo song in form and a personal song of faith in content. And in spite of the "we" style and the original title, "A Mighty Fortress Is Our God" (exactly like Zwingli's "Guide, O Lord, Thy Chariot Now") is, we now discover, a very personal hymn of consolation and trust. We set up mental blocks for ourselves against these hymns when we try to see them as roaring congregational chorales of a warlike multitude of Protestants — here of Lutheran, there of Zwinglian, persuasion. First of all, we have to see in both songs men charged with a responsibility that goes beyond human strength, men who struggle on their knees in the hour of dark temptation: Luther with the words of the divine promise of the Bible on his lips, Zwingli in suppliant prayer.

Contrary to common assertion, the martial character is not the chief content and concern of Luther's and Zwingli's so-called Reformation hymns. The term *Trutzlied* ("hymn of defiance") is, to say the least, easily misunderstood. The questionable use of Luther's hymn in the last two world wars makes even a non-German ashamed to talk about it *in extenso*. This approach hinders the comprehension of these songs in no small degree. Even W. Stapel, who otherwise has a sensitive ear, speaks [19] of a "battle hymn." To be sure, weapons, the enemy, fighting, and the battlefield are mentioned. But these are images that continue to develop the Psalter's picture of a fortress. The last stanza may mislead us to apply this fight to the confessional or ideological, or perhaps even to the physical, encounter. But I dare to assert that the first three stanzas contain nothing of this. Only the personal struggle is their subject matter. Not a word is wasted in describing the struggle; it is dealt with in pictorial and general terms. Luther shows clearly where our help lies in times of trial, namely, in our trust; he also indicates what we cannot and should not rely on. In my opinion, nearly the whole of Luther's theology of trial, as written by Paul Bühler, could be developed on the basis of this hymn.[20] The hymn is not directed against the Roman Church. It does not belong among the "Reformation songs" of the hymnbook (a doubtful section anyway!). It belongs among the hymns of consolation and trust,[21] and it belongs there at the beginning — whether one arranges the hymns in a chronological or topical order. It outweighs a dozen Pietistic hymns of consolation and trust because it gives witness to the fighting trust. As far as heaven is from earth, so far is this hymn removed from all the stoic influences that manage to assert themselves so brazenly and deceptively in this section of the hymnal, disguised in the cloak of Christian behavior.

That Luther starts from a psalm when he wants to sing of the victorious battle in times of trial must not surprise us, for the Psalter became comprehensible to him only in such a time.[22] Zwingli likewise chose the Psalter in times of trial. It is obviously no coincidence that he set into rhyme Psalm 69, the song of a person in time of trial.

That Luther's personal hymn of consolation and trust could — legitimately — become a congregational hymn is due to Luther's understanding of the struggle in times of trial as a struggle in the company of saints. To be sure, he does not talk of this expressly in the hymn; however, he did write this personal hymn in the first person plural.[23] With this he takes into account the second stanza of the psalm in Hebrew (vv. 5-8), which speaks of the city of God. This city with all its streams is to remain joyful because God sustains it in trial. In his pamphlet against "A Mighty Fortress Is Our God," the Jesuit Hartmann Grisar calls to our attention that Psalm 46 "was always a favorite in the Catholic liturgy as a prayer of need, addressed to the divine Helper in time of affliction. Even today it is prescribed to be used by the clergy in difficult times of the church." [24] Luther must have seen the psalm in this light also. With his personal trials he turned to the church and found consolation and security there, and on the other hand the trials which, amid the intellectual conflict, threatened the Protestant church had a way of becoming his own personal trials.

The beginning of Zwingli's hymn,[25] "Guide, O Lord, Thy chariot now, Or our cause will surely fail," is an exact parallel to "With might of ours can naught be done, Soon were our loss effected." No fighting spirit is evident here. By human standards, only hopelessness is apparent. Only one thing will help; the Lord Himself must interfere! "God, exalt Thy holy name!" — "Of Sabaoth Lord, And there's none other God!"

Luther's "Children's Song Against the Two Archenemies of Christ and His Holy Church — the Pope and the Turk" corresponds even more closely to the Kappel Song. Although it is completely impossible that Luther even remotely knew Zwingli's hymn, the train of thought in the two songs is the same, down to details. In the first stanza the supplication for God's assistance is presented. Only this assistance of God (that He may keep us in His Word) can do something against the enemies of God and of His church who would like to dethrone Christ, against the *Widerpart, der dich veracht so freventlich* ("the enemies" who "blaspheme Thy holy name"). In the second stanza the supplication for protection against external dangers follows: *Beschirm dein arme Christenheit* ("Protect Thy Christendom") — *Wehr und straf der Bösen Grimm* ("By destruction of their work"). In Luther's hymn, which is arranged according to the Trinity, this is the Christ stanza. Zwingli must have thought of Christ here also, for he sings: *Weck die Schaf mit deiner Stimm, die dich lieb haben inniglich* ("Strengthen us so we'll not shirk To defend Thy holy name"), John 10:4, 27. The third stanza concludes with the supplication for unity within. With the "old loyalty," for the return of which the prayer asks, Zwingli does not mean loyalty to God but the trust and love of Christians to one another, the "peace and unity" that God is asked to give to His people already here on earth. Both poems terminate with an outlook toward eternal life. A purer unison of completely independent voices can hardly be imagined! Is this concord between brothers then separated not an ecumenical sign? Is this not already an answer to the supplication in both third stanzas?

Both these hymns are Reformation hymns more than "A Mighty Fortress Is Our God." Yet they, too, are not battle songs, in spite of the original second line in Luther's song ("And curb the Turks' and papists' sword"). They contain the supplication of ecumenical unity so necessary at Reformation festivals in our own day. Since Pope Paul VI at the beginning of the second session of Vatican II — though in a very muffled tone — asked for pardon for the injustice his church may have done to other Christians, we have double reason, precisely on Reformation Day, to join in Luther's and Zwingli's petition for the unity of the church of Jesus Christ here on earth and for the return and renewal of the "old loyalty."

NOTES FOR CHAPTER 6

1. It is a well-known fact that Calvin obeyed necessity and not his own impulse when he in 1539 set into rhyme five psalms, the *Canticum Simeonis*, and the Ten Commandments and used melodies which were sung in Strasbourg. But those poems were immediately superseded by those of Clément Marot. Already in 1542 the first Geneva edition no longer contains a piece by Calvin; Calvin's rhymes maintained themselves for a while only in the tradition of the French-speaking congregation in Strasbourg. The only thing which church music of today owes to Calvin (with exception of the "idea" of the full Psalter as a congregational hymnbook) is the use of the tune of Greitter's Psalm 119 (*Es sind doch selig alle die*) for Psalm 36. In this single case Marot did keep for his poem the meter chosen by Calvin. Thus this tune from Strasbourg moved over, almost without any change, into the definitive edition of the Geneva Psalter, where Beza used it still later also for Psalm 68. In this specific combination of word and melody the tune was to become known in the 18th century as the "Marseillaise of the Huguenots" — for the French-speaking Protestants what "A Mighty Fortress" was for the Lutherans.

2. Both hymns can be found today in the German-Swiss hymnbook. The DEG (German Evangelical Hymnbook) had allotted space to the Kappel Song; the EKG (Evangelical Hymnbook) unfortunately does not include it but relegates it to the appendixes of certain provincial editions. With regret we must consider this an act of retrocession. Following in Spitta's footsteps, the new Alsatian Lutheran Hymnbook again included the hymn. Spitta had raised it to honor in his hymnbook of 1899. Before Spitta, Ebrard had taken it up in his Palatinate hymnbook. However, it did not have a tune of its own. Outside

16th-century Switzerland the Kappel Song was printed only occasionally in hymnbooks of the Palatinate, Strasbourg, and Bonn. As far as I know, the Pestilence Song did not spread beyond Switzerland at all (exception: the prayer appendix of the Frankfort hymnbook of 1928), neither did the hymn on Psalm 69, which in Switzerland, too, was even less common than the Pestilence Song. Only these two hymns by Zwingli have been translated into English. The Kappel Song is in *The Hymnal* of the Reformed Church (Philadelphia, 1927), No. 605. The Pestilence Song is in Oskar Farner, *Zwingli, the Reformer: His Life and Work*, trans. D. G. Sear (New York, 1952), pp. 35—37. For this information I am indebted to Dr. Armin Haeussler, Glenview, Ill.

3. A critical edition of Zwingli's hymns is unfortunately still lacking. I hope to be able to publish such an edition in the near future. Concerning the Pestilence Song and Psalm 69, consult for the time being the advance publication from my edition in H. Reimann, "Zwingli, der Musiker," *Archiv für Musikwissenschaft*, 1960, pp. 132—135. It is also printed in the 144th *Neujahrsblatt der Allgemeinen Musikgesellschaft* (Zurich, 1960), pp. 8—13. For the Kappel Song, see the reprint of the text of Wackernagel and at many other places and *Zwingliana*, XI, 181 (the distribution of the text as it is indicated here is the only correct one). As far as the question of further lost hymns of Zwingli is concerned, consult Zwingli's works, XI, 163, 7—9, and 316, 13—15 (Capito's letters to Zwingli). The other tunes I would like to ascribe to him are those of Nos. 10, 31, and 45 in my *Geschichte des deutschschweizerischen evangelischen Gesangbuches im 16. Jahrhundert* (Basel, 1962).

4. It seems that the Easter *Leise*, of which no earlier version is known, is an exception. I am, however, convinced that Luther, even here, used an earlier model that has not as yet been discovered and probably never will be.

5. I believe that Luther changed none of the *ordinarium* pieces into hymns. Luther's authorship of the *Gloria* hymn *All Ehr und Lob soll Gottes sein* must be denied for other reasons (see my *Geschichte d. deutschschweizerischen . . . Gesangbuches*, mentioned in n. 3 above, pp. 269 f., No. 250). But the liturgicomusical principle of Luther's noted here represents an additional support for denying the authorship referred to.

6. Zwingli's works, IV, 19.

7. H. J. Moser, "Der Zerbster Lutherfund," *Archiv für Musikwissenschaft*, II, 1920/1, 237 ff.

8. *Das Chorwerk*, Book 7 (Wolfenbüttel/Berlin, 1930), pp. 6 f., measures 55—66.

9. Available in many practical editions, for instance, *Gesellige Zeit*, I (Kassel, 1933), No. 49.

10. Cf. for the time being E. Egli, *Analecta Reformatoria*, I (Zurich, 1899), 108.

11. Cf. M. Jenny, "Zwinglis mehrstimmige Kompositionen," *Zwingliana*, XI, 164 182.

12. Zwingli's works, II, 602, 13 f., and 603, 7 f.

13. Cf. J. Kulp, *Luthers Leben im Spiegel seiner Lieder*. Welt des Gesangbuches, Book 3 (Leipzig and Hamburg, 1935).

14. J. Stumpf, *Chronica vom Leben und Wirken des Ulrich Zwingli*, 2d ed. (Zurich, 1932), 19 f., 145. *Heinrich Bullingers Reformationsgeschichte* (Frauenfeld, 1838 and 1840), I, 28 f.; II, 182.

15. A. Rich, *Die Anfänge der Theologie Huldrych Zwinglis* (Zurich, 1949).

16. G. Wolfram, *Ein feste Burg ist unser Gott. Die Entstehungszeit und der ursprüngliche Sinn des Lutherliedes* (Berlin and Leipzig, 1936).

17. W. Stapel, *Luthers Lieder und Gedichte* (Stuttgart, 1950), p. 214.

18. *Geschichte des deutschschweizerischen evangelischen Gesangbuches im 16. Jahrhundert* (Basel, 1962), p. 186.

19. Stapel, p. 214.

20. P. Bühler, *Die Anfechtung bei Martin Luther* (Zurich, 1942). *Ein feste Burg* is quoted only once (p. 78)!

21. H. Steinlein, "Zur neuesten Aussprache über 'Ein feste Burg,'" *Theologische Blätter*, 1937, Cols. 101 ff., and *Der Kirchenchor* (Kassel, 1957), pp. 74 f.

22. Bühler, p. 203.

23. Bühler, pp. 148—178: "Die Kirche als Hilfe in der Anfechtung."

24. Hartmann Grisar, *Luthers Trutzlied "Ein feste Burg" in Vergangenheit und Gegenwart* (Freiburg i. B., 1922), p. 4.

25. The full text of Zwingli's Kappel Song, trans. and arr. by Henry C. Knott and George Stibitz, in *The Hymnal* (Philadelphia, 1927), No. 605:

Guide, O Lord, Thy chariot now,   God, exalt Thy holy name
Or our cause will surely fail,   By destruction of their work;
And our enemies prevail   Strengthen us so we'll not shirk
To blaspheme Thy holy name, Lord.   To defend Thy holy name, Lord.

Grant that all the bitterness
May depart from our fair land;
Let us all united stand
And bring praises to Thy name, Lord.

7

POLYPHONIC SETTINGS OF THE GENEVAN PSALTER: ARE THEY CHURCH MUSIC?

Pierre Pidoux

In the music encyclopedia *Musik in Geschichte und Gegenwart,* Vol. X, col. 1706, Ludwig Finscher writes on the subject of the polyphonic psalms of the 16th century:

> Titles and prefaces claim that even the motet settings of Bourgeois and Goudimel are intended for performances at home devotions. In the face of their technical requirements, this is, to say the least, doubtful. At the latest since about 1580, the infiltration of the motet and simple psalm settings into the Reformed Church in Switzerland must have taken place. The performance of the simple settings could be realized in such a way that the congregation sang the cantus firmus (in octaves corresponding to their natural vocal disposition), while a church choir or instrumentalists performed the remaining parts. For the motet settings the vocal or vocal-instrumental performance must have been rendered by professional church musicians employed for this specific purpose.

The purpose of our study is to demonstrate that these affirmations as well as hypotheses cannot be applied to the French-speaking churches, which originated through Calvin's reform movement. Our information is based essentially on the following works, almost all of which were published recently. Once again they have taken up the problem of the Reformed psalm singing. These are E. Nievergelt, *Die Tonsätze der deutschschweizerischen reformierten Kirchengesang-bücher im XVII. Jahrhundert* (Zurich, 1944); Markus Jenny, *Geschichte des deutschschweizerischen Gesangbuches im 16. Jahrhundert* (Basel: Bärenreiter-Verlag, 1962); Jacques Burdet, *La musique dans le Pays de Vaud sous le régime bernois,* 1536–1798 (Lausanne: Payot,

1963); P. Pidoux, *Le Psautier huguenot du XVIe siècle*, 2 vols. (Basel: Bärenreiter, 1962). In the framework of these few pages it is not possible to give references to these works in every case. The reader will either have to believe our statements or refer to these volumes.

Concerning music in the church, the Calvinistic doctrine is absolutely clear. It is found in Calvin's preface to the collection of essays "The Form of Prayers and Ecclesiastical Chants" of 1542, the preface he completed the following year for a new edition, as well as in some pages of the "Christian Institutions," particularly Book 3, Chapter 20, Sections 30 to 33. The doctrine consists of the unison singing of the Psalms by the entire congregation without accompaniment. Figural music performed by a choir school as well as the participation of instruments is excluded. Calvin answers those who cite the Old Covenant use of instruments thus: in those times the use of instruments was tolerated in the same fashion as one allows a toy to be used to retain the attention of children, but this is no longer valid, since the children have become adults (Calvin, *Commentaries on the Book of Psalms*, passim). Figural and polyphonic music has, above all, the defect of making the comprehension of the text difficult (a sufficient reason to restrict its usage). How could the simple worshiper answer Amen to a text he had not understood clearly? Since this music was executed by a choir, the worshiper was left entirely passive!

These two reasons, which belong together — we will see the specific importance of the second reason — justify for Calvin and his contemporaries the exclusion from the service of everything that risks being only "pleasure for the ears." The goal which Calvin pursued is clearly defined in the preface of 1542/43 — to make the active participation of the entire congregation possible in the course of the Protestant service. The chant must allow the congregation to become associated with the "public prayers." This will be done when the Psalms are sung, the Psalms being models of prayer. Just as the pastor *speaks* the prayer of invocation, of confession of sins, of supplication, in the name of the assembled congregation, the congregation sings the prayers of praise and thanksgiving in the form of the rimed (metrical) psalm, using the vernacular language to melodies "which have weight and majesty" and "which are appropriate to be sung in the church."

Since experience has shown that prayers spoken exclusively by the officiating clergy leave the faithful "cold," says Calvin, the psalm which is prayed by means of the song will stimulate "the ardor of praying"! This sung psalm is not an *ad libitum* element but an essential part of the service. Were it not there, the element of praise and of adoration would be absent in the service; and the whole assembly would be lowered to the simple role of an audience.

The role which this psalm singing should play is shown best by the fact that choosing them is not left up to the officiating clergy but is prescribed by a table (often printed in the psalters). We learn from this table that in Geneva all the Psalms, with all their stanzas, were sung in the course of 25 weeks, accompanying the different "sermons" which were given both on weekdays and Sundays. On the one hand, this says that the singing of the Psalms was autonomous, independent of the subject of the sermon, and on the other hand, that the liturgical function of the congregation had important consequences. It implied familiarity with the total output of texts and melodies of the Psalter (150 psalms were sung to 124 melodies), just as many for the common man of the congregation as for the college student, who had to guide the singing according to the directions of their cantor (precentor). Under the conditions of this evidence, the singing of the assembly could only be pure and simple unison! Before asking whether another form of execution would have been possible, we should ask how a congregation could measure up honorably to its liturgical — and musical — obligations, when its musical elements were a minority.

The melodies of the French Reformation are so well known that it will not be necessary to describe them. Let us reveal, however, that even though the 19th century found them gloomy and academic, this was in no way the opinion of the 16th century, which received them with a stupendous enthusiasm. The contemporaries were not satisfied with singing them in the churches; they sang them at their work, in the fields, on the streets, in their homes, and even in the cabarets — such is the price of popularity! But not only the common man received psalm melodies favorably; the average musician was by no means the last to sing and to play them. A sufficient proof of this would be to enumerate the list of compositions for various voices — compositions literally thrown on the market by music printers all through the 16th century. Not only their number is striking (the author of this article has found more than 1,200 in score!) but also the quality of the composers who write on these themes — let us quote at random Louis Bourgeois, Arcadelt, Certon, Jannequin, Jambe de Fer, Goudimel. All these compositions belong strictly to the repertoire of chamber music.

Not one of their authors ever dreamt that they could be sung in the church. Does this affirmation seem too categorical? It is necessary that we support our assertions with proof.

1. Excepting certain of the grand motets of Goudimel, in which the complete text of the psalm is set to music *(durchkomponiert)*, almost all the polyphonic compositions treat only the first stanza. They treat this first stanza in such a way that it is impossible to sing the text of the other stanzas to this music. Only the melody, which functions in the composition as a cantus firmus, can bear all the texts, but this implies an instrumental execution of the other parts. Since the liturgical utilization of the Psalter implies the singing of all the stanzas and since the Calvinistic doctrine excludes the utilization of instruments, it is difficult to see how these polyphonic compositions could have been utilized in the church!

2. No texts in the archives prior to the 18th century, and no testimonies of contemporaries, make the slightest allusion to the liturgical performance of the psalm written for various voices. When the students of the College of Geneva took the risk of singing "in parts" — at the occasion of the visit of some notable at the time of school festivals, or at a theatrical presentation — they did not sing psalms but performed works fit for the occasion, generally of a very elementary musical style of writing; just look at the musical intermezzi of the "Tragédies Saintes" by Des Masures (Geneva, 1566)! Moreover, even if they had wanted to sing the Psalms "in parts," it is difficult to see how they could have performed compositions that call for *Bass* and *Tenor* (and sometimes *Contra*) parts written for changed voices. The collegians would have sung the *Superius* only, and sometimes the *Contra*, which were generally accompaniment parts and not bearers of the traditional melody. Where would the men's voices necessary to balance the considerable group of sopranos have come from?

Until a formal and material proof of the contrary can be given, one is thus led to admit that the polyphonic psalms served exclusively "at home" for the recreation and edification of musicians. We are astonished today when we realize what people were capable of in the 16th century. Often the compositions provided for singers and musicians present very serious difficulties; nevertheless, the abundance of the publications provided for them forces us to admit that in spite of these difficulties these works were executed frequently, otherwise the editors' reason for printing them is not to be understood.

These editors came mainly from Paris, Lyon, and Antwerp in good part because music printing required workshops and specialized composer-typographers. This does not stem from a prohibition imposed on the Geneva printers to keep them from publishing psalters for several voices! In Geneva in the middle of the 16th century there was only one single printer able to launch himself into this kind of printing — still with rather primitive apparatus — Simon du Bosc, who published a series of motets in French as well as in Latin, plus the grand psalms of Goudimel, between 1554 and 1556. If such publications were authorized in Geneva (among them Latin motets by Clemens non Papa!), it is difficult to imagine that it might have been forbidden for the Genevans to sing motets on Biblical texts in French prose by François Gindron or those by Barthélémy Le Bel and Claude Goudimel on the texts of Marot's Psalter, all of which came off Du Bosc's press in Geneva. This point has been withheld, but it has its significance; it proves that neither the authorities of the city nor Calvin personally had any objection to the part singing of religious works in the homes. Accordingly, we may get along without the theory advanced by A. E. Cherbuliez (*Die Schweiz in der deutschen Musikgeschichte*, Frauenfeld/Leipzig, 1932, p. 197), which states that the publication of Goudimel's psalms for four voices (Geneva, 1565) by the heirs of François Jaqui would not have been possible at this date since Calvin had died in the preceding year!

We have sketched the chronology of some of the editions of the psalters of Goudimel (*Revue de Musicologie*, Paris, December 1958, Vol. XLII), and we have tried to show that the Jaqui edition which became so famous was indeed only a Genevan reprint of the Parisian editions of Le Roy and Ballard of 1564 and 1565. Let us here briefly recall the contents of these publications. Goudimel offers the musicians two types of compositions: (1) for each of the 125 melodies a note-against-note harmonization of easy execution, (2) for those of the melodies which are employed repeatedly, compositions with a more embellished style that admits thematic imitations, passing notes, and a declamation of a text independent in every voice; in other words, music which is difficult to perform.

The first Parisian edition, in four booklets (one per part), gave only some stanzas of the text, and a space was left empty to be filled with the musical notation. The second Parisian edition constituted an important supplement as a continuation of the tenor booklet, since it gave the remaining stanzas which had not found a place under the music. The originality of Jaqui's re-edition consisted, on the one hand, of putting together in one small volume the four voices which Paris offered in separate booklets, and on the other hand, of printing the complete text in its proper place. To this should be added that Jaqui included in his psalter (at least in a certain number of copies which are known to us) the "form of the prayers" and the "catechism" used in the church of Geneva, that is, the texts which the worshipers usually found in the collections of one-voice melodies, which they took with them in order to participate in the Sunday service. This psalter, made complete by its appendixes, thus could be used like the one in the church. Would the faithful then begin to sing "in parts" at the public service? In order to remove any temptation, the printers printed an important prefatory note on top of their publication:

> We have added three parts to the psalm tunes in this volume: not that they may be sung thus in the church, but that they may be used to rejoice in God particularly in the homes. The one part which should not be at fault, inasmuch as it is the tune used in the church, remains in its entirety as if it were the only part.

There are many reasons for believing that the author of this note to the reader is the Genevan printer and not Goudimel; moreover, it may be asked: did Goudimel not know of this Genevan reprint of his work, and was it not made with the consent of the Parisian editors Le Roy and Ballard? In any case the intention of the printers is clear: if this little book can be used at the service (to sing there in unison), it is above all destined to be utilized "particularly in the homes," that is to say, "in private." One should understand the word *particularly* in its ancient meaning "privately" and not in the modern meaning of "especially."

Observe that a notice of the same kind, expressed in almost the same terms, figures in two other psalm collections for four voices written in a strict note-against-note style. That of Richard Crassot (Lyon, 1564) says: "You will be admonished (benign readers) that the part which one sings in church remains pure in its entirety." That of Hugues Sureau (1565) says: "You will be admonished, dear reader, that the part which one usually sings in church is here guarded (kept) in its entirety." In his preface the same Sureau recommends his work when he writes: "You have, then, what seems to be sufficient to give honest contentment to the Christians who will help themselves with this book, bringing it to the general assemblies, and singing [the

Psalms] according to the customary fashion as well as using it for private enjoyment."

Since the three compositions we quoted above include all the texts of all the psalms, with the melodies strictly conforming to the ecclesiastical usage, it is not pure coincidence that makes the users of these volumes avoid the temptation of singing in church any other part but "the usual chant!"

Curiously enough, none of these homophonic versions, although very simply executed, seem to have enjoyed what today one would call a bookstore success. The only version which caught the public eye was that of Goudimel, but as a result of events that we are going to sketch briefly. If one consults the bibliography of editions of the Reformed psalter as presented by O. Douen in the second volume of his work on *Clement Marot and the Huguenot Psalter* (Paris, 1878/9), one finds that the "Goudimel-Jaqui" was not reprinted in the 16th century. Douen cites two editions of psalms for four voices by Goudimel (which he has not seen and which no one seems ever to have found?). These appeared in Charenton in 1607 and Delft in 1608. Were these editions reprints of the Jaqui edition? What is significant in Douen's work, however, is that between 1601 and 1664 he lists 13 editions of 4- and 5-part settings by Claude Le Jeune! Thus it seems that singers favored the more modern, more poetic, but often more difficult harmonies of this composer.

It was quite a different matter in German countries. Translated into German by Ambrosius Lobwasser, Marot's and Beza's psalms appeared in Leipzig in 1573 with the Goudimel-Jaqui harmonies. This was a stupendous success. These "German" psalms spread very fast in German Switzerland, but not without becoming modified in a very pronounced way; they were set according to the taste of the day or simply adapted to practical needs. The above quoted work by E. Nievergelt gives a very good survey of this evolution. Because of its consequences, the most important of all revisions was no doubt that of Joh. Ulrich Sultzberger, "director of music and cornet player of the venerable city of Bern." In 1675 he issued a Lobwasser edition for four voices (Goudimel is no longer mentioned!) in which he had "transposed" the original versions in order to print all of them for the same key — for reasons of simplification. For the same reason — and because the part best represented in congregations is the *Tenor* — he transferred to the *Tenor* all those melodies which in Goudimel had been in the *Superius* part. Finally, with the same perspective of simplification in mind, the embellished harmonizations were eliminated in favor of versions with note-against-note harmonizations.

In this form, which was no longer that of Goudimel but which still conserved its qualities (quality of harmony, natural bass leading, exactly correct rhythm . . .), the multiple editions of the *Transponiertes Psalmen-Buch* of Sultzberger were an enormous influence in German-speaking Switzerland. Through them the singing of four voices was progressively introduced in the Reformed churches. One of the main motives for organizing the *Collegia Musica* was the desire to sing these 4-part psalms. Groups of wind instruments were established for the accompaniment of the congregational singing before the organs, which the 16th century had driven out, made their return into the churches.

What happened in the French-speaking part of Switzerland during this time? When the first enthusiasm had gone, one usually sang the Psalms in unison. And this routine soon led the congregations to singing the melodies without regard for the strict notation of the original rhythm — as if they were dragging! All the notes were sung with an equal time duration, and this was called "singing the Psalms in *plain chant* fashion"! As for Goudimel's harmonizations, first they seem to have been eclipsed by Claude Le Jeune's settings, then later they were forgotten in general. But toward the middle of the 17th century a new movement came into being. In Geneva (1667, 1668, and 1690) editions by the printer from Tournes appeared which reproduce exactly the Jaqui edition of 1565, excluding the psalms written with an embellished counterpoint, to be sure. And in the Land of Vaud, which had belonged to Bern since 1536, the 4-part psalms were about to make their entrance — imitating what was done in German-speaking Switzerland and above all in Bern! In imitation of the *Collegia Musica,* "sacred music" societies were established that organized the amateurs who wanted to cultivate the singing of 4-part psalms before they were introduced into the church service; in the same way, as an imitation of what had happened in Bern, people were going to introduce groups of "church trumpets" and later, organs. For these different ensembles Goudimel editions in the Sultzberger version were going to appear with a French text! This "Sultzberger French" was constantly reprinted, first by the presses in Bern (1721, 1759, 1774), then in Lausanne (for the first time in 1777, then in 1801, 1803, 1812, 1818, 1824, 1829, 1850, and until 1862).

In Geneva and Neuchâtel the version of the printer from Tournes referred to above was reproduced during this time; it had six editions during one century, and the last edition known to us dates from 1755.

The reader will perhaps think all these publications mean that in the course of the 18th and, above all, in the 19th century the 4-part performance practice had progressively become the rule in the churches of French-speaking Switzerland. This was most certainly not the case, since during the 18th century there are almost 100 known editions of the Psalter with the melody only, these for French-speaking Switzerland alone! If, in the 19th century, the proportion of editions for four voices is a little greater, this does not prove that unison singing was not the rule and 4-part singing the exception. Harmony was given more and more to the organ; the organ replaced the groups of the "sacred music" societies and the "church trumpets." This leads us to the modern period. Since 1866 three collections — still called "psalters," although they contain a majority of canticles — show the strict 4-part harmonizations, which are presented in piano score with the melody in the soprano part. They always recommend: to be sung . . . in unison!

Why this long parenthesis on the singing of the worshipers in the course of the last centuries? Because it seems to us to be appropriate to confirm what we found already in the 16th century, that is, the persistence of unison singing in spite of attempts to install a general practice of 4-part harmonization. The Goudimel-Jaqui Psalter enjoyed popularity only in narrow circles, but it was not used by the people in the church. Does it, then, require long argumentation to show that polyphonic music of the 16th century had almost no chance of getting a hearing in French-speaking Switzerland that would have allowed it to come into the foreground? Once the 16th century had passed, all these marvelous compositions fell into a long uninterrupted slumber. Not until the publications of Henry Expert (1894, 1896, 1897), in his *Master Musicians of the French Renaissance*, did Goudimel's version of the embellished psalms reappear (that of 1568 and 1580). In 1935 a facsimile reproduction of the Jaqui edition of 1565 was issued by P. Pidoux and Konrad Ameln (Kassel: Bärenreiter); in 1953, a facsimile reproduction of the "150 Psalms" of P. de l'Estocart of 1583, by P. Pidoux and H. Holliger (Kassel: Bärenreiter); in 1962, a critical edition of the "24 Psalms" of Loys Bourgeois, 1547, by P. André Gaillard (Basel: Bärenreiter). Some rare isolated pieces have appeared in practical editions, but all the other great collections still await publication. The fact that these polyphonic compositions have never been reprinted since their original publication is the most evident proof that this kind of music has never been used in the worship service of the French-speaking Reformed congregations.

If we have not said anything in reference to France, no doubt the reader will have understood that it is because of historical circumstances (religious wars, persecutions, revocation of the Nantes edict, etc.) that the establishment of the Reformed Church and the creation of a continued liturgical tradition in France was hindered. Switzerland has not known any of the great revolutions that have endangered the existence of Reformed congregations. Her churches have been able to live a normal uninterrupted existence. Musical tradition of the French churches in Switzerland was not swayed violently from one side or from another. It seems to us, therefore, particularly significant in its evolution.

8

LEONHARD LECHNER IN HIS TIME

Konrad Ameln

I. NATIVE COUNTRY, LIFE, AND ENVIRONMENT

The life of the composer Leonhard Lechner began in Etschtal (South Tyrol), where he was born around 1553; it ended in Stuttgart in 1606. Little is known about his youth; we know neither the day nor the place of his birth, nor to which of the numerous families he belongs. The name Lechner or Lehner ("one that has an estate in fee") can be traced back to the 13th century in the German borderland at the upper Etsch. That Lechner came from there is proved beyond doubt by the designation *Athesinus,* which he always added to his signature and to his name on the title pages of his works.[1] It is not known where he went to school and where he obtained his first musical instruction. He himself reports only that he "had since his youth a great desire and inclination for music."[2] Probably he attended a Latin school and as a boy was a singer in the choir of a parish church; he distinguished himself by a beautiful voice and good musical talent. One of the agents sent out by the Bavarian court to hire singers for the court band conducted by Orlando di Lasso took note of him.[3] An entry in a book of accounts of 1570 indicates that he left the band of the successor to the throne at Landshut as a choirboy with a dismissal payment of 10 guilders. In the same year the band in Landshut was dissolved for reasons of economy; the dismissed choirboys were "sent to the monasteries" to obtain further education there. Lechner, however, apparently went his own ways;[4] he himself reports that he wandered far and wide through many different regions.[5] According to the fashion of traveling students, he probably attended higher schools of learning to continue his studies in composition.[6] During the years 1570–1575 he probably lived in Italy, too, for a time. He possessed a comprehensive knowledge of the repertory of Italian composers and even in his early works evidenced an unusual mastery of Italian composition technique and idiom.

What he learned at this time is evident in his first publication, *Motectae sacrae*, a collection of thirty-one 4-, 5-, 6- and 8-part Latin motets, which are at times rather extensive (preface dated Oct. 28, 1575). This collection at once placed him among the most important composers of his time. Like almost all the printed works of Lechner, this collection was published in Nuremberg, where he was active as a "school servant" (teacher) in the parish school of St. Lorenz since 1575. On Oct. 8, 1576, he married a daughter of a middle-class family of Nuremberg — Dorothea Lederer (b. 1549), the widow of the town piper Friderich Kast. He lived at St. Katharina, where at the end of December 1578, his only son Gabriel was born; the child was baptized on New Year's Day, 1579, at St. Lorenz Church.

We do not know anything about Lechner's activity as a teacher; he himself did not think very highly of it. This is confirmed by his remark [8] that he does not want to be regarded and judged as a school assistant but as a musician and composer; musical composition, he maintains, is the real substance of his life. In Nuremberg he had abundant opportunity to compose. For the "Musical Societies," to which councilmen and patricians belonged, he composed the 3-part *Newe teutsche Lieder . . . nach art der welschen Villanellen* (two parts 1576–77), the 4- and 5-part *Newe Teutsche Lieder* (1577), the 5-part *Newe Teutsche Lieder* on melodies of Jacob Regnart and three Italian madrigals (1579), and 5- and 4-part *Newe Teutsche Lieder* (1582), altogether 113 compositions, many of which are multisectional. He dedicated them to the leading members of the city council and obtained from them commissions for the composition of festival music. Thus, for instance, he composed music for the festival inauguration of the high school in Altdorf (1575), for the weddings of the Augsburg patrician Sebald Welser and of Joh. Christoph Gugel, son of a Nuremberg jurist (1582), and for that of the Coburg councilor Christoph Andreas Gugel (1583). In the dedication of a motet honoring Duke Joachim Ernst of Anhalt (1582) Lechner called himself *Archimusicus* of Nuremberg. The direction of the municipal musical culture was apparently connected with this title. Already in 1577 the council had given him the same salary as the cantor because he was "such a tremendous composer and musician." Nevertheless, the subordinate position of a school assistant was not sufficient for him. The bonds of relationship and friendship, even the feeling of gratitude for favors received could not keep him permanently in Nuremberg. The dedication of the motet honoring the duke of Anhalt and a letter of recommendation written by Lasso March 21, 1582, to Elector August I of Saxony, to whom Lechner had already dedicated a motet at an earlier time, show that he applied repeatedly for the position of court conductor. Upon the recommendation of the Nuremberger Dr. Dretzler (Drezel), who lived at the court of Hechingen as Count Eitel Friedrich von Hohenzollern's counselor and overseer, Lechner was invited there in the fall of 1583 and presented by the count with princely gifts. After he dedicated a collection, called *Liber missarum* (3 Masses and 10 Introit motets) and dated Jan. 1, 1584, to the count, the count employed him as court conductor.

Thus Lechner came to the court of a pomp-loving Renaissance prince and in the spring of 1584 assumed the direction of a court band which, although small, was capable of good performance. Jacob Meiland had organized this band in 1577 and conducted it half a year before his untimely death (Dec. 31, 1577). His successor was Johannes Nanquette (1578–1581). The years following that the bass singer Jacob Flori seems to have taken charge of the tasks of the *Kapellmeister*. Lechner's activity, which began under favorable omens, ended after little more than a year; in July 1585 he secretly left the Hohenzollern residence during the count's absence, having previously taken his wife and child to the safety of Nuremberg. First he fled to Tübingen. His reply to the count's letter calling him back was very bold and showed little respect. Lechner alluded to the weak power and the unpopularity of the count; he threatened to publish in a printed pamphlet all that had happened at the court of Hechingen and what had driven him away from the court. However, in this letter he does not mention the reason for his flight. Neither is the reason for the quarrel mentioned in the numerous letters the count addressed to the sovereigns of the surrounding territories as well as to the councils of Nuremberg and Ansbach, letters in which the count pressed for the capture and extradition of his runaway *Kapellmeister*. Lechner went to see Duke Ludwig of Württemberg. Although the Hohenzollern count had requested the duke not to support Lechner in any way nor to admit him into his court band, and, above all, to avoid everything which was directed against the count's "reputation," Ludwig protected the composer and supported his application for the position of conductor at the court of Electoral Saxony.

This failed since Lechner, because of the count's threats, did not dare to undertake the trip to Dresden to present himself in person. In his circular letter the count had called him a perjurer, slanderer, infamous calumniator, and "inexperienced schoolmaster from Nuremberg," whose excessive haughtiness and pride are much greater than his art; the elector would not gain anything, he warned, by employing him. Lechner had to consider himself lucky to find a modest living as a tenor in the court band of Stuttgart. Thanks to the benevolence of the duke, his family was united with him again, and the fight with the count of Hohenzollern was settled in an amicable way in January 1586; Lechner apologized to the count.

Many compositions originated in the following years; however, only a few of them appeared in print. We know of many of them only through entries in the court account books of the years 1586–1600. These certify that Lechner was paid "honoraria" of different amounts (from 6 to 20 guilders) for works which he had dedicated to the sovereign; the works themselves have been lost, with a few exceptions. The compositions which have come down to us are, however, so important that they must be considered the most valuable ones of his time. In print appeared: *Neue lustige Teutsche Lieder, nach Art der Welschen Canzonen, mit 4 Stimmen* (1586 and 1588), *Septem Psalmi Poenitentiales 6 vocibus compositi* (1587), *Neue Geistliche und Weltliche Teutsche Lieder mit 5 und 4 Stimmen* (1589), and two 6-part *Epitaphia* on the emperor Friedrich Barbarossa and his spouse Beatrix for an academic festivity (Tübingen, 1593). Also, a printed edition of Lechner's St. John Passion (Nuremberg, 1594) is listed in catalogs of masses, but no copy has come down to us. This important work, the most excellent in the history of the German motet passion, is transmitted to us in a manuscript choir book which is mentioned for the first time (1613) in the inventory of the court band of the landgrave of Hessen at Kassel.[9] Lechner's last compositions have been handed down to us in a posthumous manuscript of 1606, which was likewise found in the possession of the court band at Kassel. It contains among other compositions the two cycles of the *Hohelied Salomonis* and *Deutsche Sprüche von Leben und Tod* — song motets which represent the high point in the development of this genre.

Beginning in 1586, Lechner could call himself "Composer and Musician of the prince of Württemberg." However, he became the court conductor only after Balduin Hoyoul's death from the plague in 1594; he obtained his final appointment in April 1595 and conducted the band until his death. It distinguished itself under his direction at various festive occasions, although sickness and many other difficulties hindered Lechner. In 1604 he created a large-scale composition, *Laudate Dominum* (15 voices in three choirs), for the celebration of the wedding of a princess of Württemberg to the successor to the throne of Electoral Saxony. This composition has been preserved for posterity in the *Landeshauptarchiv* at Dresden. Because of his illness, Lechner was not able to travel with the court band when it accompanied the princess to Dresden for the wedding festivities.

Lechner died on Sept. 9, 1606; on Sept. 11 his mortal remains were buried with high honors close to the altar in the "Hospital Church." A great number of people attended the funeral. The inscription of the original monument is preserved; the monument itself is no longer there. At the reconstruction of the Hospital Church (1958), mostly destroyed by bombs during World War II, no trace of the monument or of the tomb was found. In November 1961, a memorial tablet was unveiled and placed on the wall of the nave to keep alive the memory of this great composer.

II. TEACHERS AND CONTEMPORARIES

During his whole life Leonhard Lechner showed over and over again his gratitude, veneration, and love for his teacher Orlando di Lasso, whom he called [10] the "one and outstanding unique musician," [11] whose works showed the seal of divine talent.[12] Lasso repeatedly took his student's side and gave him letters of recommendation when he applied for the position of the court conductor in Dresden. In those letters Lechner is characterized as a "well-known, good composer and musician" who has experience and understanding in everything a conductor must be able to do. Lechner showed his devotion to Lasso in that wherever he worked, he made people buy editions of Lasso's works; he also edited two collections of Lasso's works, arranged in such a way that they could be used in Protestant congregations.

When Lechner was a choirboy in Landshut, the court band of the successor to the throne was directed by Ivo de Vento (ca. 1540 to 1575) and from 1569 on by Anton Gosswin (1540–1594). How far these two composers influenced Lechner in a direct way cannot be established easily, because both were strongly influenced by Lasso.[13] In the years of travel, between 1570 and 1575, Lechner undoubtedly studied various models, for he tells [14] of "distinguished artists whose student he professed to be"; however, he mentions no names. Probably one can look for the names of these artists among the composers of the motet collection *Harmoniae miscellae cantionum sacrorum* (Nuremberg, 1583), which Lechner edited and dedicated to his friend Paul Dulner. Next to Lasso, Palestrina, Gosswin, Andrea Gabrieli, and Cypriano de Rore are the most significant among the older of the 22 composers represented in this collection. When Lechner uses as models for his three masses works of other masters, this must be considered a sign of his respect for them too. Those models are: O. di Lasso (Psalm *Domine, Dominus noster*), L. Marenzio (1553/54–1599) (sacred madrigal *Nun fu mai cervo si veloce*), and C. de Rore (1516 to 1565) (madrigal *Non e lasso martire.*) Of these, Marenzio and Lechner are the same age. Also belonging to this generation were, among others: Johann Eccard (1553–1611), likewise from 1571–1573 a Lasso student and a band singer in Munich, Ferdinand di Lasso (ca. 1560–1609), who became Lechner's successor at the Hohenzollern court, and Giovanni Gabrieli (ca. 1555–1612), who belonged to the band of the court at Munich about 1575–1579. Since Andrea Gabrieli as well as C. de Rore were Lasso's friends, it is clear that Lechner owed his knowledge of their works and also his personal acquaintance with living contemporaries to Lasso. In Nuremberg he no doubt knew Hans Leo Hassler (1564–1612), who, like Lechner, left this city in 1584. He may even have helped him with his musical studies. It remains doubtful that he met personally Teodore Riccio (ca. 1540 to 1600), who was active in Ansbach from 1575 to 1578, and again from 1586 until his death. The same is true of J. Eccard, who became a member of the court band at Munich only after Lechner's departure.

III. EMPLOYERS AND PATRONS

As a choirboy at the Bavarian court Lechner served the dukes *Albrecht* and *William of Bavaria.* The last-named was a great music lover, who played the lute and other musical instruments with great skill.[15] Six, later seven, choirboys belonged to the court band he established as the hereditary prince at the Trausnitz castle in Landshut, 1568. The prince and his court conductor themselves usually participated in the Italian comedies Lasso performed there. The wall paintings of the *Narrentreppe* even today give an ingenious impression of the persons who took part in the *commedia dell'arte*. In contrast to the brilliant and colorful life at a typical Renaissance court, Lechner worked as school assistant in Nuremberg in far more modest circumstances. His immediate superior was Andreas Beheim, who since 1571 was the rector of the parish school at St. Lorenz; but his real superior was the council of the free city of Nuremberg, represented by the councilman Hieronimus Baumgartner, Jr., who was responsible for the church and school system. The young composer dedicated to him his first printed work as a sign of gratitude for the "exceedingly great blessings, heaped upon an absolute stranger who did not deserve them." [16] Numerous members of the Nuremberg council belonged among Lechner's patrons. To many of them he dedicated compositions, to some of them even entire collections of his works. In addition to those whom we have already named as people who commissioned wedding and other festival music,[17] special mention must be made of the following: the famous goldsmith and member of the smaller council, Wenzel Jamnitzer (1508–1585), to whom Lechner dedicated his *Newe Teutsche Lieder*, 1582, the patricians Hans Pfintzing (d. 1582), Philipp Geuder (d. 1581), Anton Geuder (1539–1604), Niclas Nützel (d. 1585), Joachim Nützel (1531–1607), and Christoph Fürer (1541–1610). Most of these men belonged to the music societies of Nuremberg for which Lechner created his song collections from 1576 to 1582. He took part in their meetings, and he may have directed them as well.[18] When he left these circles to become court conductor, his new superior was Count Eitel Friedrich von Hohenzollern (1545 to 1605), who had ruled his small county since 1576 and at the residence of Hechingen had organized a splendid court of the muses. He was considered a special authority and promoter of the arts and sciences and was enthusiastically supported in such endeavors by his second spouse Sibyl, countess of Zimmern (1558–1599), who loved music.[19] Yet the count was a choleric and stubborn lord, who ruled his small county with an iron fist. He suppressed with unrelenting severity a peasant revolt that erupted in 1584 over quarrels concerning the hunting of deer; his servants were afraid of him because of his sudden outbursts of anger. Since the count was a zealous partisan of the Counterreformation and Lechner an equally zealous Protestant, difficulties over the execution of the church service in the chapel of the castle and in the cathedral were bound to arise because of the increasingly conspicuous confessional hostilities of these years. The fact that Lechner fled from the county shows how much his working conditions, which originally were in such good standing, had declined. He escaped to Duke Ludwig von Württenberg, who ruled from 1568 to 1593. The duke received Lechner in a friendly fashion and helped him in any way he could. Lechner's direct superior there was the court conductor Ludwig Daser (ca. 1525–1589) and after Daser's death Balduin Hoyoul (1547/48–1594); later Lechner followed him in the office. Curator of the court band and the superior of the conductor was the theologian Lucas Osiander (1534–1604), since 1567 court preacher in Stuttgart and member of the consistory.[20] As the former teacher of Duke Ludwig, Osiander was his intimate adviser, but he lost this influential position under Ludwig's successor, Duke Friedrich, who ruled from 1593 to 1608. Thus it happened that from 1593 the music of the court band became increasingly secular in character. In the first draft of regulations for the conductor, April 30, 1595, Duke Friedrich with his own hand deleted most of the regulations that referred to the duties of the band in church and to the Christian education of the band's choirboys. When Lechner, because of illness, was no longer able to work full time, the duke, it seems, lost interest in him. Lechner's complaint of 1604 that the contralto singer Tobias Salomo without an appointment styled himself vice-conductor was dismissed with the laconical note: "the duke received it [the complaint] but gave no orders."

IV. FRIENDS AND ANTAGONISTS

In the records of the Bavarian court band the names of the choirboys are only rarely mentioned; furthermore, since no reports are extant concerning Lechner's travel years, we know nothing about the friends of his youth. In Nuremberg, however, there were persons among his acquaintances who evidently were his friends. First to be mentioned is the poet Paul Schede (Melissus) (1539–1602), who at the age of 25 was crowned as *poeta laureatus* and knighted by Emperor Ferdinand in Vienna. He made many trips and studied, among other places, in Wittenberg, where he lived as a guest in Paul Eber's home and was active as a composer. His best friend there was magister Laurenz Dürnhofer, who later became a preacher at St. Egidien in Nuremberg. Melissus probably visited him in Nuremberg and met Lechner there through him. In a letter from Padua, July 31, 1577, Melissus asked Lechner to set to music some poems with lines of 11 syllables.[21] Melissus thanked him with a Latin poem of praise and later dedicated several epigrams to Lechner in which he praises Lechner because he "adorns his music with a lovely harmony of the voices and because proper words inspire corresponding music in his imagination." [22] Both felt united in striving for a new expression of affects through poetry and music. Further epigrams that Melissus wrote in honor of Lechner, a sophisticated Latin answer that Lechner wrote and set to music, and Melissus' poems for epithalamiums that Lechner composed for weddings of patricians in Nuremberg give witness to their friendship. A third person belonging to this group of friends was the goldsmith Paul Dulner (d. 1596), to whom Lechner dedicated the 1583 collection of motets as to his "godfather, patron, and best friend." [23] Dulner had provided him with most of the texts for his collection of German song motets of 1582. These motets, formally influenced by the Italian madrigal technique, in power of language and strength of imagery surpassed by far all other contemporary German poetry. Melissus also honored Dulner in a laudatory poem as a poet who has created something of eternal value.[24] On March 30, 1582, Lechner wrote in the autograph album of the Nuremberg minister Georg Werner (1563–1624):

> Hic scopus omnis erit, cunctis prodesse, nocere
> Nemini, amare bones, & tolerare malos.[25]

Whether a friendship can be deduced from this evidence is difficult to say. There is greater probability of a friendship with the councilman Dr. Johann Dretzler (Drezel), who established Lechner's contact with the Hohenzollern court in Hechingen; but even this cannot be proved through the archives. Because of his leaving the court as if in flight and because of the bold challenge of his letter, Lechner had made Count Eitel Friedrich his personal adversary; he was forced to ask for forgiveness in order to be reconciled with him.[26] Apart from quarrels with the instrumentalists of the court band, from which hardly any conductor of that time was exempt, no note regarding personal enmity can be found in Lechner's entire life history.

When Lechner stayed in Tübingen after his flight in 1585, he asked for and received advice and help in his dispute with the count of Hohenzollern from his friend, Prof. Nikodemus Frischlin (1547 to 1590). The belligerent humanist evidently advised Lechner ill when he encouraged him to write a letter of challenge.[27] However, Frischlin's recommendation to Duke Ludwig, written while he was still in his favor, may have helped to prompt the duke to take care of Lechner. In Stuttgart Lechner is supposed to have kept himself distant in his association with the personnel of the band; [28] perhaps this was caused by his illness, which frequently forced him to seek relief in health resorts. Prof. Martin Crusius (1526–1607) of Tübingen, a great music lover, knew Lechner personally and exchanged greetings and letters with him.[29] Lechner was on friendly terms also with Magister Samuel Mageirus, a music survey lecturer at the theological seminary in Tübingen. In a letter dated Aug. 8, 1583, Lechner calls the much younger man his "intimate friend," and recapitulates a conversation concerning the church modes that he had had with him once on a walk.[30] Magister Erasmus Grüninger (1566–1631) rendered the last services of friendship to the composer, who, with the mark of death upon him, lived in a "wearisome weakness." Grüninger had been a music survey lecturer at the theological seminary in Tübingen from 1590 to 1591 and pastor at St. Leonhard in Stuttgart in 1594. As the court preacher, he held the funeral sermon at the Hospital Church on Sept. 11, 1606,[31] and in it he reports in detail on Lechner's last days and his last hour. The epitaph of another friend, Magister Georg Johann Kanzius, is appended to the funeral sermon; it celebrates the deceased as a very famous, highly honored man, well versed in music and in history:

> Hic dulcissima Musica quiescit,
> hic mirabilis Harmonia gliscit.

V. SPHERE OF ACTIVITY AND FAME AFTER DEATH

Since in the first one and one-half decades of his activities almost all of Lechner's compositions appeared in print, some collections in two and more editions, his works quickly obtained a wide distribution. Numerous contemporary inventories of court bands, of princely or municipal *Kantoreien,* of schools and libraries list sacred and secular printed editions. In addition, not infrequently we also find copies of his works, either in part books or in tablatures. Very frequently account entries also indicate that sums of money have been paid to Lechner as a recompense for compositions submitted by him. Lechner's works were also incorporated in other collections, frequently as examples in text books and theoretical works. It is reported in Augsburg that Lechner's motets were sung by the *Kantoreien* on the streets, and in a "little handbook," bound in one volume with the Zwickau copy of the L. Stiphelius *Geistlich Gesangbuch* (1612), are listed the *Missa prima* and nine motets by Lechner, to be sung either on "Sundays and festival days all the year round," at weddings and other festivities, or "in the churchyard," that is, at funerals.

There are two reasons why Lechner and his work were nevertheless almost completely forgotten: (1) The most mature works (written after 1590) are too advanced for their time and in their form do not have parallels. These works were not printed and were known only to the circle of the composer's closest friends; most of them are lost.[32]

(2) However, the main reason is the basic stylistic change which began about 1600 with the introduction of the figured bass. The process was not different from one observable today: compositions of a stylistic period that had just come to a close were considered out of date and obsolete. To be sure, J. G. Walther remembered Lechner once more with a short chapter in his *Musikalisches Lexikon* (1732). He even listed some of his works. But this remained unnoticed when about 1870 music research began to deal with Lechner's works. Insufficient knowledge of sources led to misinterpretation and misjudgments. Only the rediscovery of some of his magnificent late works through young unprejudiced musicologists and the courage of a young publisher who dared to publish the works of an almost unknown composer prepared the way for a just appreciation of this great master of German choir music [33] whose fame radiates anew today.

NOTES FOR CHAPTER 8

1. [*Athesinus* (from Lat. *Athesis*, It. *Adige*, Germ. *Etsch*): "from the Etsch river valley" — Ed.]

2. In the preface to *Der ander Teyl Newer Teutscher Lieder* (Nuremberg, 1577). Similarly in the preface to *Motectae sacrae* (Nuremberg, 1575): *Ego ab ineunte aetate vel natura, vel usu et assuefactione praeter ceteras artes Musicam amavi.*

3. In 1562 and 1656 travels were made through Italy for this purpose. They led through the Etsch valley.

4. At this time he had already changed to the Lutheran Church, as the court preacher E. Grüninger informs us in his funeral sermon of 1606.

5. In the preface of the second book of his *Sacrarum Cantionum* (Nuremberg, 1581): . . . *qui longe lateque regiones peragraverunt.* . . .

6. In the preface of the *Motectae sacrae* (1575): . . . *ut ipse aliquid Musici operis conficere atque componere possem.*

7. About where the Municipal Conservatory of Music now stands.

8. In the preface to *Motectae sacrae*, 1575.

9. In *Die Musikforschung*, IV (1953), pp. 156 ff., I showed that this choir book was prepared in 1593 by Heinrich Leitgeb, the bass of the Stuttgart court band.

10. In the preface of the collection edited by him, "*Selectissimae Cantiones* . . . *compositae per excellentissimum musicum Orlandum di Lassus* (Nuremberg, 1579).

11. *Unius atque unici . . . Musici excellentissimi.*

12. . . . *divinum . . . ingenium referentes.*

13. K. Huber, *Ivo de Vento* (diss. Munich, 1918), p. 67, says: "In the Italian external musical form as well as in the German inner national spirit Lechner is based above all on Vento's song style, which he only expands." This thesis (doubted by A. Sandberger, among others) would have to be examined once more without prejudice.

14. In the preface to his *Sanctissimae Virginis Mariae Canticum 4 vocibus compositum* (1578): . . . *dedit Deus* . . . *artifices praestantissimos. Eorum ego me profiteor esse discipulum* . . .

15. Cf. Massimo di Trojano, *Die Vermählungsfeier des Herzogs Wilhelms V. von Bayern* . . . *zu München im Jahre 1568*, trans. F. Würthmann (Munich, 1842), p. 30.

16. In the preface of 1575: . . . *pro ingentibus beneficiis, quibus a Tua Amplitudine homo peregrinus, nihilque tale meritus, cumulatus sum.*

17. See above p. 76.

18. U. Martin, "Die Nürnberger Musikgesellschaften," *Mitteilungen des Vereins für Geschichte der Stadt Nürnberg*, 49 (Nürnberg, 1959), 185—225.

19. E. F. Schmid, *Musik an den schwäbischen Zollernhöfen der Renaissance* (Kassel, 1962).

20. Through his *Fünfzig Geistliche Lieder und Psalmen* (Nuremberg, 1586), he decisively influenced the development of Protestant church music.

21. Cf. U. Martin, pp. 208 f. These poems are probably Italian madrigals.

22. . . . *quia tu vocum lepidis concentibus ornas, verbaque dant aptos sensibus apta modos.*

23. . . . *affini, fautori et amico suo optimo.*

24. Cf. U. Martin, "Der Nürnberger Paul Dulner als Dichter geistlicher und weltlicher Lieder Leonhard Lechners," *Archiv für Musikwissenschaft*, XI (1954) 315—322.

25. See the facsimile reprint in *Musik und Kirche*, XXIV (1954), 193, and in the encyclopedia *Die Musik in Geschichte und Gegenwart*, VIII (Kassel, 1960), 434.

26. See E. F. Schmid, pp. 216 ff.

27. Frischlin later violently attacked the aristocracy in an academic lecture and in a lampoon insulted his own sovereign; he was put into prison and died while trying to escape.

28. G. Bossert, "Die Hofkapelle unter Herzog Friedrich," *Württembergische Vierteljahrshefte für Landesgeschichte*, Neue Folge, XIX (1910), 329 f.

29. G. Reichert, "Martin Crusius und die Musik in Tübingen um 1590," *Archiv für Musikwissenschaft*, X (1953), pp. 185—212.

30. See G. Reichert, pp. 206, 210—212.

31. Published in Tübingen in 1607 by Phillip Gruppenbach.

32. Probably they were burnt in the fire of the Lusthaus theater in Stuttgart on January 19/20, 1902, when many valuable theater and music manuscripts were lost.

33. Since 1954 a complete edition of the works of Leonhard Lechner, planned to contain 15 volumes, is being published by the Bärenreiter-Verlag, Kassel-Basel-London-New York. Other editions and the most important literature are given in *Die Musik in Geschichte und Gegenwart*, VIII (1960), 437 f.

9

THE UNPARTHEYISCHES GESANG-BUCH

J. Murray Barbour

In the summer of 1963 a friend presented me with a copy of an American Mennonite hymnbook, *Unpartheyisches Gesang-Buch* ("Unpartisan Hymnbook"). This, the 5th edition of the work, containing three *Anhänge*, had been published, as had other editions, in Lancaster, Pa., in 1841. Later I was to learn that this hymnbook had run to 15 editions between 1804 and 1887, with further editions in 1903, 1923, and 1941, these last being demanded by the ultra-conservative Old Order Amish. Condensations of the UGB were published during the 19th century also, such as *Ein unpartheyisches Gesang-Buch* (Canton, 1839), and, particularly, *Eine unparteiische Lieder-Sammlung* (Lancaster, 1860). The latter is "das dünne Büchlein" of the Old Order Amish, who honor it next to the *Ausbund,* to be discussed later. *Die gemeinschaftliche Liedersammlung* (Berlin, now Kitchener, Ont., 1836) has drawn two thirds of its hymns from the UGB, and S. D. Guengerich's *Unparteiische Liedersammlung* (Elkhart, 1892) about half.

I wondered how typical the UGB was of German-American hymnody in the middle of the 19th century. Earlier, such hymnbooks could not have been distinguished from their counterparts abroad. For example, the Reformed Church's *Neu-vermehrt- und vollständiges Gesang-Buch* (2d ed., Germantown, 1763) contained the Psalms of David in Lobwasser's translation and 730 hymns. Conrad Doll's *Sammlung geistlicher Lieder* (Lancaster, 1798) is noted chiefly for the presence of the elegant, florid tunes that cheapened 18th-century German hymnody. *Das neue und verbesserte Gesangbuch* (3d ed., Germantown, 1807) contained both hymns and psalm paraphrases, the latter being compiled from Lobwasser, Spreng, and the Herborner *Gesang-Buch.* So these Reformed hymnbooks before and at the beginning of the 19th century contained collectively metrical psalms from several sources and tunes that included both the sturdy 16th-century chorales and the more florid 18th-century type.

By the middle of the 19th century, although the language was still German, these German-American hymnbooks had, in general, been greatly influenced by Anglo-American hymnody. Characteristic was J. G. Schauk's *Deutsche Harmonie* (2d ed., Philadelphia, 1847). It contained a section of harmonized chorales, a section of *Chorgesänge* arranged from well-known Continental and English composers, and a section of bilingual hymns. The second and third sections owed much to Lowell Mason. Contemporary with *Deutsche Harmonie* was Heinrich Staub's *Die Kirchen-Harfe* (Circleville, Ohio, 1851), official hymnbook of the United Brethren in Christ. Its texts are unabashed translations of English hymns in such a collection as Walker's *Southern Harmony.* Some of these are very amusing in their German garb. "Von Grönlands Eisgestaden, Von Indiens Perlenstrand" rubs elbows with "Dort ist ein Vaterland, weit, hoch und schön." No tunes are printed in this collection, but "Blast die Trompete, blast" must have been sung to the popular fuguing tune *Lenox,* and "Wie prächtig ist der Nam'! Brüder, singt! Brüder, singt!" to the traditional *Captain Kidd* tune. Although the Old Order Amish in Pennsylvania cleave to all of the old texts in their "dünnes Büchlein," they often enliven their services by singing Neander's "Himmel, Erde, Luft und Meer" to the tune of "Christ the Lord Is Risen Today," or Rinkart's "An Jesum denken oft und viel" to the tune of "Ive Reached the Land of Corn and Wine."

The UGB reveals no such compromise with its American environment as was shown by the hymnbooks named above. Its first edition consisted of 62 metrical psalms and 390 hymns. The first *Anhang* (1808) added 35 hymns, the second (1820) added 32, and the third (1829) 14 more, for a total of 471 hymns. We had noted above that the psalms in *Das neue . . . Gesangbuch* had been drawn from several different psalters. But the conservative UGB drew its psalms solely from Lobwasser's venerable translation of the French Psalter, first published in 1573. One exception, interestingly enough, is Psalm 130, "Zu dir von Herzensgrunde." It is sung to Hassler's popular song, "Mein G'müth ist mir verwirret" (1601), which, as everyone knows, was shortly thereafter taken into sacred use, to Knoll's hymn, "Herzlich thut mich verlangen." In the UGB the Hassler tune is used for 33 hymns, including Gerhardt's "O Haupt voll Blut und Wunden." Psalm 134 ("Ihr Knecht des Herren allzugleich") was soon borrowed for

Psalm 100, and we still call the tune *Old 100th*. (Psalm 142, with no tune of its own in the Genevan Psalter, is here also sung to the tune of Psalm 134.) For completeness' sake one should mention that two hymns in the UGB are to be sung to the Genevan tune for Psalm 140, printed as Tune 48, although the text of Psalm 140 does not occur in this collection. There is also a paraphrased psalm, which is printed with the hymns rather than with the psalms. This is Wolfgang Meusel's well-liked translation of Psalm 23, "Der Herr ist mein getreuer Hirt" (1531). Made 40 years before Lobwasser's clumsy version ("Mein Hüter und mein Hirt ist Gott der Herre"), it could of course have had no place among the translations from the French. Significant of a change of taste during the 19th century is the fact that none of the four condensations of the UGB mentioned earlier has included Lobwasser psalms.

The melodies in the UGB are printed without harmony, using the alto clef, either with no key signature or with one flat. As given, these melodies are singularly free of ornamentation; there are a very few passing notes, but often the line is even plainer than in 16th-century hymnbooks. No rhythm is indicated for the melodies, which proceed uniformly in half notes save for a whole note to mark a cadence.

The *Mennonite Encyclopedia* states quite fallaciously that the UGB contains only a few psalm tunes. It is true that the rival Mennonite publication, *Die kleine geistliche Harfe der Kinder Zions* (Germantown, 1803) printed a few tunes for its psalms, but had no printed hymn tunes. Moreover, no other Mennonite hymnbook provided printed tunes until *Hymns and Tunes for Public and Private Worship* (Elkhart, 1890). But the hymns in the UGB are completely supplied with tunes. The hymns are grouped according to stanza form into 62 numbered categories, the appropriate tune for each category being printed once. In addition, 34 of the Genevan psalm tunes printed in the book are not included in numbered categories. For 27 hymns there is printed an "eigne Melodey." The last two stanzas of Hymn 38, "Heut fänget an das neue Jahr," are directed to be sung to the known tune "Ich liebe dich herzlich." In the *Anhänge* there are no printed tunes, but eight of the tunes are indicated by the proper text and can be found in Zahn's *Die Melodien der evangelischen Kirchenlieder*, sometimes with a choice of tunes. Altogether there are 123 printed tunes in the UGB, and nine more are clearly indicated. I was able to find all of the Genevan Psalter tunes, of course. All of the remaining tunes were located in Zahn, except for seven of the 62 numbered tunes and eight of the 27 "eigne Melodien."

The striking thing about the tunes in the UGB is that the majority of those in the numbered categories come from the 16th century, the earliest period of Lutheran and Reformed hymnody. Sixteen Genevan tunes and 13 others from this period are found in the numbered categories, as well as the 34 unnumbered Genevan psalm tunes already mentioned. Three hymns "in eigner Melodey" also come from this period, and one listed in the third *Anhang*. This makes in all 67 tunes of the 16th century. Often these tunes are modal, such as the Dorian Tune 36, "Vater unser im Himmelreich" (1539), and Tune 41, "Ich ruf zu dir, Herr Jesu Christ" (1535). They are all characterized by a noble simplicity, such as Tune 21, Walter's "Gelobet seist du, Jesu Christ" (1524), and Tune 37, Isaac's "Innsbruck, ich muss dich lassen" (1539).

The next largest number of tunes in the numbered categories in the UGB are tunes from the 17th century. Included among these 20 tunes are two familiar Crüger melodies, Tune 15, "Nun danket alle Gott" (1649), and Tune 40, "Jesu, meine Freude" (1653). There are also seven hymns "in eigner Melodey" from the 17th century, one listed in the second *Anhang* and the "Ich liebe dich herzlich" tune previously mentioned. This makes 30 tunes in all from this century.

Only six tunes in the numbered categories are from the 18th century; these include Tune 23, "Wunderbarer König" (1719), and Tune 39, "Seelenbräutigam" (1704). Not unexpectedly, 10 of the "eigne Melodien" are also from this century, as well as six of the eight tunes indicated by name in the three *Anhänge*. This makes a respectable total of 21 18th-century melodies. Even so, the 16th century clearly predominates when one considers that 48 hymns are to be sung to Tune 3 ("Nun freut euch, lieben Christen g'mein") and 42 more to Tune 12 *(Old 100)*. It seems probable that at least 10 of the 15 unidentified tunes also belong to the 16th century, since they are settings of texts of this period.

Sixty-four of the 16th-century hymns in the UGB come from the *Ausbund* (Paragon), the oldest German Mennonite hymnbook. Its first known print, held uniquely at Goshen College, has the title *Etliche schöne christliche Gesänge* and the date 1564. It contains 50 hymns written by Swiss Brethren who, fleeing from persecution in Moravia, had been imprisoned for five years (1535–40) in the dungeons of Passau. These hymns breathe out a calm spirit of resignation and hope for heaven, so well expressed in the final stanza of Hans Betz's "Gelobt sei Gott im höchsten Thron": "Wir bitten dich, o Herre Gott! Erlöss all dein' gefangen, Thu ihn'n Beistand in aller Noth, Dass sie die Kron erlangen." Twelve hymns by Betz are in the *Ausbund,* seven of these being taken over into the UGB. Of 11 *Ausbund* hymns by Michael Schneider, four are found in the UGB, including "Es hatt' ein Mann zween Knaben," the parable of the Prodigal Son expanded into 33 8-line stanzas.

With the Passau hymns as a nucleus, the complete *Ausbund* appeared in 1583 with 130 hymns, 10 more being added early in the 17th century, including the beloved "O Gott Vater, wir loben Dich," a translation from the Dutch of Leenaert Clock. Several hymns in the expanded *Ausbund* relate, often in gory detail, stories of Anabaptist martyrs, as in Hymn 187, which begins prosaically enough: "Als man zählt tausend fünf hundert jahr sieben und fünfzig eben." This narrates the flaming death of the Neapolitan Anabaptist, Algerius, in Rome in 1557.

The most fascinating of the martyr hymns is the 32-stanza *Hasslibacherlied,* "Was wend wir aber heben an." This tale of the Swiss Anabaptist, Hans Hasslibacher, appears as Hymn No. 140 in the *Ausbund* and was not taken into the UGB until the third *Anhang.* It has all the crudity and naiveté of the folk ballad, complete with a miraculous laughing head, a bloodred sun, a fountain gushing blood.

The UGB and its condensation, *Eine unparteiische Lieder-Sammlung,* are the only Mennonite hymnbooks to have included a substantial number of the *Ausbund* hymns. In Europe, as the bloody days of the 16th century became remote, congregations were no longer interested in singing about the Anabaptist martyrs. In Walther H. Hohmann's list of the 17 most popular German Mennonite hymns in Europe and America not one is from the *Ausbund.* It is strange, therefore, that these hymns should have retained such an appeal to Mennonites in Eastern Pennsylvania, where they were free to worship according to the dictates of their conscience and where their pacifistic ideas were fully shared by their neighbors, the Quakers.

Like Schneider's "Es hatt' ein Mann" and the *Hasslibacherlied,* a great many of the *Ausbund* hymns were of inordinate length, so that the 140 hymns filled a book of over 800 pages. It is no wonder that the Old Order Amish, who still use the *Ausbund* today, call it "das dicke Buch." In the days of persecution these interminable hymns were used for meditation rather than for singing. Today they are always sung in small segments. It is to be observed that the 37 *Ausbund* hymns in "das dünne Büchlein" have been pruned ruthlessly, and this is true in the other condensed versions of the UGB also. A dozen of the hymns that I have not yet identified average 25 stanzas, and if length is taken as the criterion, they are probably by Mennonite poets. Three of the five hymns by Christopher Dock ("Mein Lebensfaden läuft zu Ende," for example) also fall into this category. Dock was a German-born Mennonite, who came to Pennsylvania in 1714 and taught school in the Philadelphia region, dying there in 1771.

The Mennonites did not hold a monopoly on longwindedness, however. Paul Gerhardt's "Wir singen dir, Immanuel" has 20 stanzas, and his "Sollt ich meinem Gott nicht singen" is in twelve 12-line stanzas. The UGB contains altogether 17 of the hymns of Gerhardt (1607–1676), the most popular Lutheran hymnodist after Luther himself. Ranked just below Gerhardt as a religious poet is Johann Heermann (1585–1634), 10 of whose hymns (such as "Zion klagt mit Angst und Schmerzen") are present. Among the Reformed hymnodists, Joachim Neander (1650–1680) is represented with 15 hymns ("Sieh hier bin ich," for example), and the mystic Gerhard Tersteegen (1697–1769) with 12 ("Gott ist gegenwärtig"). The Pietists include Benjamin Schmolck (1672–1737), who contributed 10 hymns, and Laurentius Laurenti (1660–1722) with eight. Five hymns were added by the Lutheran-turned-Catholic Johann Scheffler (1624–1677), Pastor Johann Rist (1607–1667), and Burgomaster Johann Franck (1618 to 1699).

Only four hymns by Martin Luther appear in the UGB, but these include "Gelobet seist du, Jesu Christ" and "Vom Himmel hoch." The tune of "Ein' feste Burg" is mentioned, but the hymn itself was apparently too militant to be chosen by a group that has always been strongly pacifistic. Luther's direct followers, Paul Eber and Bartholomäus Ringwaldt, also contributed four hymns each. Johann Walter's "Herzlich thut mich erfreuen" was the sole Lutheran hymn taken over from the *Ausbund*.

Altogether I have located 286 of the UGB hymns in the standard German Protestant repertory, hymns by the poets just listed and by many less noted than they. There are still 121 hymns to be identified by author; I believe that most of these, except for the group of a dozen long hymns previously mentioned, are also part of the main current of German hymnody.

And so the *Unpartheyisches Gesang-Buch* has a bewilderingly eclectic character, especially in its texts. In fact, "unpartheyisch," in its present context, might even be translated "eclectic." One need not hold a brief for Lobwasser's translation of the Psalms in order to enjoy the Genevan melodies to which these psalms and a host of the hymns were sung. And if many of the *Ausbund* hymns have become more curious than devotional with the passing of time, the sturdy chorale melodies to which they had been sung were retained for the more congenial hymns of Gerhardt, Neander, and Schmolck.

The first Mennonite hymnbook in English appeared in 1832, and of course English has been the language of the standard hymnbooks of the denomination for decades. The change to English, however, opened the way to the inclusion of a great many trivial gospel songs of the Moody-Sankey type, before the end of the century, as well as to a discarding of the precious Franco-Teutonic melodic heritage. During all of this time, however, the melodies of the UGB remained an ever-steady beacon light for reverential worship. Finally a reaction has set in, and *The Mennonite Hymnary* (1940), for example, has included 104 German tunes, of which 58 are the old chorale melodies. Thus the UGB, planned and produced by a little band of Mennonites in Eastern Pennsylvania, 160 years ago, has exerted a leavening influence far beyond the narrow confines of its place and time of origin.

10

MICHAEL PRAETORIUS
ON CONCERTATO STYLE

Harold E. Samuel

Of the important innovations occurring around 1600 in Italian music, the German Lutheran composers quickly adopted basso continuo and *concertato* style, both of which, along with the already traditional close relation of music and text *(musica poetica),* dominated Lutheran music throughout the 17th century. The chief theoretical source for *concertato* style is Part III of Michael Praetorius' *Syntagma musicum* (Wolffenbüttel, 1619), which is all the more important because Praetorius, with his vast knowledge of Italian music and theory and their German counterparts, wrote "from the practice for the practice." [1] His description of *concertato* style was intended as an aid for the establishment of this practice in the German churches and courts. [2] The description was so thorough, and the practice in the 17th century was so fixed, that it was unnecessary for later German writers to be concerned with the subject. A clear outline of *concertato* style can be established from Part III of *Syntagma musicum;* an understanding of this tradition is essential to the editor and performer of Lutheran Baroque music.

Much has been written recently about the etymology of the term "concerto," [3] which needs only to be summarized here. Until about 1600 the Italian word *concerto* was identified with the Italian verb *concertare,* "to proportion or accord together, to agree or tune together, to sing or play in concert." [4] This originated from the Latin *conserere* (whence the Italian parallels *conserto* and *consertare*), "to join or fit together, connect." [5] Along with its Spanish and English equivalents, *concierto* [6] and *consort,* [7] the term "concerto" was similar in meaning to *symphonia*, that is, "agreement or concord of sound."[8] Praetorius writes:

Die Engelländer nennens gar *apposite a consortio* ein *Consort*, Wenn etliche Personen mit allerley *Instrumenten* . . . zusammen in einer *Compagny* unnd Gesellschafft gar still, sanft und lieblich *accordieren*, und in anmutiger *Symphonia* mit einander zusammen stimmen.[9]

The English call the opposite of a *consortio* a Consort, that is, when several people with diverse instruments come together and accord quietly, softly, and charmingly; they play together in pleasant *Symphonia*.

But after 1600, with the advent of *concertato* style, concerto was identified with the Latin *concertare*, "to contend zealously, dispute, debate."[10] Praetorius writes:

Daher auch das Wort *Concerti* sich ansehen lest, als wann es vom Lateinischen *verbo Concertare*, welches mit einander scharmützeln heist, seinen Ursprung habe. Fürnemlich und eigendlicher aber ist dieser Gesang ein *Concert* zu nennen, wenn etwa ein niedriger oder hoher Chor gegen einander, und zusammen sich hören lassen.[11]

Therefore the word "concerto" appears as if it had had its origin from the Latin verb *concertare*, which means to skirmish with one another. Strictly speaking, however, a vocal work is to be called a concerto if perhaps a low choir and a high choir are heard together and in opposition to each other.

Throughout the Baroque era German theorists associated "concerto" with opposition or rivalry. Johann Andreas Herbst, in his *Musica practica* (Nuremberg, 1642), writes:

1. *Concerto*, ist erstlich *in genere* so viel als ein jegleiche Motetta, oder *Symphonia*. 2. *In specie* aber heist es so viel als *Concertatio*, wenn gleichsam die Stimmen mit einander *certiren*.[12]

1. Concerto in general, first of all, is like a motet or symphonia. 2. In a special sense, however, it means the same as *Concertatio*, that is, when the voices oppose one another.

Johann Mattheson, in *Critica musica* (Hamburg, 1722), writes:

Unter den Concerten verstehe ich gleichfalls alle *species cantionum* die mit einander certiren.[13]

I interpret the term "concerto" as all the kinds of song (in which the voices) oppose one another.

Johann Walther, in his *Lexicon* (Leipzig, 1732), defines *concerto* as "to perform in rivalry" (". . . in die Wette spielt").[14] In the middle of the 18th century Leopold Mozart referred to the "concertist" (the name given to the solo performer in *concertato* style) as a virtuoso;[15] at the beginning of the 19th century Heinrich Christoph Koch gave the present meaning of concerto: a composition for solo instrument(s) with orchestral accompaniment.[16]

But the new, seemingly opposite meaning, "opposition," is not entirely incompatible with the older meaning, "cooperation." For a definition including both senses of concerto, Handschin suggests "agreement with simultaneous contrasts." [17] To state this differently, it could be said that *concertato* style is the sounding together in opposition of different voices or instruments or groups of voices or instruments.

A technique devoted to contrast naturally led to a great variety of combinations of voices and instruments. But *concertato* style in Baroque vocal music can be reduced to two species: contrast between choirs *(Concerto per choros)* and contrast between solo voices (solo *concertato* style).

1. CONCERTO PER CHOROS

Juxtaposition of vocal groups, a trait that can be traced back to the 15th century, became an important element in the antiphonal style of Adrian Willaert's (d. 1562) *cori spezzati*. His pupil Andrea Gabrieli (ca. 1510–1586) abandoned Willaert's practice of identical groups for both choirs and introduced colorful and varying combinations of voices and instruments. And Andrea Gabrieli's pupil and nephew, Giovanni Gabrieli (1555–1612), extended the technique by contrasting solo voices with a vocal ripieno and with instruments.[18]

It is a combination of the *concertato* style in the works of Giovanni Gabrieli, its further development after his death, and innovations added by Praetorius that is described by the latter in *Syntagma musicum. Concerto per choros*,[19] the first of the two species of *concertato* style, is a contrast, a rivalry, an alternation between choirs. Three types of choirs are set in opposition to each other: a choir of solo voices *(Coro favorito)*, a choir consisting of several voices to a part *(Chorus pro capella)*, and a choir of instruments *(Chorus instrumentalis)*.[20] Heinrich Schütz's *Gesang der drei Männer im feurigen Ofen*, exemplifies these choirs. Here the *(Chorus pro) capella* is doubled by a choir of violins; there are two instrumental choirs, one of trombones and one of small *cornetti*.

a. CORO FAVORITO

From the entire company of musicians (i. e., *capella*) the best or "favored" voices were selected for the choir of solo parts. The Baroque demand for an intelligible statement of the text could best be accomplished by these solo voices, which were not to be doubled by instruments. In addition to being constrasted with reiterations of the text by the *Chorus pro capella* or with a *Chorus instrumentalis,* the solo voices were put in opposition to each other. Praetorius describes the *Coro favorito* [21] as follows:

So nennt nun der *Hieronymus Jacobi* [22] . . . die *Parti Concertate, voci Concertate* oder *Concertat-Stimmen* . . . welche in einem *Concert* absonderlich zum Singen und nicht zum *Instrumenten* gerichtet und *Componiret* seyn: . . . Ich nenne es *Voces Concertatas, vel potius Concertantes;* die gleichsam einander *Respondiren,* und untereinander *Concertiren* und streiten, wer es unter ihnen zum besten machen könne. Darumb man denn zu solchen Stimmen die besten Cantores und Sänger ausslesen, bestellen und ordnen mus, die nicht allein *perfect* und gewiss seyn, sondern auch auff itzige newe Manier und Weise ein gute *disposition* zu singen haben, also das die Wörter recht und deutlich *pronunciret,* und gleich als eine *Oration* vernehmlich daher ursachen es die Itali auch bissweilen *Chorum recitativum* nennen.[23]

Hieronymus Jacobi [22] defines the *Parti Concertate, voci Concertate* or *Concertato* voices . . . as those which are arranged and composed for voices alone and not for instruments: . . . I call them *Voces Concertatas,* or rather *Concertantes;* they answer back and forth one to another as it were and *Concertiren,* that is, rival one another to see who among them can do the best. Therefore the best *Cantores,* that is, singers, must be selected, appointed, and organized for these parts. These singers must not only sing with true voices, but must also have a good aptitude to sing in the current new manner and style; that is to say, the words are to be correctly and clearly pronounced and projected as if they were an oration. It is for this reason that the Italians sometimes call it a *Chorum recitativum.*

Heinrich Schütz uses the term *Coro favorito:*

Cori Favoriti werden von mir die jenigen Chor und Stimmen genennt, welche der Capellmeister am meisten *favorisiren,* und auffs beste und lieblichste anstellen soll, da hingegen die *Capellen* (i. e., *Chori pro capella*) zum starcken Gethön und zur Pracht eingeführet werden.[24]

I call *Cori Favoriti* those choirs and voices which the *Capellmeister* favors most and which he wants to use for the best and tenderest passages, whereas the *Capellen* (i. e., *Chori pro Capella*) are brought in for a large sound and for splendor.

Johann Andreas Herbst, in his *Musica practica* (Nuremberg, 1642), also uses the term *Coro favorito:*

Favorito ist ein Chor welcher mit den besten Vocalisten und Singern muss bestellet werden, da dann entweder eine Stimm allein (oder zwo, drey, ec.) in ein Orgel Werck gesungen wird, und gleichsam mit einander *certiren,* und einen sonder-

Favorito is a choir which must be filled with the best singers, for here either a single part or two, three, etc., will be sung to the accompaniment of an organ; it is as though these voices were rivaling one another and were seeking a special

lichen *favor* und Ruhm erlangen, darauff als dann die Capella zum starcken Gethön und Pracht mit einfällt.[25]

favor and honor. Thereupon the Capella joins in for a large sound and for splendor.

Although solo voices were already an important element in Giovanni Gabrieli's concertos, the invention of the basso continuo was necessary before the composer had complete freedom in his use of solo voices. In Germany, by 1620 (e. g., Praetorius' *Polyhymnia caduceatrix* and Schütz' *Psalmen Davids,* both published in 1619) the *Coro favorito,* with its intelligible and expressive statement of the text, had become the most important of the three types of choirs; the full sound of the pompous *Chorus pro capella* contrasted effectively with the solo voices.

b. CHORUS PRO CAPELLA

The chief contrast used in *concertato* style is that between solo and tutti sections. As seen above, the best voices of the company of musicians were selected for the *Coro favorito.* The remaining vocalists and instrumentalists, who were referred to as the *capella,* were combined to perform the tutti sections, "which then offered an excellent ornament, splendor, and pomp to such music." [26]

The number of vocal and instrumental parts in a composition were adjusted by the *Kapellmeister* to the size of his company of musicians. Almost any combination of vocal and instrumental parts was possible, of course, though all combinations can be reduced to three types; these types are described by Praetorius as three uses of the term *capella:* [27] (1) a choir of voices doubled by instruments, (2) a choir of voices only, and (3) a choir of instruments only.

(1) The choir of voices doubled by instruments is described by Praetorius as follows:

. . . wenn . . . etliche unterschiedene Chor mit allerley *Instrumenten* und Menschen Stimmen angestellet werden, dass alsdann noch ein absonderlicher *Chorus* aus diesen allen heraus gezogen, und *Chorus pro Capella* genennet worden . . . Und wird solche *Harmonia* noch mehr erfüllet, und mit grösserer Pracht erweitert, wenn man dabey eienen grossen Bass-Pommer, doppelt Fagott, oder grosse Bass-Geygen *(Italis, Violone)*

. . . if . . . a few sundry choirs of various instruments and voices are appointed, then a special choir is formed from them and is called *Chorus pro Capella* . . . And this *Harmonia* (i. e., concord) is yet better realized and extended with greater splendor, if one adds a bass shawn, a contrabassoon, or a double-bass viol (called *Violone* by the Italians). If other instruments in addition to these are available, they can

Auch wol andere *Instrumenta,* wo deren uberig vorhanden, zu den Mitteln und OberStimmen ordnet.[28]   also be used with the middle and upper parts.

Herbst, who restates Praetorius' three uses of the term *capella,* describes the first use as follows:

Capella, ist erstlich ein sonderlicher Chor, welcher zu gewisser Zeit in den *Clausulis,* gleich wie die *Ripieni,* zur Stärckung und Pracht der Music einfällt.[29]   *Capella* is first a special choir which, like the *Ripieni,* enters at a certain time at the cadences to add strength and splendor to the music.

(2) *Capella,* meaning a choir of voices only, became the most frequent use of the word during the Baroque era. The *capella* (abbreviation for *Chorus pro capella*) was contrasted with one or more instrumental choirs, as well as with the *Coro favorito.* Praetorius describes this second use of *cappella* as

... der *Chorus,* welche mit *Cantoribus* und Menschen-Stimmen muss besetzet werden; als wenn in einem *Concert* der eine Chor mit *Cornetten,* der ander mit Geigen, der dritte mit Posaunen, Fagotten, Flöitten und dergleichen Instrumenten ... So ist meistentheils noch ein Chor darbey, do alle vier Stimmen mit *Cantoribus* besetzt werden.[30]   ... the choir that must be made up of voices; when in a concerto there is a choir with cornetti, a second choir with violins, a third with trombones, bassoons, flutes, and similar instruments ... there is usually also a choir in which all four parts are for voices.

Herbst describes the second use of *capella* as follows:

Beym *Joh.* Gabr.: und Joh. Leo Hasl.: ist *Capella* so viel als *Chorus Vocalis,* welche allezeit mit Menschen stimmt, starck solle besetzt werden.[31]   With Giovanni Gabrieli and Hans Leo Hassler *Capella* means the same as *Chorus Vocalis,* which consists of voices, several to a part.

It would be contrary to Baroque practice for the modern conductor to restrict himself to the particular voices and instruments prescribed by the composer. The conductor simply makes the best use of the musicians at his disposal. The *Coro favorito* parts are essential; if there are only enough voices available for a *Coro favorito,* the remaining parts can be played by the organist.[32] If extra voices and instruments are available, they can combine to form a *Chorus pro capella,* or a choir of voices can be contrasted with a choir of instruments, or the *capella* can consist of only instruments. The latter, Praetorius' third use of the word *capella,* is the *Chorus instrumentalis.*

c. Chorus Instrumentalis

The third use of the term *capella* is described by Praetorius as follows:

Nunmehr aber nennen etliche auch dieses eine *Capellam* wenn man zu einem *Choro Vocali,* einen *Chorum Instrumentalem componirt* und setzet.[33]

Today, however, some also use the term *Capella* for a *Chorus instrumentalis,* which is composed in addition to the *Chorus vocalis.*

Unlike the essential *Coro favorito,* the *Chorus instrumentalis* can be omitted if there is a shortage of instrumentalists. Herbst writes:

Ist *Capella* ein *Chorus Instrumentalis,* sonsten *Capella fidicinia* genannt, so absonderlich in dem *Concert Componirt,* und in einem besondern Ort in der Kirchen gestellet wird, kan auch in manglung der Personen gar ausgelassen werden.[34]

The composer may write expressly for a *Capella* or choir of instruments (sometimes called a *Capella fidicinia*), which is separately placed in the church, and which can even be left out altogether if there is a shortage of personnel.

If more singers are available than instrumentalists, the instrumental parts can be sung by voices:

Demnach aber in Schulen und sonsten, do man die *Instrumenta* nicht darbey haben kan, die *Instrumentales Chori* entweder ganz aussgelassen, oder aber *humanis Vocibus* bestellet werden mussen.[35]

However, in schools and other places where one does not have the instruments, either the choir of instruments must be left out altogether or else voices must be substituted for them.

An awareness of the text should be maintained in the *Chorus instrumentalis.* Praetorius describes a type of instrumental choir that includes at least one voice:

. . . als wenn in einem *Concert* der eine Chor mit Cornetten, der ander mit Geigen, der dritte mit Posaunen, Fagotten, Flöitten und dergleichen *Instrumenten* (besetzt ist), doch dass bey jedem Chor zum wenigstens eine *Concertat-* das ist, eine Menschen Stimme darneben geordnet.[36]

. . . when in a Concerto one choir is for cornetti, the second for strings, the third for trombones, bassoons, flutes, and similar instruments, at least one *concertato* voice, that is, a vocalist, must be set to every choir.

In Herbst's description of *Chorus instrumentalis* (given above) he identifies this choir with *Capella fidicinia,* that is, a choir of stringed instruments. Praetorius writes:

Dass ich diese *Capellam* darumb *Fidiciniam* genennet, dieweil es bes-

This *Capella* I call *Fidicinia* because it is better to put stringed instru-

ser ist, mit besaiteten *Instrumenten*
. . . dieselbige *Capellam* zu bestellen. Denn der *Sonus* und *Harmonia*
der *Violen* und Geigen *continuiret*
sich immer nach einander mit son-
derbahrer Lieblichkeit ohne einige
respiration, deren man uff Posaunen
und andern blasenden *Instrumenten*
nicht entrathen kan.[37]

ments together in the same choir.
For the sound and concord of the
strings can be sustained most
sweetly and without pauses for
breathing, such as are necessary
with trombones and other wind
instruments.

In *Concerto per choros* practice the choirs were placed in different
parts of the church. At Venice, the influential center in the early development of *concertato* style, the church of St. Mark has a floor plan
of a Greek cross, which was especially convenient for the placing of
contrasting organs and choirs in each of its four galleries.[38] Praetorius's *Urania* (Wolfenbüttel, 1613) consists of settings *per choros*
of chorales and includes instructions for the placing of two, three, or
four choirs in various parts of the church.[39] In this practice each of
the choirs had its own continuo instrument, or if sufficient instruments
were not available for each of the choirs, at least one extra basso continuo instrument could be placed away from the main organ. Praetorius writes:

Wenn man *per Choros* musiciren,
und bey etlichen unterschiedenen
Choren sonderliche Organisten oder
Lautenisten ordnen wil: So zweiffelt
mir nicht, es werde ein jeder, ohn
mein erinnern, wissen, dass der
General-Bass so offt muss abge-
schrieben, und einem jeden Chor
darinnen mit roter oder anderer Din-
ten unterstrichen werden, was ein
jeder bey seinem Chor schlagen
solle.[40]

When one is performing *per Choros*
and wants to place special organists
or lutenists with some of the various
choirs, there is no doubt in my mind
that everyone knows without my re-
minding him that copies of the basso
continuo part must be made for
each (of these instruments). The
portions that each (organist or lu-
tenist) has to play with his choir
must be underlined in his part with
red or some other ink.

As pictorial evidence for the placing of choirs, the frontispiece of
Part III of *Syntagma musicum* is well known.[41] Similar evidence of
this practice in Nuremberg has been preserved in a copper plate included in Johann Klaj's *Geburtstag Dess Friedens* (Nuremberg,
1650).[42] Klaj describes the Peace Festival Banquet held in Nuremberg on Sept. 25, 1649, celebrating the end of the Thirty Years' War.
The plate shows four choirs on elevated platforms in the four corners
of the hall.

2. SOLO *CONCERTATO* STYLE

The second species of *concertato* style, which like *Concerto per
choros* also resulted in a type of Baroque composition, is "solo *con-*

certato style." The first instance of solo *concertato* style can be easily dated, since it appeared in a collection of music published by Lodovico Viadana in Venice in 1602, *Cento Concerto Ecclesiastici*. Viadana states in the preface that he wrote some of the concertos "five or six years ago when in Rome." These concertos, based on the contrapuntal technique of the 16th-century motet, are compositions for one or more solo voices with basso continuo accompaniment.

The basso continuo technique was necessary before the composer had complete freedom in his use of solo voices. German Baroque theorists incorrectly attribute the invention of basso continuo to Viadana (1564–1645).[43] To the already established practice of *bassus pro organo (basso seguente)*, that is, an unfigured bass line (excerpted from the lowest vocal part) from which the organist completed the harmony, Viadana merely added the practice of making the basso continuo part independent — not excerpted from the voices — and hence indispensable to the composition.[44]

The invention of basso continuo also made possible the use of a *Coro favorito* within a *Concerto per choros;* one or more solo voices, supported by a continuo instrument, could alternate with a *Chorus pro capella* or with a *Chorus instrumentalis*. While the voices in Viadana's concertos are accompanied only by a basso continuo, later composers used other instruments as well. Such concertos could be described as compositions for a *Coro favorito* and a *Chorus instrumentalis*, but without a *Chorus pro capella*. Solo concertato style can be described as a contrast, opposition, or rivalry between solo voices, between the voices and the basso continuo, or between them and the instruments.

Early German solo concertos are modelled after Viadana's.[45] The style, the basso continuo accompaniment, and the spatial disposition of the solo voices are described by Praetorius as the third of 12 possible types *(Arten)* of *concertato* style:

Die Erste Manier, ist auff des *Ludovici Viadanae, Joan. Damasceni, Antonii Cifrae, Jacobi Finetti, Seraphini Pattae* und anderer unzehlicher *Italorum Musicorum* itzige Art gerichtet; darinnen man zwo, drey oder vier *Concertat*-Stimmen, so man entweder beyeinander oder voneinander, damit eine Stimm für der andern fein deutlich, unnd unter-

The first method is prescribed according to Ludovico Viadana, Giovanni Damasceni, Antonio Cifra, Jacobi Finetti, Seraphin Patta, and other innumerable Italian musicians devoted to the new style. Here one places two, three, or four *concertato* voices near the organ or near a *Regal*, and the organist must accompany from the basso continuo part.

schiedlich vernommen werden kön-
nen, bey die Orgel oder ein *Regal*-
Werck ordnen, und der Organist,
auss dem *General-Bass* darzu schlagen und spielen muss.[46]

The singers can be placed either together or apart, so that each voice
can be heard clearly and distinctly
from the others.

An accompaniment of only basso continuo, which lacked a colorful instrumental contrast, was not popular among the German composers. In Praetorius' words:

Dieweil etlichen unter uns Teut-
schen, so der jetzigen newen Italiän-
ischen *Invention,* do (*i. e.,* wo) man
bissweilen nur eine *Concertat*-
Stimme allein, zu zeiten zwo oder
drey in eine Orgel oder Regal singen
lest, noch ungewohnet, diese Art
nicht so gar wol gefället, in Mey-
nung, der Gesang gehe gar zu bloss,
und habe bey denen, so die *Music*
nicht verstehen, kein sonderlich ansehen oder *gratiam.* Darumb ich
dann uff dieses Mittel bedacht seyn
müssen, dass man einen *Chorum*
oder *Capellam* mit 4. Stimmen
darzu setzte, welcher entweder mit
Posaunen oder Geigen allzeit zu-
gleich mit einstimmen köndte.[47]

Some of us Germans are unaccus-
tomed to the present new Italian
technique, where sometimes only
a single *concertato* voice or at times
two or three sing with an organ or
with a *Regal.* This method does not
especially please us, because we believe that the composition is too bare
and is not especially appreciated by
those who do not understand music.
I have therefore had to consider the
remedy that one add to this a choir
of four voices, which together with
either trombones or strings can always join in.

During the course of the 17th century the solo concerto form was
extended until it developed into the solo cantata. But, as with the
solo concerto, the German composers were not especially attracted to
the solo cantata either. They preferred the choral cantata, in which
they incorporated solo *concertato* style, either as a separate solo movement or as a *coro favorito within* a choral movement. Thus there was
a union of the two species of *concertato* style, a union of solo *concertato* style with *concerto per choros.*

Handschin has suggested that the Baroque era be labeled "the
period of the *concertato* style" (*die Zeit des konzertierenden Stils*),[48]
as Riemann some 50 years earlier had labeled it "the basso continuo
period" *(das Generalbasszeitalter).*[49] Both *concertato* style and basso
continuo, as well as a close relation between music and text, are important elements of most Baroque vocal music, and no one term properly
denotes them. But Handschin's suggestion does serve to emphasize
the importance, the uniformity, and the universality of contrast in the
music of this era.

The Peace Festival Banquet in Nuremberg on September 25, 1649

NOTES FOR CHAPTER 10

1. Max Schneider, "Die Besetzung der vielstimmigen Musik im 16./17. Jahr-hundert," *Archiv für Musikwissenschaft*, I (1918/19), 206: "Der fleissige braunschweigische Hofkapellmeister [i. e., Praetorius] schrieb aus der Praxis für die Praxis."

2. See the Dedication and the Introduction to *Syntagma musicum*, III. Through-out this paper reference will be made both to the modern edition of *Synt.*, III, ed. Eduard Bernoulli (Leipzig, 1916), and to the facsimile edition, ed. Wilibald Gurlitt (Kassel, 1958). Pages 104—128 in the original edition (and in the facs. ed.) were erroneously printed 124—148.

3. Jacques Handschin, *Musikgeschichte im Ueberblick* (Lucerne, 1948) pp. 284 to 288; Franz Giegling, "Sinn und Wesen des Concertare," in *Report of the Fourth Congress of the International Musicological Society* (Basel, 1949), pp. 129—132; Hans Heinrich Eggebrecht, "Zur Geschichte des 'Konzert'-Begriffs," in *107. Niederrheinisches Musikfest in Aachen, Jahrbuch* (Aachen, 1952), pp. 63—70, and *Heinrich Schütz, Musicus poeticus* (Göttingen, 1959), p. 15; David Boyden, "When is a concerto not a concerto?" in *Musical Quar-terly*, 43 (1957), 220—232, and Part I of the article "Konzert," in *Die Musik in Geschichte und Gegenwart*, VII, 1556 f.; Harold E. Samuel, Chapter IV of *The cantata in Nuremberg during the seventeenth century* (diss. Cornell, 1963).

4. *The Oxford English Dictionary* (Oxford, 1933), II, 764, "concert," second entry.

5. Ibid.

6. Ibid.

7. Ibid., p. 868, part 3 of the second entry of "consort": "The accord or harmony of several instruments or voices playing or singing in tune."

8. Ibid., X, 370, "Symphony."

9. *Synt.*, III, 19 (facs. ed., p. 5).

10. *Oxford English Dictionary*, II, 764.

11. *Synt.*, III.

12. P. 54.

13. Vol. I, p. 306. In *Der vollkommene Capellmeister* (Hamburg, 1739; facs. ed., ed. Margarete Reimann, Kassel and Basel, 1954), p. 222, Mattheson writes: ". . . the name *(Concerto)* comes from *certare*, to rival." (". . . der Nahm von *centare*, streiten, herkommt . . .")

14. Facs. ed. (Kassel: Bärenreiter Verlag, 1953), p. 179.

15. *Versuch einer gründlichen Violinschule* (Salzburg, 1756; modern ed. by Bernhard Paumgartner, Vienna, 1922) p. 263, para. 20.

16. *Musikalisches Lexikon* (Frankfort a/M, 1802), p. 350. Koch also defines baroque, *concertato* style; see p. 351, *concertirend* on p. 355 f., *concerto grosso* on p. 357, and *ripieno* on pp. 1260 f. For the definitions of concerto as a public concert and as a company of musicians see Eggebrecht, *"Zur Geschichte des 'Konzert'-Begriffs."*

17. P. 286: "Zusammenwirken mit gleichzeitigen Sichabheben."

18. For general information about the development of the polychoral style in Italy see Erich Hertzmann, "Zur Frage der Mehrchörigkeit in der ersten Hälfte des 16. Jahrhunderts, *Zeitschrift für Musikwissenschaft*, XII, (1929/30), 138—147; H. Zenk, "Adrian Willaerts 'Salmi spezzati,'" *Musikforschung*, II (1949), 97—107; and the excellent, recent studies made by Denis Arnold, especially

the articles "Andrea Gabrieli" and "Giovanni Gabrieli" in *MGG*, and "The significance of 'cori spezzati'," *Music and Letters*, XL (1959), 4—14. For the parallel German development of polychorality see Friedrich Blume, *Die evangelische Kirchenmusik* (Potsdam, 1931), pp. 94f.

19. The term *per choros* ("by choirs," or "choirwise") is from Praetorius; see *Synt.*, III, p.76 (facs. ed., p. 99).

20. During the baroque era the three choirs were given various designations, which Praetorius conveniently lists in a table on pp. 93f. (facs. ed., pp. 138f., i. e., 118). The table is reproduced in the article "Chor," by Walter Blankenburg, in *MGG*, II, 1241f.
    The spelling "capella" is found in all the German sources and has been retained here for the term *"Chorus pro capella."*

21. Other designations frequently used for this choir are *Chorus Vocalis, Voces Concertatae*, or *Chorus der Concertat-Stimmen* ("choir of *concertato* voices"). See *Synt.*, III, 82 (facs. ed., p. 126, i. e., 106).

22. This musician, who is identified by Praetorius (p. 82; facs. ed., p. 126, i. e., 106) as *"Capellmeister"* at St. Petronio's in Bologna," is listed in Eitner's *Quellenlexikon* (IV, 230) as "Giacobbi, Girolamo (Hieronymus Jacobus und Jacobbi)." Eitner gives his dates as c. 1575—1630.

23. *Synt.*, III, 82 (facs. ed., p. 126, i. e., 106).

24. In the foreword to his *Psalmen Davids*, II, 5 of his collected works.

25. Page 54. Walther, in his *Lexicon*, p. 179, designates the singers of the *Coro favorito* "Concertisten."

26. *Synt.*, III, 89 (facs. ed., p. 133, i. e., 113): "Welches dann ein trefflich Ornamentum, Pracht und Prangen in solcher Music von sich gibt."

27. *Synt.*, III, 88—91 (facs. ed., pp. 133—135, i. e., 113—115). In Baroque music the term "a capella" means "for the entire company of musicians," not "an unaccompanied, purely vocal composition" (see the article "a capella" by Hermann Zenck in MGG, I, 70—75).

28. Pp. 88 f. (facs. ed., pp. 133 f., i. e., 113 f.).

29. *Musica practica*, p. 54. See also Schütz's foreword to his *Psalmen Davids*, p. 5, par. 4, and Mattheson's *Der vollkommene Capellmeister*, p. 221, par. 70.

30. *Synt.*, III, 89 (facs. ed., p. 134, i. e., 114).

31. *Musica practica*, p. 54.

32. *Synt.*, III, 152 (facs. ed., p. 189).

33. *Synt.*, III, 90 (facs. ed., p. 135, i. e., 115). See also pp. 82f. (facs. ed., pp. 127f., i. e., 107f.).

34. *Musica practica*, p. 54. See also *Synt.*, III, 65 (facs. ed., p. 87) and 89 (facs. ed., p. 134, i. e., 114).

35. *Synt.*, III, 77 (facs. ed., pp. 100f.). For an example of an editor's experiment with underlaying a text to instrumental parts, see Spitta's ed. of Schütz's *Gesang der drei Männer im feurigen Ofen* (Ex. 1, above), in the collected ed. of Schütz's works, vol. XIII², pp. 177f. (see also Spitta's remarks on p. xiv).

36. Ibid., p. 89 (facs. ed., p. 134, i. e., 114). See also Schütz's foreword to his *Psalmen Davids*, II, 5, of his collected works; Schütz suggests the same practice as Praetorius and gives examples from his works. See also No. 4 on p. 5, where Schütz remarks that his choirs labeled *capella* (i. e., *Chorus pro capella*) are usually intended for "Zincken and other instruments": "however it is all the better, if one can also add singers."

37. Ibid., pp. 91f. (facs. ed., p. 136, i. e., 116). *Fidicinia* is from the Latin *fides*, meaning "a stringed instrument." (A *fidicen* is a lute player, a harper.) For German Baroque examples of *Concerto per choros* see Praetorius' "*Vater unser im Himmelreich*," in *Polyhymnia caduceatrix* (collected works, 17², 433—476); any of the concertos of Schütz's *Psalmen Davids*, but especially *Jauchzet dem Herren* (III, 239—282) and *Danket dem Herren* (pp. 182—216); Johann Schelle's *Lobe den Herrn, meine Seele* (*Denkmäler deutscher Tonkunst*, 58/59, pp. 122—166); the first movement of Bach cantata No. 195, *Dem Gerechten muss das Licht* (*Bachgesellschaft Ausgabe*, XIII¹, pp. 3—32); Bach cantata No. 71, "Gott ist mein König" (*BG*, XVIII, 3—56); and Bach cantata No. 110, *Unser Mund sei voll Lachens* (*BG*, XXIII, 271—304).

38. For experiments with the placing of choirs in various parts of a church for modern performances of Schütz' music, see the remarks and diagrams of Robert Unger, *Die mehrchörige Aufführungspraxis bei Michael Praetorius und die Feiergestaltung der Gegenwart* (Wolfenbüttel and Berlin, 1941), pp. 145—159. See also Hertzmann (title given above in footnote 18) and Karl Gustav Fellerer, "Raum und Klang in der Musik," *Die Musik*, 31 (1939), 289—294.

39. See the collected ed. of Praetorius' works, Vol. 16. The title reads: *Urania Oder Urano-Chorodia, Darinnen XVIIII . . . Teudtschen Kirchen Gesänge . . . Auff 2. 3. und 4. Choren zugebrauchen . . . Benebenst genugsamen Bericht und Anleitung, wie man alle andere Teudtsche Psalmen und Kirchen Gesänge . . . ohn sonderbahre Mühe und mit wenig Knaben, in 2. 3. und mehr Choren in der Kirchen an unterschiedenen Orten anordnen und gebrauchen könne.* For other instructions for the placing of choirs see *Synt.*, III, 90f. (facs. ed., p. 135, i. e., 115), 137 (172), and 144 (180); Praetorius' *Herr Christ, der einig Gottes Sohn*, in *Polyhymnia caduceatrix* (1619), in his collected works, 17², 708—719; Johann Staden's *Jesaiae dem Propheten das geschah*, in *Kirchen-Musik*, Part I (Nuremberg, 1625), No. 10 (modern ed., *Denkmäler der Tonkunst in Bayern*, VIII¹, 64—71, see especially p. x); and Schütz's foreword to his *Psalmen Davids*, p. 5, No. 2.

40. *Synt.*, III, 189 (facs. ed., p. 242); see also pp. 69f. (92) and 142f. (178f.). See also Schütz's foreword to his *Psalmen Davids*, p. 6, No. 7. The above quotation from Praetorius may partly explain the relative rarity of compositions with a separate basso continuo notated for each choir: the various continuo instruments played from copies of the same part.

41. It is reproduced in the facs. ed. of *Synt.*, II; in Kinsky, *Geschichte der Musik in Bildern*, p. 164, No. 2; and in Unger, p. 148.

42. The copy used for this study is in the Universitätsbibliothek, Erlangen, Germany. The plate is also reproduced in Kinsky, p. 174, No. 1. For a description of the seating plan of the four choirs, see Tobias Norlind, "*Ein Musikfest zu Nürnberg im Jahre 1649*", in *Sammelbände der Internationalen Musikgesellschaft*, 7 (1905/06), 111—113.

43. See, for example, Praetorius, *Synt.*, III, p. 98 (facs. ed., p. 144); J. Staden, in the Appendix to his *Kirchen-Music, Ander Theil*, Nuremberg, 1626 (see Arnold's *The art of accompaniment from a thorough-bass*, London, 1931, pp. 100f.); J. A. Herbst, *Musica practica* (Nuremberg, 1642), p. 54; Wolfgang Caspar Printz, *Historische Beschreibung der edlen Singe-Kunst* (Dresden, 1690), p. 132f.; J. G. Walther, *Musicalisches Lexicon* (Leipzig, 1732), the article "Viadana" (facs. ed., Kassel and Basel, 1953); and Johann Mattheson, *Der volkommene Capellmeister* (Hamburg, 1739), p. 221.

44. *Bassus pro organo*, the basso continuo in Viadana's solo concertos, and the

basso continuo of the *nuove musiche* are described by H. H. Eggebrecht, "Arten des Generalbasses im frühen und mittleren 17. Jahrhundert," in *AfMw*, 14 (1957), 61—82. See also H. Samuel, Chapter V.

45. Several of Viadana's concertos are available in modern editions: eleven are in M. Schneider, *Die Anfänge des Basso Continuo und seiner Bezifferung* (Leipzig, 1918), pp. 172—202; six are in F. T. Arnold, *The art of accompaniment from a thoroughbass* (London, 1931), pp. 21—33; and at least one in each of the various anthologies (Schering, Davison and Apel, Parrish and Ohl, and Wolf). For examples of German solo concertos see J. Staden's *Cantate Domino canticum novum* in his *Harmoniae variatae*, Nuremberg, 1632 (modern ed. in *DTB*, VIII¹ 3—5; Schütz's *Kleine geistliche Concerte*, Leipzig, 1636 (Collected works, vol. 6); and nos. 2 and 8 of J. E. Kindermann's *Musicalische Friedens Seufftzer*, Nuremberg, 1642 (modern ed. in *DTB*, 13, 127—31 and 145—47).

46. *Synt.*, III, 140 (facs. ed., p. 176). The third *Art* includes nine *Manieren*. For Praetorius's suggestions for placing the solo voices in various parts of the church, see also *Synt.*, III, 137 (facs. ed., p. 172) and 146 (182).

47. *Synt.*, III, 91 (facs. ed., p. 136, i. e., 116).

48. *Musikgeschichte im Ueberblick*, p. 285.

49. See the foreword, p. vi, Vol. II², of his *Handbuch der Musikgeschichte* (Leipzig, 1912).

11

BACH'S CHORALE CANTATAS

Alfred Dürr

Composers of Protestant church music have always considered the polyphonic arrangement of the Protestant chorale their main task. This polyphony reaches its climax in the work of Johann Sebastian Bach. No composer before or after him possessed a closer relationship to the chorale; hardly another composer blended his work so intimately into it. At a time when composers begin to lose their interest in the chorale arrangement, Bach does not grow tired of arranging it in constantly new formal patterns. While Bach's contemporaries frequently observe a noticeable distance to the given church tune in their chorale arrangements, Bach amalgamates it with his composition in the closest possible way. With Philipp Spitta (II, 991) we find this to be a genuinely Protestant feature in Bach, "when he treats the chorale tune with great freedom."

An especially characteristic form of chorale arrangement of Bach is the chorale cantata, that is, the composition of a whole church cantata on the basis of one single chorale. To be sure, chorale cantatas were composed in great numbers already in the 17th century, and among them true master works were created; yet even this form of composition finds its climax in Bach. At the same time Bach developed a new, specific application of this form by combining chorale arrangements with the aria and recitative, forms which he took over from the opera.

The manifold forms of the Bach cantata make it necessary first of all to define what we mean by "chorale cantata" in this discussion. We take for granted that we deal with a chorale cantata when the entire work or essential parts of it are oriented according to one single chorale, the text and music of the stanzas of which are either retained in an unchanged fashion or only partly preserved and partly composed in a free fashion. The following works do *not* fall under the category of the chorale cantata: (1) works that use only an occasional chorale stanza, (2) works that incorporate in their texts several, or even many, stanzas from various chorales, and (3) works which dovetail two different movements of the work through the same chorale melody (as Bach frequently manages to do through instrumental chorale quotations in his Weimar cantatas), without shaping the greater part of the work according to this chorale in text and melody. Nevertheless, an exact classification is hardly possible. Thus one will hardly call *Cantata BWV 138*, "Warum betrübst du dich, mein Herz," a chorale cantata since only 3 of the 14 stanzas of the hymn are utilized, and since the remaining text of the cantata does not show any connection with the chorale. On the other hand, *Cantata BWV 10*, "Meine Seel' erhebt den Herren," after a Biblical text (Luke 1:46-55), may still be considered a chorale cantata since this text, together with the melody of the ninth psalm tone, here takes the place of the chorale.

Under these assumptions the following cantatas of Bach can be designated as chorale cantatas. We shall list the cantatas in their probable chronological order [1] and at subsequent mention refer to them with the numbers of this list. We do this in order to facilitate their location in the following chart.

No.	Season	BWV [2] Text Beginning	Text Author [3]	Melody Zahn No.[4]	Year
About 1708:					
1	Easter	4 "Christ lag in Todesbanden"	M. Luther, 1524	7012a	1524
1715/after 1723:					
2	Reformation	80 "Ein feste Burg"	M. Luther, 1528/29 S. Franck, 1715	7377d	1528/ 1529
1724:					
3	Trinity I	20 "O Ewigkeit, du Donnerwort"	*J. Rist,* 1642	5820	1642/ 1653
4	Trinity II	2 "Ach Gott, vom Himmel sieh darein"	*M. Luther,* 1524	4431	1524
5	St. John, Baptist	7 "Christ, unser Herr, zum Jordan kam"	*M. Luther,* 1541	7246	1524
6	Trinity III	135 "Ach, Herr, mich armen Sünder"	*C. Schneegass,* 1597	5385a	1601/ 1613
7	Visitation	10 "Meine Seel erhebt den Herren"	*Luke 1:46-55*	Psalm tone IX	
8	Trinity V	93 "Wer nur den lieben Gott lässt walten"	*G. Neumark,* 1657	2778	1657

9	Trinity VII	107	"Was willst du dich betrüben"	J. Heermann, 1630	5264b	1563
10	Trinity VIII	178	"Wo Gott der Herr nicht bei uns hält"	J. Jonas, 1524	4441a	1529
11	Trinity IX	94	"Was frag ich nach der Welt"	Kindermann, 1664	5206b	1679/ 1698
12	Trinity X	101	"Nimm von uns, Herr"	M. Moller, 1584	2561	1539
13	Trinity XI	113	"Herr Jesu Christ, du höchstes Gut!"	B. Ringwaldt, 1588	4486	1593
14	Trinity XIII	33	"Allein zu dir, Herr Jesu Christ"	K. Hubert, 1540	7292b	1545
15	Trinity XIV	78	"Jesu, der du meine Seele"	J. Rist, 1641	6804	1662
16	Trinity XV	99	"Was Gott tut, das ist wohlgetan"	S. Rodigast, 1675	5629	1679
17	Trinity XVI	8	"Liebster Gott, wann werd' ich sterben"	C. Neumann, before 1697	6634	1695
18	St. Michael	130	"Herr Gott, dich loben alle wir"	P. Eber, about 1561	368	1551
19	Trinity XVII	114	"Ach lieben Christen, seid getrost"	J. Gigas, 1561	4441a	1529
20	Trinity XVIII	96	"Herr Christ, der ein'ge Gottessohn"	E. Kreuziger, 1524	4297a	1524
21	Trinity XIX	5	"Wo soll ich fliehen hin"	J. Heermann, 1630	2164	1576/ 1627
22	Trinity XX	180	"Schmücke dich, o liebe Seele"	J. Franck, 1653	6923	1649
23	Trinity XXI	38	"Aus tiefer Not"	M. Luther, 1524	4437	1524
24	Trinity XXII	115	"Mache dich, mein Geist, bereit"	J. B. Freystein 1697	6274a	1694
25	Trinity XXIII	139	"Wohl dem, der sich auf seinen Gott"	J. C. Rube, 1692	2383	1605/ 1628
26	Trinity XXIV	26	"Ach wie flüchtig"	M. Franck, 1652	1887b	1652/ 1661
27	Trinity XXV	116	"Du Friedefürst, Herr Jesu Christ"	J. Ebert, 1601	4373	1601
28	Advent I	62	"Nun komm, der Heiden Heiland"	M. Luther, 1524	1174	1524
29	Christmas I	91	"Gelobet seist du, Jesu Christ"	M. Luther, 1524	1947	1524
30	Christmas II	121	"Christum wir sollen loben schon"	M. Luther, 1524	297c	1529
31	Christmas III	133	"Ich freue mich in dir"	K. Ziegler, 1697	5187	——
32	Sunday after Christmas	122	"Das neugeborne Kindelein"	C. Schneegass, 1597	491	1609

1725:

33	New Year	41	"Jesu, nun sei gepreiset"	*J. Herman, 1591*	8477a	1591
34	Epiphany	123	"Liebster Immanuel, Herzog der Frommen"	*A. Fritsch, 1679*	4932c	1698
35	Epiphany I	124	"Meinen Jesum lass ich nicht"	*C. Keymann, 1658*	3449	1658
36	Epiphany II	3	"Ach Gott, wie manches Herzeleid"	*M. Moller, 1587*	533a	1602/ 1625
37	Epiphany III	111	"Was mein Gott will, das g'scheh allzeit"	*A. v. Branden- burg(?), 1547*	7568	1529/ 1572
38	Septuagesima	92	"Ich hab in Gottes Herz und Sinn"	*P. Gerhardt, 1647*	7568	1529/ 1572
39	Purification	125	"Mit Fried und Freud ich fahr dahin"	*M. Luther, 1524*	3986	1524
40	Sexagesima	126	"Erhalt uns, Herr, bei deinem Wort"	*M. Luther, 1524/J. Jonas*	350	1543
41	Estomihi	127	"Herr Jesu Christ, wahr' Mensch und Gott"	*P. Eber, 1562*	2570	1551
42	Annunciation	1	"Wie schön leuchtet der Morgenstern"	*Ph. Nicolai, 1599*	8359	1538/ 1599
43	Trinity XII	137	"Lobe den Herren, den mächtigen König"	*J. Neander, 1680*	1912a	1665

1726 or 1727:

44	Trinity	129	"Gelobet sei der Herr, mein Gott"	*J. Olearius, 1665*	5206b	1679/ 1698

1730:

45	(none)	192	"Nun danket alle Gott"	*M. Rinckart, 1636*	5142	1647

1731:

46	Trinity XXVII	140	"Wachet auf, ruft uns die Stimme"	*Ph. Nicolai, 1599*	8405	1513/ 1599
47	Misericordias	112	"Der Herr ist mein getreuer Hirt"	unknown poet Augsburg, 1531	4457	1539

1728/1731:

48	(none)	117	"Sei Lob und Ehr dem höchsten Gut"	*J. J. Schütz, 1675(?)*	4430	1523

1732:

49	Trinity IV	177	"Ich ruf zu dir, Herr Jesu Christ"	*J. Agricola, 1529(?)/31*	7400 (5689)	1527/ 1529

1734:

50	(none)	97	"In allen meinen Taten"	*P. Fleming, 1642*	2293c	1505/ 1605

1735:

51	Epiphany IV	14	"Wär Gott nicht mit uns diese Zeit"	*M. Luther, 1524*	**4434**	1524
52	Trinity VI	9	"Es ist das Heil uns kommen her"	*P. Speratus, 1524*	4430	1523
53	(none)	100	"Was Got tut, das ist wohlgetan"	S. Rodigast, 1675	5629	1679

Bach's chorale cantatas can be subdivided according to the text as follows:

a) The text of the chorale has been left unchanged and retained without any inserts (Nos. 1, 9, 43–46, 48–50, 53).

b) The text of the chorale has been retained unchanged, but between stanzas inserts of free texts are found (Nos. 2, 46).

c) The wording of the text of the chorale has been partly retained, partly written anew or provided with free inserts. These poetic paraphrases sometimes follow the chorale text very strictly, sometimes, however, they imitate more freely and thus cannot always be distinguished from free inserts (Nos. 3–8, 10–42, 51, 52).

Three different phases of Bach's occupation with the chorale cantata can be also distinguished according to the time they were composed. The first phase, around 1708, comprises only the cantata "Christ lag in Todesbanden" (No. 1), which Bach sets to music still according to the old-fashioned form of the chorale arrangement *per omnes versus,* and which he later, notwithstanding this, included in the cycle of his chorale cantatas. Textually it belongs to group a).

The second group falls into the narrow time limit from Trinity I, 1724, to the Annunciation, 1725 (Nos. 3–42). During this time Bach composed the famous annual set of his chorale cantatas, providing them Sunday after Sunday in succession; later supplements refer only to cantatas that for some reason were omitted within the mentioned time interval, or that, according to their purpose, fall in the time between Easter and Trinity. According to their textual form, the cantatas of this phase belongs almost exclusively to group c); only No. 9 is set to music with an unchanged hymn text, or in the manner of group a). Possibly this was caused by the lack of a paraphrased text.

The chorale cantatas composed *after* this series belong to the third phase. In part these were afterwards inserted into the set already mentioned (Nos. 43, 44, 46, 47, 49, 51, 52, probably also 2); in part, they do not have any church-year designation at all and

therefore do not seem to be connected to any set (Nos. 45, 48, 50, 53).
All these cantatas belong only in small part to the text form of group
c) (Nos. 51, 52), in one case to group b) (No. 47), mostly, however,
to group a) (Nos. 43–46, 48–50, 53).

Composing cantatas on unchanged chorale texts coincides for the
most part with a time when Bach had already abandoned the systematic composition of entire annual sets of cantatas. Apart from the
sacred parody of some occasional secular works, it therefore exhibits
the general characteristics of Bach's later cantatas. Philipp Spitta dated
the annual set of the chorale cantatas around 1740. He understood
the literal retention of the text as a transitory solution, which could
not satisfy Bach in the long run and thus led him to the text group b).
This order presents itself to us today in a reversed way: the freer text
form of group b) appears to be embedded in the composition of Sets I
(1723–1724) and III (1725–1727), which were not conceived as
chorale cantatas, while the literal retention of the text of the chorale
characterizes the real *final phase* of Bach's cantata compositions.

The section of Bach's chorale cantatas that is numerically largest
belongs to the cycle of 1724/1725 and to the texts of group b). The
composing of entire annual cycles of chorale cantatas was not new;
it was practiced already at various times in the 17th century. Not only
musical intentions but the sermon as well may have motivated it.
In those days the service was in many places still under the domination
of the pericopes. The Gospel of the morning service was at the same
time the text for the sermon, and the imagination of the preacher
strove to vary the annually recurring themes as much as possible.
Thus, one hit upon the chorale sermons; the pastor selected a chorale
suitable to the Gospel, and this, next to the Gospel itself, was chosen
as the subject of the sermon. Nothing was more appropriate than
to use this chorale also for the Sunday church music. This can be
proved, for instance, from Johann Schelle's activity as canter at Saint
Thomas in Leipzig.

In 1690 the pastor of St. Thomas, Johann Benedict Carpzov, published his *Lehr- und Liederpredigten* ("Instructive Chorale Sermons"),
delivered during the preceding year. In the preface he remarked that
on each Sunday of the past year he had expounded the Gospel for the
day plus "a beautiful, old Protestant and Lutheran hymn . . . and also
had ordered that the chorale discoursed upon be sung by the congregation right after the sermon." He went on to say that he would
deliver similar discourses in the coming year and that "the famous

musician, Mr. Johann Schelle, had kindly offered to compose pleasant music around each chorale and to perform it before the sermon in order to make the service even more inviting and the pious listeners even more eager to hear." [5]

We do not know whether Bach's compositions of the chorale-cantata cycle, or at least the texts, go back to a similar motivation. It is certainly possible.

The chorales which Bach chose belong mostly to those songs which a special index in the hymnbooks of the time recommended as suitable for the Gospels of the individual Sundays. In numerous cases this recommendation is obvious — for Advent I the chorale "Nun komm, der Heiden Heiland" or for Christmas I the chorale "Gelobet seist du, Jesu Christ"; in certain other cases chorales were chosen that habit had assigned to certain Sundays, though the authors had not specifically made this assignment — for Trinity XVIII "Herr Christ, der ein'ge Gottessohn" or for Trinity XXI "Aus tiefer Not schrei ich zu dir"; in some other cases, as far as this is evident in the hymnbooks of Bach's time,[6] a given hymn is neither assigned specifically for a certain day nor listed in a category of hymns useful for that day (Jesus-Hymns, for instance) — for example, "Liebster Immanuel, Herzog der Frommen" for Epiphany. Therefore the statement which one encounters occasionally, that Bach always set to music the hymn for the day in his chorale cantatas, is not quite correct. These chorales were in the first place for the congregation, and Bach may have seen no reason to take them away from the congregation regularly. Thus, for instance, the chorale "Warum betrübst du dich, mein Herz" was usually identified with the Trinity VII. On that Sunday in 1724 it was probably sung in its entirety by the congregation, while the chorale "Was willst du dich betrüben?" — similar in content but not expressly recommended for this particular Sunday in most of the hymnbooks — was heard in the cantata (No. 9).

As one surveys the *poets* of the hymns used, one is impressed by the considerable percentage of Reformation hymns, especially those of Luther. While the other poets are represented by no more than two hymns, Luther's name is found right at the beginning of the cantata compositions (No. 1), then in connection with Salomon Franck's poetry of 1715, which was expanded to the "Ein feste Burg" cantata at an unknown date. (No. 2), further, eight times in the cantatas of 1724/1725 (Nos. 4, 5, 23, 28–30, 39, 40), and once more at the end of the series in perhaps the last week of this kind, "Wär Gott nicht mit uns diese Zeit" (No. 51). The remaining poets represented by more than one text are Justus Jonas (Nos. 10, 40), Paul Eber (18, 41), Martin Moller (12, 36), Cyriacus Schneegass (6, 32), Philipp Nicolai (42, 47), Johann Heermann (9, 21), Johann Rist (3, 15), and twice with the same hymn Samuel Rodigast (16, 53). All other poets are represented only by one text. A chronological table showing the dates of origin of the hymn texts presents the following picture:

(Biblical text:)	1 cantata
1524 – 1550:	17 (11 of which are texts by Luther)
1551 – 1600:	12
1601 – 1650:	8
1651 – 1697:	15
After 1697:	—

On the one hand, there is certainly an emphasis on the Reformation period and the decades that followed it immediately, and on the other hand a stress on the second half of the 17th century. The period of the Thirty Years' War remains untouched completely. This can be seen above all from the fact that there is only one chorale (No. 38) by the representative poet of these decades, Paul Gerhardt. In the same way, the contemporary sacred poetry of the Bach period is missing completely, and not only the poets of the Freylinghausen hymnbook but also those of the Orthodox movement, such as Erdmann Neumeister, Salomon Franck, or Benjamin Schmolck, are not present.

As one examines the melodies Bach used, a similar result is observed. Here, however, still other factors must be taken into consideration. First of all, one may assume that Bach in most cases followed the melody used locally. He was thus committed already by the selection of the text. Furthermore, one must consider that our knowledge about the origin of the melodies is often very incomplete, so that the year assigned often represents only the *terminus ad quem*. Finally, many melodies are altered in many ways to such an extent that the altered and the original melody often can hardly be distinguished. If, in spite of this, one attempts to undertake a chronological chart of the melodies used by Bach, the following distribution results:

Gregorian:	1 cantata
Before 1550:	25
1551 – 1600:	6
1601 – 1650:	9
1651 – 1700:	11
After 1700 (?):	1

Thus here, too, the two centers of gravity are in the Reformation period (including the hymn repertory of the pre-Reformation era) and the second half of the 17th century. Here again the absence of chorales from the period 1550–1650 and from the era of Pietism is noteworthy, chorales that were later represented throughout the Schemelli hymnbook (1736).

Notable, however, is the use of a new melody for "Ich freue mich in dir," a tune then probably still unknown in Leipzig. It is well known that Bach notated this melody for himself for the first time in connection with the composition of the cantata of the same name (No. 31), sketching it on the score of the *Sanctus* (BWV 232) at Christmas in 1725. There is no reason to assume that Bach composed this melody himself; but it is not found in print until 1738 (J. B. König, *Harmonischer Lieder-Schatz*). This is an example of our defective knowledge of the history of the melodies of that time! Here Bach actually took up an unknown melody and introduced it to the Leipzig congregation through his setting of the chorale cantata. On the whole, however, this case represents an exception.

The chorale cantatas show how closely tradition and modern writing go hand in hand in Bach's work. The concertizing arrangements of old-fashioned chorale melodies and, above all, the settings of chorale texts in the form of recitatives and arias prove this. To conclude, it would be advisable to ask cautiously whether Bach himself, in the course of his life, was not exposed to a change and in the 1730s turned his interest to an increasing degree to the chorale output of his own time. Already in the *Christmas Oratorio* the hymnody of the 17th century outweighs that of the Reformation period.[7] And even more in the Schemelli hymnbook the turn to the musical present time was completed. Possibly future investigations may decide whether this happened just accidentally, or whether we can here observe a change of aesthetics in Bach.

NOTES FOR CHAPTER 11

1. Cf. Alfred Dürr, "Zur Chronologie der Leipziger Vokalwerke J. S. Bachs," *Bach-Jahrbuch 1957*, pp. 5 ff.
2. The number assigned in *Bach-Werke-Verzeichnis*, ed. Wolfgang Schmieder (Leipzig: Breitkopf & Härtel, 1950).
3. If the author's name is in regular type, the text is his own composition; if the name is in italics, the person named has altered the text in part, and the original author is unknown.
4. The number in Johannes Zahn, *Die Melodien der deutschen evangelischen Kirchenlieder*, 6 vols. (Gütersloh, 1888—93; reprint: Hildesheim, 1963).
5. See Arnold Schering, *Denkmäler Deutscher Tonkunst*, 58/59, p. XXXIII.

6. See Werner Neumann, "Zur Frage der Gesangbücher J. S. Bachs," *Bach-Jahrbuch 1956*, pp. 112 ff.

7. See *Neue Bach-Ausgabe*, Series II, Vol. 6, *Kritischer Bericht*, pp. 196 f.

12

KIERKEGAARD AND MOZART: A STUDY

Gerhard M. Cartford

KIERKEGAARD – THE STAGES OF LIFE'S WAY

One of the basic elements in Søren Kierkegaard's philosophy is his doctrine of the three spheres of human existence, which he calls the "stages of life's way." The first, the aesthetic, is the one most common to man. It calls for him to realize as completely as possible his own capacities for self-fulfillment. The second, the ethical stage, introduces into life an "ought," the idea of duty beyond that of mere self-realization. God appears in this stage, but only as a sort of universal, underlying principle. In the third stage, the religious stage, God breaks through the universal ethical to establish contact with man. This contact results in man's sensing God's "otherness." He feels a sense of guilt and suffers for it. This is as far as he can get in what Kierkegaard terms Religion A, or immanent religion. In Religion B, transcendent religion, man's sense of guilt is revealed to him as sin because he recognizes God's total, awful "otherness," His eternity as against man's temporality. The gulf between the two is infinite, unbridgeable – except by the leap of faith.

The three stages are not mutually exclusive. They overlap to a greater or lesser degree. Although Kierkegaard places the aesthetic stage at the lowest level and the religious at the highest, in terms of relative value, he holds that the aesthetic, as well as the ethical, ought to be incorporated as a disciplined part of the religious.

The discussion in the following pages deals with one aspect of the aesthetic stage, as Kierkegaard saw it embodied in the legendary figure of Don Juan.

THE BANQUET

"To be good, a thing must be at once, for 'at once' is the most divine of all categories" (*Stages*, p. 39). Victor Eremita was addressing his companions as they sat speaking about a projected banquet in which they were all planning to take part. He was objecting to having a banquet because he did not think it could be carried out properly. And if this were to be the case, it would be better not to have one at all. In any case, it was a mistake to speak about it beforehand because that would rob it of its spontaneity, its freshness, its immediacy.

Ideally, the banquet ought to appear suddenly, complete in every detail, so that the banqueters could sit down to it in immediate delight, without having to give it any prior thought. The fruitfulness of the earth would be in lavish supply in front of them, "as though everything were sprouting the very instant appetite desires it." Even if it could not all be there, the possibility of it, "more seductive than the sight," must be. There would be ceaseless animation, like a bubbling fountain. Life would sparkle, and everyone's full enjoyment would be the key of the hour. Conversation would flow freely, and music would fill in the gaps that might occur. Speeches would be made only when one's tongue was sufficiently loosened by the plentiful wine so that one's mind was absolved of the responsibility of guiding its utterances.

Only in this fashion should a banquet take place. That it could take place was much to be doubted. After having imagined it in all its details, it would be anticlimactic to try actually to bring it off — a mere repetition of the imagined banquet and consequently not desirable. Reality would probably fall disappointingly short, "for while there is no power which knows so well how to beautify all things as does imagination, neither is there any power which can so profoundly disturb everything when it fails one upon coming into contact with real life." (*Stages*, p. 42)

It is not the purpose of this paper to discuss further the banquet with which Kierkegaard (or his pseudonymous author) illustrates his concept of the life of the aesthete, but the brief recounting above provides a fruitful point of departure for a description of it.

THE AESTHETE, DETAILED

How can the aesthetic be most fully emphasized? By living it — in immediacy, without undue reflection, except insofar as reflection will add to fulfillment of desire. The banquet described by Victor Eremita is one type of aesthetic realization. "Eat, drink and be merry, for tomorrow we may die," is the way the rich farmer in the Bible puts it. For the aesthete, the past is dead and forgotten; the future has not yet come and so warrants no immediate concern; all of life is concentrated in the present, more exactly, the present moment. "The happy moment is everything." [1] The aesthete's goal in life is to extract from every moment the maximum enjoyment. ". . . he lives . . . statically . . . on the basis of what he already is, taken immediately. He is, in other words, the natural man. Enjoyment is the accompaniment of a functioning whose organ is already adequate to its task." [2] He is sufficient unto himself. He takes life as it comes, living accidentally, adapting to circumstances in order not to subtract from his pleasure. The fulfillment of his appetites and desires shapes his habits, and he will not change them, unless by so doing he can further his pleasure. He is not concerned with any consequences of his actions, except to escape them. He is not plagued by any moral compunctions. In fact, morality does not enter into the picture at all, for that posits an authority outside the self which the aesthete refuses to recognize. His perspective is bounded by his own age, and self-realization is its total aim. He is a poet, to the extent that he can abstract from life and derive enjoyment out of the *idea* of life, without having to bore himself with all of real life's common details. Victor Eremita can enjoy the superabundance of all the good things at the table, even if they are not all there, but present only as possibilities. Don Juan enjoys the *idea* of woman as much as he relishes seducing individual women. John the Seducer, in his banquet speech, elaborated thus on this theme: "One therefore can think of a single man existing and nothing more than that. On the other hand, the idea of woman is a generality which is not exhaustively exemplified in any single woman . . . for her idea is only a workshop of possibilities, and for the erotic these possibilities are the never-failing source of enthusiasm" (*Stages*, pp. 84 f.). The possibility is as good as the reality, better if there is a chance that the reality might not be realized.

Kierkegaard describes five types of aesthetes. They are represented by the people who make up the banquet company. There is first the Young Man. He has superior intelligence and knowledge, but he cannot commit himself to anything in life. He will not take part in life but tries rather to apprehend its experiences at second hand, by means of reflection. He wants to remain unsullied by the common, the mean. The second type of aesthete is characterized by Constantin Constantius, who prepared the banquet. He has despaired of trying to repeat life's happy moments. He also is coldly intelligent, speaks contemptuously of women and treats them as a jest of the gods. The third aesthete is Victor Eremita, a reflective sort. His publishing of *Either/Or* reveals his awareness of ethical categories, but he rejects them as guides for life. John the Seducer, is the fourth type. He lives for woman in the moment, an object to be explained in order to satisfy selfish desire. The fifth type is the Dressmaker, the mad fashion designer, who derives aesthetic satisfaction from exploiting woman's vanity by creating and imposing styles that make her appear utterly ridiculous. Of the five types, the fourth, John the Seducer, is the one most nearly akin to Don Juan, the central figure in Mozart's opera *Don Giovanni*.

Don Juan

There are three stages of the Don Juan type. All three are typified by characters in three of Mozart's operas: Cherubino in *The Marriage of Figaro*, Papageno in *The Magic Flute*, and Don Giovanni (Don Juan) in *Don Giovanni*. The stages do not exist independently of each other. Kierkegaard proposes the term "metamorphosis" as an alternate for "stage," since the first two stages culminate in the last. Actually they are three manifestations of desire: dreaming, seeking, conquering.

Kierkegaard abstracts from *The Marriage of Figaro* and *The Magic Flute* in order to build his characterizations of Cherubino and Papageno. He is not describing the "accidental" Cherubino and Papageno on the stage, but what he considers to be the "essential" Cherubino and Papageno — the type. Cherubino, the first type, is characterized by a melancholy longing to consummate his desire, but his desire is never really born. He never gets beyond the dreaming stage. In this stage desire is never really born. We "both are neuter gender," male and female in the same blossom. Mozart's music for Cherubino is like a "love potion."

Stage two comes a step further. Desire in Papageno is awakened, but in awakening is immediately separated from its object. So it goes seeking its object and does so "in the manifold," that is, it is intent upon, and satisfied with, discovery — brief encounters, stolen kisses, but not consummation. Thus it is with Papageno, over and over, like his own incessant, twittering musical accompaniment, "cheerfully chirping, vigorous, sentimental." Flute music expresses him admirably.

The third stage is found only in Don Juan, and the whole opera *Don Giovanni*, not just a part of it, is expressive of him. He is thoroughly desirous, and completely and supremely successful in realizing his desire. He is not satisfied with anything less than full realization; but at the same time he is capable of being satisfied with the *principle* of desire, of becoming so engrossed with the *idea* that he becomes absolutely demonic,[3] entirely self-sufficient, so intoxicated with himself that, as the author puts it in discussing Don Juan's Champagne Aria: "If every girl in the world surrounded him in this moment, he would not be a source of danger to them, for he is, as it were, too strong to wish to deceive them; even the manifold enjoyments of actuality are too little for him in comparison with what he enjoys in himself" (*Either/Or*, I, p. 109). Here he becomes qualified no longer as the individual, but as the principle of desire, the essence of the sensuous, a state of being which is adequately expressible only in music.[4]

THE SEDUCER

The Middle Ages created Don Juan. He became the incarnation of fleshly desire. Christianity breathed life into him by positing his opposite: spirit. The church, with strong ascetic leanings, widened the breach between spirit and flesh. Don Juan, therefore, came to stand at the ultimate point of removal from all that the church stood for. He was the embodiment of pure sensuality, of eroticism, of the principle of seduction. Because he came to occupy a position of such rarified abstraction, the Middle Ages provided him with a more humane, believable companion: Leporello (Sganarelle, in the earlier story). Thus in parallel legends, Faust had his Wagner, and Don Quixote his Sancho Panza. This struck a comic balance, too, between master and servant that provided some basis for reality and for appropriating the legend, in varying forms, to everyday life.

Don Juan was therefore well established in popular history — with what Edward J. Dent calls "an unearned increment in popular history" — it remained, however, for Mozart to come along with the perfect medium in which to give expression to him: music. For music is the absolute medium for sensuous immediacy, and sensuous immediacy is Don Juan's predicate.

Kierkegaard compares Mozart's Don Juan with Molière's, in his play *Le Festin de Pierre* (1665).[6] He says that Molière's Don Juan, who quite naturally has a speaking role in the play, is for this reason out of character. For language reduces him to the level of an individual whose destiny is now affected by those around him. He no longer represents the principle of seduction. He is now only the individual seducer, interested in the accidental rather than the essential.

Language makes him reflective rather than immediate. He gets more enjoyment from the deception — the how — of seduction than he does from the satisfaction of desire. Seduction for him becomes a series of "sleight-of-hand tricks," rather than the "handspring" of the immediate seducer. To connect the individual seducer with the 1,003 conquests in Spain is ridiculous. For the true Don Juan, on the other hand, the 1,003 follow of necessity, because he represents the principle of seduction, which can only be satisfied with the totality of womanhood. The figure itself means nothing, except to indicate that it is incomplete, that Don Juan is a man in a hurry. The immediate Don Juan hovers between actuality and idea. His essence is energy, life, and his life is at the same time the moment and the sum of all the moments. He cannot properly be described or seen. He is best heard. Herein lies Mozart's genius, that he made Don Juan come alive by wedding him to music.

Some people have held the opinion that Molière's Don Juan is more moral than Mozart's. If this be so, it speaks well for the opera, which does not seek to be moral. These people merely reveal that they have their categories mixed up. They are dragging in the ethical where no one wants it, least of all Don Juan, who even refuses to admit of any ethical imperative as he is being dragged down to hell.[7] Furthermore, to criticize an opera as immoral reveals ignorance on the part of the critics, who have lost sight of its totality in viewing its details.

On the contrary, seen in its proper category, *Don Giovanni* expresses Don Juan admirably, because, as music, it is a "perpetual vanishing," "a disappearance in time," just like Don Juan's love. He is the great unfaithful lover, loving each girl only in the moment, then leaving her for the next one. It is a stroke of genius to have Don Juan try to seduce Zerlina in the opera, because she is just a peasant girl with no particular attraction, except that, in Leporello's words, "she wears a petticoat" and therefore is legitimate prey for the Don. (*Pur chè porti la gonella voi sapeta quel chè fa.*) He loves them all, poor and rich, young and old, noble and peasant. To him "every girl is woman in general, every love affair an everyday story." In a drama, where the characters confront each other as individuals, it would hardly do justice to the dramatic action to allow the hero to waste time on a peasant girl. He would have to involve himself with the noble lady. But, expressed in music, Don Juan is not interpreted as an individual, but as principle, as power, as the "whole infinitude

KIERKEGAARD AND MOZART: A STUDY

of passions." Music allows him to be true to his essential nature, to express the general, always confident of victory, always triumphant, exuberant, bursting with *joie de vivre*.

DON JUAN IN THE OPERA

A drama tends to "pull apart" because the action and dialog set the characters against each other as individuals, dramatically. By contrast, an opera "pulls together" by virtue of its music, which unites its different elements, lyrically.[8] Unity in an opera is provided by a keynote. Here it is Don Juan himself. He is not, in one sense, a character in the opera, but the principle of life itself — therefore musical. "Det D. Juanske Liv er egl. musicalsk . . ." [9] He, or his presence, his idea, dominates the opera from the beginning to the end. All interest centers in him. The others derive their interest from him. His life is the life principle in them. His passion sets theirs in motion. He is the common denominator. Compared with his, their existence is derived. He is heard through the utterances of all the others. He is the lyrical one, concerned only with *the* golden moment. His point of highest lyricism comes in his Champagne Aria, where he is totally lost in his own identity as the embodiment of the sensuous.

The reason Don Juan is so completely the center and substance of the opera is that he is the only absolutely musical subject there is. In uniting music and Don Juan, Mozart achieved the ultimate in classic expression: perfect union of form and content, the most abstract medium and the most abstract idea. "There can, of course, be a number of classical musical productions, but there will never be more than the one work of which it is possible to say that the idea is absolutely musical, so that the music does not appear as an accompaniment but reveals its own innermost essence in revealing the idea. It is for this reason that Mozart stands highest among the Immortals, through his *Don Juan*." (*Either/Or*, I, p. 46)

Music can also lend expression to what lies within the realm of spirit, but it does so only imperfectly. Its proper realm is the sensuous. "The genius of sensuality (sensuousness) is hence the absolute subject of music. The sensual (sensuous) genius is absolutely lyrical, and it comes to expression in music in all its lyrical impatience. It is, namely, spiritually determined, and therefore, it is force, life, movement, constant unrest, perpetual succession;[10] but this unrest, this succession, does not enrich it, it remains always the same, it does not unfold itself, but it storms uninterruptedly forward as if in a single breath. If I desired to characterize this lyrical quality by a single predicate, I should say: it sounds; and this brings me back again to the sensual (sensuous) genius as the one that appears immediately musical." (I, p. 57)

MOZART – LIFE AND MUSIC

Mozart was really the first of the child prodigies. Since his time, there have been a number of others, but none with quite the same hold on the popular imagination, or, for that matter, with the same genius. His early successes as a *Wunderkind* were indicative of the facility with which he handled music all his life. After only 35 years he died. Yet he left behind a prodigious amount of music, a normal lifetime's worth, which had been written for all the existing media of his time. Furthermore, most of it is music of the highest artistic level. Music almost literally flowed from his fingers. In addition, as Karl Barth remarks, another vast storehouse of Mozart's music died the moment it was born: all of the music which he improvised on the spur of the moment,[11] which, to our knowledge, was never subsequently written down.[12] Mozart wrote to his father on July 31, 1778: "You know that I am, so to speak, soaked in music, that I am immersed in it all day long and that I love to plan works, study and meditate." [13] Edward J. Dent, the British opera historian, says: "(Of musicians) Mozart is commonly believed to have been the most divinely inspired, the most completely instructive and the most utterly mindless." [14] Paul Henry Lang, in *Music in Western Civilization,* speaks of Goethe's admiration for Mozart: "Whenever Goethe spoke of the nature of genius – which he did especially in his later years – he mentioned Mozart, who appeared to him as the human incarnation of a divine force of creation." [15] In this same vein, the following entry in Kierkegaard's Journal, 1849, though not referring to Mozart, is thoroughly descriptive of him: "Every genius is predominantly immediacy and immanence" (X[1], A 266, p. 176). Encased in Kierkegaard's prose, this definition of genius acquires a ring of finality that seems to sum up what has been said above regarding Mozart.

Mozart composed apparently intuitively. He seemingly did not have to labor over many successive drafts of a work, as Beethoven, for example, did in order to bring it to perfection.[16] Although he was affected by external circumstances – such as temperamental singers, difficult church authorities, constant need for money – basically, he was uncomplicated, optimistic. He enjoyed life but did not concern himself very much with it. He never evinced any interest in the sciences or other arts. Nature remained an unopened book for him, as though he was always too preoccupied with his music to notice it. In any event, he never dwells on observations of his natural or physical surroundings in his letters, in spite of his rather extensive travels. If he had any interest in the causes of his day, he did not show it. He ignored politics, and the French Revolution passed him by completely. "When he sat down to compose, he had no axe to grind, no social or artistic theory to advance. The message of the music itself was sufficient. Indeed, to attempt to analyze Mozart in terms of meaning is a barren project. As you proceed, it only becomes clearer that his music means just one thing, and that is beauty — beauty in the abstract." [17] Lang sums up Mozart thus: "Mozart is the greatest musico-dramatic genius of all times. This unique position he owes to a temperament which approached everything, every situation, and every human being with absolute objectivity. He did not want to become the German nation's teacher and eulogist, as did Wagner; he did not, like Beethoven, want to reach the highest ideal tone; nor did he, like Handel, want to be God's voice. Every situation and every individual appeared to him as music, his whole conception was purely aesthetic, and music was his language" (Lang, p. 674). Barth says: "Mozart's music, in contrast to that of Bach, has no message and, contrary to that of Beethoven, involves no personal confession. His music does not give rules, even less does it reveal the composer himself. . . . Mozart does not want to say anything at all; he just sings and sounds." (Barth, p. 69)

Socrates once said that in order to be a good poet a man must be able to write both comedy and tragedy, in other words, to mirror life. One of the most frequently remarked characteristics of Mozart's music is his gift to express both the comic and the tragic, oftentimes in close proximity, even in juxtaposition (e. g., Acts I, Sc. v, Elvira sings her aria of lament while Don Juan and Leporello are jesting in the background, all singing together). Egon Wellesz, writing in *The Music Review* (May 1943), characterizes Mozart as "a passionate composer." His moods changed abruptly from serenity to outbursts of irony. He was an example of emotional instability often found among Austrian artists. In opera this disposition enabled him to change in a few bars from tragic to comic, from joy to passion. *Don Giovanni* gave Mozart his best medium to express this inborn state of mind.[18]

Mozart once said: "I deem nothing human alien to me." He found
the essence of life to be in its manysidedness. An English contemporary of his, when asked if he thought Mozart was ever really happy,
replied: "Never." "Don't forget that whenever you mention the 'cheering' character of his music!" (Barth, p. 67). It is this "cheering character" that Franz Schubert noted in his diary on June 13, 1816, and,
despite Barth's words, it is probably this characteristic with which
people most often classify the music of Mozart: "A light, bright, fine
day this will remain throughout my whole life. As from afar the
magic notes of Mozart's music still gently haunt me. How unbeliev-
ably vigorously, and yet again how gently, was it impressed deep,
deep into the heart by Schlesinger's masterly playing. Thus does our
soul retain these fair impressions, which no time, no circumstances
can efface, and they lighten our existence. They show us in the dark-
ness of this life a bright, clear, lovely distance, for which we hope
with confidence. O Mozart, immortal Mozart, how many, oh, how
endlessly many such comforting perceptions of a brighter and better
life hast thou brought to our souls!" [19]

"A great deal of gaiety leads to foolery; and Mozart had a share
of both. The double influence of Italian *opera buffa* and Viennese
taste encouraged it in him. It is his least interesting side, and one
would willingly pass it by, if it were not part of him. It is only natural
that the body should have its needs as well as the spirit; and when
Mozart was overflowing with merriment, some pranks were sure to
be the result. He amused himself like a child; and one feels that characters like Leporello, Osmin, and Papageno gave him huge diver-
sion." [20] In some respects Mozart remained a child all his life. He
took great pleasure in jokes. He engaged in word play. He would
shuffle the letters of his name about when he signed letters — e. g.,
Romatz, or in cancrizans: "Oidda, Gnagflow Trazom, Neiw, ned 12
tsugua 3771." He juggled words in greetings to his father: "Ich gute
eine wünsche Nacht!" He used rondo-like repetitions of a word or
sound within the text of a letter: "Er soll bald dazu *thun,* damit er
mir die Freude *thut* machen, dass ich ihm einmal *thue* accompa-
gnieren. An alle andere gute Freunde und Freundinnen *thue* meine
Empfehlungen machen und *thue* gesund . . ." [21] He liked to tell
stories with surprise endings. These crept into his music as well
(e. g., in *The Marriage of Figaro* when Susanna appears from behind
the door where we are expecting to see Cherubino). He wrote an
instrumental piece which he called the Musical Joke *(Musikalischer*

Spass). "Mozart often laughed, but certainly not because there was much for him to laugh about. Rather he laughed (and that is something absolutely different) because he was allowed and able to laugh in spite of all" (Barth, p. 67). His letters to his cousin reflect a response to the cruder aspects of life that strike one strangely at first when one considers that their author is also the composer of the *Requiem,* the *G Minor Symphony,* and the *C Minor Quartet.* But all these things merely show the "roundedness" of the Mozart personality. Winternitz feels that Mozart's balance is apparent even in his manuscripts. The "space aura" that surrounds his notes, Winternitz claims, was not deliberately achieved on Mozart's part, because he wrote too fast. So it must have been intuitive. Such everyday aspects of a man's life, when examined in the totality of his life, are found to be symptomatic of his personality. (Winternitz, p. 200)

Mozart "never knew a doubt. . . . This is the strangely exciting and appeasing aspect of his music; it comes unmistakably from a height where everything is known and from where the right and left side of existence, happiness and pain, good and evil, life and death have all been perceived in their reality as well as in their limitation" (Barth, p. 67). Mozart cheerfully accepted the disciplines and limitations of his art and found his freedom within them. A. Hyatt King says that the increasing interest in Mozart's music reflects an increased interest in formalism in the other arts. The music of Mozart that has the widest appeal is that which shows the greatest certainty of form. He warns, however, against becoming too serious and introspective about it: "There is indeed some danger, particularly in English- and German-speaking countries, that Mozart's music may be taken over-seriously for its ultimate good. It would be sad if sheer enjoyment of its technical skill, its wit, and humanity should be submerged in a welter of interpretation and annotation. It would be ironical if its vitality, having survived the partial neglect of the nineteenth century were to be endangered by the mummifying assiduity of the twentieth." Later, King points up the close analogy that exists between the spirit of Mozart and the spirit of the Greeks. The chief qualities are restraint and proportion; purity of line and thought; consciousness of genius but freedom from excess egoism; searching for the values of life with a happy serenity born of self-knowledge and tempered by a just sense of sadness and inscrutability at man's brief destiny; a generous frankness; simple, ardent seriousness; a sense of wonder and pleasure in experiment; balance of mind and perfect control of emotion; balance of passion and purity.[22] Barth enlarges on this theme:

> Mozart is universal. One admires again and again everything that speaks in his work! heaven and earth, nature and man, comedy and tragedy, passion in all its forms and deepest inner peace, the Virgin Mary and the demons, the High Mass of the Church, the strange solemnity of the Freemasons and the ballroom, the stupid and the clever people, the cowards and the (real or apparent) heroes, the faithful and the unfaithful, the aristocrats and the peasants, Papageno and Sarastro. And he always seems to provide for each in turn not only partially but entirely, rain and sunshine for all alike. If I hear correctly, this is mirrored in the extremely affectionate way (which, however, appears always to be an unintentional necessity) in which Mozart forms and regulates the relation between the human voice or (in the concerti) between the dominating solo instrument and the accompanying (yet, regularly never only accompanying) strings and wind instruments. You cannot listen enough to what happens, lives and moves in Mozart's orchestra, to what unexpectedly and always is mobilized at the right place and is honored in its special height or depth and timbre. It is as if a small part of the universe is singing. (Barth, p. 68)

"He was (and I quote Grillparzer's beautiful words) the musician 'who never did too little, and never did too much, and who always arrived at but never went beyond his goal.'" (Barth, p. 76)

It has been said of Mozart that, although he was enamored of several women on various occasions, he never really loved a woman — with an exception: "Dame Music" (Barth, p. 67). "The only passions that Mozart knew well were anger and pride. The greatest of all passions — 'the entire Venus' — never appeared in him. It is this lack which gives his whole work a character of ineffable peace" (Rolland, p. 358). From what we know of his life, and from his own words in a letter to his father (quoted on p. 128), we know that his waking hours were almost entirely absorbed in the composing and performing of music. In another letter to his father, Oct. 10, 1777, he says: ". . . And I am happier when I have something to compose, for that, after all, is my sole delight and passion" (Letters, p. 446). He was not a good manager of his home affairs, and his wife was no great help to him in this respect. He was constantly on the edge of outright poverty. The marvel is that he was able to maintain his sense of objectivity and good humor.

An interesting comparison can be made with Mozart's great successor in the musical world of the turn of the 19th century — Beethoven. Beethoven also was afflicted with adverse conditions of existence. But, although their life spans overlapped, a great change had taken place in the world between the productive years of the two. Mozart still stood within the comparative serenity of the 18th-century world. Beethoven on the other hand stood at the door of, and ushered in, the 19th century with its attendant moralism, romanticism, and nationalism. He lived in a new atmosphere of introspection and self-analysis. Dent, in discussing the music of Mozart in the light of the romantic movement, says: "He knows all depths of human emotion, but he is always Italian and strictly realistic" (Dent, p. 186). One might paraphrase Dent and describe Beethoven thus: He knows all depths of human emotion, but he remains German and uncompromisingly idealistic. This objective (especially considering its date of writing) appraisal of the two masters appeared in *Amiel's Journal* on May 14, 1853:

> The quartets were perfectly clear and easy to understand. One was by Mozart and the other by Beethoven, so that I could compare the two masters. Their individuality seemed to become plain to me: Mozart — grace, liberty, certainty, freedom, and precision of style, — the health and talent of the master both on a level with his genius; Beethoven — more pathetic, more passionate, less perfect, more feeling, more intricate, more profound, more the slave of his genius, more carried away by his fancy or his passion, more moving and more sublime than Mozart. Mozart refreshes you like the Dialogues of Plato: he respects you, reveals to you your strength, gives you freedom and balance. Beethoven seizes upon you: he is more tragic and oratorical, while Mozart is more disinterested and poetical. Mozart is more Greek, and Beethoven more Christian. One is serene, the other serious. The first is stronger than destiny, because he takes life less profoundly: the second is less strong, because he has dared to measure himself against deeper sorrows. His talent is not always equal to his genius, and pathos is his dominant feature, as perfection is that of Mozart. In Mozart the balance of the whole is perfect, and art triumphs; in Beethoven feeling governs everything, and emotion troubles his art in proportion as it deepens it.[23]

W. J. Turner, in a lyrical mood, tries to describe Mozart's music in these words:

> There is no "waste" in Mozart — no overlapping, no exaggeration, no strain, no vagueness, no distortion, no suggestion. He is so pure that he seems often meaningless. His music *disappears*, like the air we breathe on a transparent day. All those who have really appreciated Mozart will admit that at one time or another they have felt certain Mozart masterpieces as one would feel a still, bright perfect, cloud-

less day. Such a day has no meaning, none of the suggestiveness, the "atmosphere," the character of a day of cloud or storm, or of any day in which there is a mixture of warring elements whose significance has yet to appear. Such a day does not provoke or in the faintest degree suggest one mood rather than another. It is infinitely protean. It means just what you mean. It is intangible, immaterial — fitting your spirit like a glove.[24]

Karl Barth, the theologian who wrote music into his doctrine of creation (and who says that he begins every day with an hour of recorded Mozart music), gives his reaction to Mozart in these words: "Play, too, belongs to daily bread. I hear Mozart, both the young and the old Mozart, play as nobody else can play. Yet playing is such a high and serious matter that it must be mastered. Mozart's art of playing sounds to me quite different from that of every other person. Beautiful playing presupposes a knowledge of the center of all things — including the knowledge of their beginning and their end. I hear Mozart make music from this beginning, this center, this end" (Barth, p. 61). Again he reaches for words which will nail down what he feels to be the essence of the Mozartean sound: "Is it not rather possible that the original sound (Urton) of the early and late Mozart (which cannot be confounded with any other) is identical with the original sound of music as such? Did he find and touch it in its timeless form?" (Barth, p. 65). It remains, finally, for Alfred Einstein to strain the language in his attempt to capture Mozart: "It is as though the world-spirit wished to show that here is pure sound, conforming to the world-spirit." [25]

The Opera Don Giovanni

"How much ink has flowed in the effort to portray the Don Juan type! A vast mass of prosaic verbiage and a plethora of philosophical and psychological essays have been employed in the effort to bring down the firebird. Can he be portrayed except by implication?" [26] Don Juan probably gives us the most valuable clue to his own character when he says in response to Leporello's plea to reform: "Leave the girls alone? I need them more than the bread I eat or the air I breathe" (Acts II, Sc. i). And again: "I love them all. He who is true to one is cruel to all the others" (Act II, Sc. i). And in the banquet scene Don Juan drinks a toast to "women and wine, they nourish and gratify all mankind" [27] (Act II, Sc. xiv). Dent calls him a profligate and a blasphemer, but treats him, on the whole, in the lighthearted manner typical of the British writers on Don Giovanni (Dent,

p. 120). He points out that for a person with the Don's reputation for having his way with women, he is singularly and repeatedly unsuccessful in his attempts in the opera. (Dent, p. 158)

Joseph Kerman, in his book *Opera as Drama,* says that Mozart failed to characterize Don Juan, although he characterized all the other characters. This is precisely what Kierkegaard feels to be a strength, since Don Juan invades and informs all the other characters in the opera (see above, p. 127). But Kerman contends that this is to argue *ab vacuo;* in opera we trust what is done most firmly by the music. The very blankness of Don Juan's characterization indeed was most likely what attracted romantic critics. "Their daydreams and idealizations could sprout and flourish in Mozart's relative void." [28] He continues to take Kierkegaard to task:

> Kierkegaard first spoke of a magic "marriage" between the genius of Mozart and the subject matter of Don Juan, and many have followed him in this view. I could not disagree more completely; the whole basis of the Don Juan legend seems to me curiously out of Mozart's intellectual, ethical, and metaphysical style. Very few people nowadays see Mozart as a "daemonic" composer, even if they think of music as a daemonic art. In a work like the g minor Quintet, we sense an exquisitely constrained pathos, in the Piano Concerto in c minor a controlled foreshadowing of Beethovenian tragedy, in the Requiem mass a certain frustration strikingly symbolized by its noncompletion. As an opera composer, Mozart had dwelt more profoundly than anyone else on man in relation to other men and women, never in relation to God and the universe. Then suddenly theology was thrust on him at the end of *Don Giovanni* — right at the end, when things were getting rushed, as usual. He did his best, a very wonderful best, but everything we know or feel about Mozart should assure us that the inflexible view of sin and death set forth in the legend must have been distasteful to him. Mozart never saw man's will as inevitably opposed by the will of God. He conceived an essential harmony expressed by human feelings; his terms were brotherhood and sympathy and humility, not damnation and defiance. The magic marriage is *The Magic Flute.*
>
> And with *The Magic Flute* anyone might be tempted to echo Kierkegaard about the consuming desire of Genius for Idea. What an extraordinary subject, after all, as compared with the traditional claptrap of Don Juan. (Kerman, pp. 122–123)

Barth echoes Kerman in rejecting Kierkegaard's interpretation of *Don Giovanni* in this single comment: ". . . and *Don Giovanni* has nothing to do with the myth of the eternal libertine (as Kierkegaard asserted)." (Barth, p. 75)

Alfred Einstein enters the lists by saying: "We can best appreciate Mozart's boldness in deciding to set Don Giovanni to music not by drawing for our knowledge upon Søren Kierkegaard's fantasies on Don Juan, say, or other books of the nineteenth or twentieth centuries, but only by considering the attitudes of the eighteenth century toward this subject." He says that attitude was summed up by Carlo Goldoni, the author of *Il Convitato di Pietra* (an Italian counterpart of Molière's *Le Festin de Pierre*), who maintained that the whole subject was in very bad taste, but who wrote his version of it because he had seen Molière's and decided "to regale my own country with the same subject" (Einstein, p. 434). Gerald Abraham, writing in the chapter "The Operas" in *The Mozart Companion*, expresses the opinion that all the discussion about *Don Giovanni* would probably only bewilder Mozart or just leave him cold. "Mozart could never have written a systematic explanation for his aesthetic of opera; he was an empiricist of genius, guided by the sure instinct of his genius." [29] Perhaps the freshest breath of air on the subject is that which comes from Ernest Newman, in the introductory essay to Vol. I of the Mozart Opera Society's recording of *Don Giovanni*:

> It would save a great deal of trouble, and help to avoid much unclear thinking, if it were frankly recognized that *Don Giovanni* has all the irremediable faults of a work hastily patched together for an immediate purpose, and then rather stupidly hacked about later by its authors for a further purpose. Neither librettists nor composers in that epoch took the solemn historical view of themselves that we are inclined to take of them today. They knew comparatively little of the past of music, and did not worry very much about the future; nothing was further from their thoughts than to try to create works that would someday take their place, for critics and historians, in a long line of aesthetic evolution.
>
> They concerned themselves very little with theories; they just settled down like honest workmen, to do the job of the moment, putting what talent or genius they had into the doing of it. And for both Da Ponte and Mozart the commission to write an opera for Prague in 1787 was merely a careful job like any other . . . To discuss *Don Giovanni* as if it were a carefully thought-out work of art, aiming at organic unity from first to last . . . is to be the dupe of a false historical perspective.[30]

Kerman comes to much the same conclusion: "The Romantics worshipped it as a unique masterpiece, the only opera in which Mozart touched the daemonic roots of reality. From E. T. A. Hoffmann and Kierkegaard to Bernard Shaw and Richard Strauss, Don Giovanni has been idealized into a Faust or a superman, a shining knight of the *ewig Weibliche* if not the life-force itself. Only in the twentieth century has historical scholarship labored to interpret the opera as an ordinary farce with supernatural additions, clumsily grafted together and blessedly over-composed." (Kerman, p. 117)

There is one aspect of the opera that Kierkegaard touches upon only in passing. That is the final judgment scene. He mentions it when he is talking about the aesthetic kingdom of the Venusberg: "The first-born of this kingdom is Don Juan. That it is the kingdom of sin is not even mentioned . . . Not until reflection enters does it appear as the kingdom of sin, but by that time Don Juan is slain, the music is silent" (*Either/Or*, I, p. 73). This leads one to wonder if the productions of *Don Giovanni* with which Kierkegaard was familiar retained the epilogue (in which a comic sextet, made up of the rest of the characters, points the moral of Don Juan's life, and in general relieves the tragic mood induced by the immediately preceding scene), or if they ended with the judgment and demise of Don Juan. Whatever the case, Kierkegaard's basic premise about the relation of music as an expression of the immediate, sensuous genius embodied in Don Juan remains unaffected. Don Juan's fate is really irrelevant, because Kierkegaard is treating music as a purely aesthetic expression, into which the question of ethicality does not enter.

However, none of Mozart's other critics and analysts have adopted such an elemental interpretation of *Don Giovanni* as did Kierkegaard, and they are driven to try to rationalize Don Juan's doom. We recall Joseph Kerman's irritation at having theology suddenly "thrust" upon an unsuspecting Mozart (see above, p. 135). Earlier he says that we have been led to sympathize with the Don, only to have him unexpectedly damned out of hand. However, Don Juan saves the situation by rising to the occasion, remaining true to himself (like another celebrated rake: Peer Gynt), and refusing to repent (Kerman, p. 122).[31] Paul H. Lang says that Don Juan perishes "because his passions flare beyond the limits of life, challenging the powers that reign beyond" (Lang, p. 662). Egon Wellesz feels that *Don Giovanni* should be considered a tragedy because it is that element which predominates in the opera, as it did in the old puppet play. Mozart has here brought it back. But the compelling reason for calling it a tragedy, in his opinion, is the fact that Mozart himself left out the epilogue in the Vienna production of the opera on May 7, 1788 (Wellesz, p. 124). Annette Kolb ventures the opinion that Don Juan does not consign himself to the flames as the "justly punished profligate" at all, but rather as the phoenix. (Kolb, p. 209)

Christopher Benn, on the other hand, holds that the sextet in the epilogue conforms to the original idea in the opera. It restores a balance that would not be there if the opera ended with Don Juan's demise. Ending with his death would make of the opera a tragedy, as though Don Juan were to be mourned. But this is hardly the case. The world has survived his eclipse. Life goes on.[32] "*Don Giovanni* is not really a moral drama; the real terror of the hero's end is dispelled by the ironic humor of the final commentary" (Abraham, p. 286). This is most succinctly expressed by Leporello in his remark about going down to the tavern to find a better master. Dent agrees with this view of the opera: "And so . . . they bring the opera to an end with a copybook maxim starting off as if it was going to be an elaborate fugue, but turning almost at once into a proper Italian finale, with just a few pretenses at counterpoint thrown in — who could have done anything so much as to forget that they have been thoroughly well amused." (Dent, p. 174)

If we sum up these views, we get the following interesting result: among writers on Mozart, the English and the French treat *Don Giovanni* as a farce, the Germans as a tragedy. Aside from labeling the score of the opera *Opera buffa in due atti*, Mozart is not of any comfort to either side, for he performed it in Prague with the epilogue, and later, in Vienna, without it, as though he himself had come to prefer the stark, tragic finish. Lorenzo Da Ponte called the libretto a *dramma giocoso*. Historically and formally speaking, the opera is *buffa* with *seria* roles. But this is inadequate to describe it. "The work is *sui generis*, incomparable and enigmatic from the evening of its first performance to the present day." (Einstein, p. 442)

NOTES FOR CHAPTER 12

1. David F. Swenson, *Something About Kierkegaard*, rev. ed. (Minneapolis, 1945), p. 176.

2. Ibid., p. 167.

3. Demonic is here used in the sense in which James Collins uses it in his book *The Mind of Kierkegaard* (Chicago, 1953), p. 59: "A demonic life is one based deliberately upon an all-absorbing idea. The demonic person relates himself immediately and individually to his leading idea, repudiating by implication the ordinary conventions and attachments of the human community."

4. Valter Lindström fortifies this point in the following quotation: "I fråga om Don Juan är detfor övrigt något misvisande att tala om en gestalt, då han för Kierkegaard framstår, icke så mycket som individ utan som en idé, den

sexuella åtrån som princip." *Stadiernas Teologi: En Kierkegaard Studie* (Lund, 1943), p. 192.

5. *Mozart's Operas*, 2d ed. (London, 1947), p. 135 — hereafter cited as Dent.

6. Romain Rolland characterizes and contrasts the Juans of the three main epochs thus: "Don Juan is here (in *Don Giovanni*) an eighteenth-century Italian, and not the haughty Spaniard of the (original) story, or the dry, atheistical little marquis (Molière's) of Louis XIV's court." *Some Musicians of Former Days*, trans. Mary Blaiklock (New York, 1915), p. 361 — hereafter cited as Rolland.

7. To make this judgment on Don Juan is like condemning the lion for eating the lamb. The lion is simply being true to himself — as is Don Juan.

8. The most striking example: Mozart's finale ensembles, which combine different texts, different passions, different people in a harmonious chorus.

9. *Søren Kierkegaards Papirer*, udg. P. A. Heiberg og V. Kuhr (Kjøbenhavn, 1935), II, A598, p. 223.

10. Cf. the description of the banquet pp. 121—122.

11. In Kierkegaard's language, literally the most immediate of all his music.

12. "Wolfgang Amadeus Mozart," *Religion and Culture. Essays in Honor of Paul Tillich*, ed. Walter Leibrecht (New York, 1959), p. 70 — hereafter cited as Barth.

13. Emily Anderson, ed., *The Letters of Mozart and His Family*, II (London, 1938), p. 871 — hereafter cited as *Letters*.

14. "Mozart. Lecture on a Master Mind," *Proceedings of the British Academy*, XXXIX (London, 1953), 181.

15. (New York, 1941), p. 646 — hereafter cited as Lang.

16. This is not entirely true, for, according to his own references to the subject in various letters, fugal writing did not come easily for him.

17. Archibald T. Davison, "Mozart: Composer for the Church," *Christian Century*, (May 1956), 615.

18. "*Don Giovanni* and the Drama Giocoso," IV, 124 — hereafter cited as Wellesz.

19. Otto Erich Deutsch, *Schubert. A Documentary Biography*, trans. Eric Blom (London, 1946), p. 60.

20. Rolland, p. 360.

21. Emmanuel Winternitz, "Gnagflow Trazom: An Essay on Mozart's Script, Pastimes and Nonsense Letters," *Journal of the American Musicological Society*, XI, 207—210 — hereafter cited as Winternitz.

22. *Mozart in Retrospect* (London, 1955), pp. 53, 190 — hereafter cited as King.

23. Quoted from King, pp. 29—30. Pub. H. F. Amiel, *Amiel's Journal*, trans. Mrs. Humphry Ward (London, 1899), p. 40.

24. *Mozart* (New York, 1938), p. 380 — hereafter cited as Turner.

25. Alfred Einstein, *Mozart. His Character and Work*, trans. Arthur Mendel and Nathan Broder (New York, 1945), p. 471 — hereafter cited as Einstein.

26. Annette Kolb, *Mozart* (Chicago, 1956), p. 209 — hereafter cited as Kolb.

27. For parallel thoughts see John the Seducer's banquet speech in praise of woman (*Stages*, pp. 81—88).

28. (London, 1957), p. 121 — hereafter cited as Kerman.

29. Ed. Gerald Abraham (London, 1956), p. 286 — hereafter cited as Abraham.

30. Quoted in Geoffrey Sharp, *"Don Giovanni:* Some Observations," *The Music Review,* IV (January 1943), 45.

31. It must be borne in mind that Kerman's book is an attempt to make out a case for opera *as drama.* He says in the introduction, on page three: ". . . opera properly is a musical form of drama, with its own individual dignity and force." This is a point of view with which we might expect Kierkegaard and Mozart to take issue, both having expressed themselves specifically on the subject. (Kierkegaard's argument is set forth briefly above on pp. 125—126.) Mozart approached the matter from the standpoint of a man who is first and foremost a musician: "He did not long trouble his head about the difficult question of the association of poetry and music in drama. He quickly decided that where music was there could be no rival. 'In an opera, it is absolutely imperative that poetry should be the obedient daughter of music.' (Oct. 13, 1781) Later he says: 'Music reigns like a king, and the rest is of no account.' . . . So poetry to Mozart simply furnished 'a well-made plan,' dramatic situations, 'obedient' words, and words written expressly for music. . . . Because he was altogether a musician, Mozart did not allow poetry to make demands upon his music; and he would even force a dramatic situation to adapt itself to his music even when there was not any sign that it would overstep the limits of what he considered good taste. 'Passions, whether violent or not, should never be expressed when they reach an unpleasant stage; and music, even in the most terrible situations, should never offend the ear, but should charm it, and always remain music' (Sept. 26, 1781)." (Rolland, pp. 352—355)

32. Frederick Christopher Benn, *Mozart on the Stage* (New York, 1947), p. 49.

II

CHURCH MUSIC
AND OUR TIME

1

THE PEACE OF GOD
(A Four-Part Canon)

Jan Bender

THE PEACE OF GOD, WHICH PASS-ETH ALL UN-DER-STAND-ING, SHALL KEEP YOUR HEARTS AND MINDS THROUGH CHRIST JE-SUS.

PHILIPPIANS 4:7

2

WHITHER CHURCH MUSIC?

Edgar S. Brown, Jr.

James Reston of *The New York Times* once described, with obvious tongue-in-cheek, a "new" invention of the Swiss. It seems that these ingenious folk constructed a rather clever device connecting one city with another by a pair of parallel shining steel rails on which was placed a large vehicle capable of propelling itself. Strung along in back, like baby chicks following a mother hen, was a line of long boxes on wheels equipped with seats. The purpose of this invention, said Reston, was the rapid transportation — at appointed hours according to fixed schedules — of great numbers of people from one city to another. Translating the name of this *thing* into English, we get the word "train." What is more, added Reston, in Switzerland trains work.

The satire was delicious, the contrast obvious. Americans comparing their own service couldn't miss the point — a looking at things as they can be and as they really are.

Another invention which deserves the same treatment is music. Once again there are lines, lines stretching across the page, and on these lines a host of little black marks march up and down in frenetic array. Given the task of interpreting these marks, an individual or a group of individuals produces what we call music. And the result can either make one soar in ecstacy or squirm in anguish.

This is true of all music. You go to a Broadway show. The story may be moving, the acting inspired, the costumes and the sets exciting, but unless you leave the theatre whistling a tune like "I'm Getting Married in the Morning" or "Ole Man River," the evening's outing just doesn't leave a lasting impression.

What about the music one hears in church? Music in the service of religion is the vehicle of grace. Now grace, in spite of the many theological differences that divide us, is still for the religious man just another way of talking about the presence of God. How then does music serve the church?

For years I've been alternately amused and annoyed by certain pages of the resort and travel section of the Sunday paper. These curios usually appear for several weeks preceding the Jewish high holy days. Page after page is filled with ads of varying size proclaiming why this lodge or that hotel is the perfect resort spot to visit on high holy days. I noticed that usually, in spite of the different sizes of these ads, all of them were remarkably alike in format. Often there was the photo of a distinguished-looking man wearing tallith and kipah. Beneath the photo were words something like these: "Hear the golden-throated tenor tones of Cantor Pompous, assisted by the magnificent choir of heavenly voices from Temple Shalom-by-the-Shopping Center." All of this was, of course, featured in heavy blackface type, at times even rivaling in size the name of the resort itself. Then, somewhere near the bottom of the ad, in type face so small as to almost require a magnifying glass for its reading, were these other words, "Assisted by Rabbi Blank."

Once, when pondering what seemed to be the sad state of worship among my Jewish friends, I came across an article in *The New Yorker*. Here, I said excitedly, is a kindred spirit. Obviously the ads had disturbed Mr. Perrin, so much so that he determined to do some digging, and the result is an interesting study in Jewish liturgical and pseudoliturgical music.

Mr. Perrin's concern finds expression in an article in *The Jewish Encyclopedia* by Rabbi Max Schloessinger. Says Mr. Perrin:

> It was Dr. Schloessinger's profound love of Jewish liturgy that made him suspicious of cantors. Cantors, he felt, were antiliturgical. (Rabbis, of course, in common with priests, Church of England clergymen, imams, and mullahs, are proliturgical.) As he likes to point out, cantors once in the past got control of the Jewish service of worship, and when they did, they made it into a kind of singing contest or Sabbath opera, to the confounding of rabbis, true religion, and good taste. He was convinced that, given half a chance, they would do so again.[1]

A harsh judgment? Perhaps, but the problem of the relation of the *domina* to the *ancilla* is still worthy of debate. Is music, as understood and practiced among us, still the "handmaid of religion," or has she begun to usurp the place of the mistress of the house?

Back in 1930 the Committee on Church Music reporting to the biennial convention of the United Lutheran Church in America had this to say:

For anthems in the Anglican sense there is little place in the Lutheran orders, though there is a distinct place for the choir in the Introit and Gradual of The Service, and in the Responsory for Matins and Vespers. But in every case the words must fit into the thought of the day and occasion, and the music must be of a kind appropriate to God's house. The anthem, as well as the rest of the service, should always be regarded as an act of worship, and should minister to edification; nor should choirs attempt to sing anthems that are beyond their ability. If an anthem is to edify, it is far better to sing a simple one well than to mutilate a more difficult one.[2]

One wonders now — some 30 years later — just how much of the music sung and played in our churches today is of "a kind appropriate to God's house." What justification is there for the choir that wants, and more frequently demands as its right, the opportunity to present its own rendition of the sort of stuff featured on TV spectaculars, complete with local imitation of all sorts of tricky sound effects? And who is to draw the line before choirs that would "attempt to sing anthems that are beyond their ability"? A preacher can at most offer his best, even if that means with nervous stammer or faltering reason, but the choir that dares to take on a Bach cantata (and even that would be a welcome change in some congregations that know only sentimental inanities) in place of a less ambitious offering will only produce a congregation of squirmers. The congregation is, it is true, a captive audience, but why must it be made to suffer just because there are eager but unqualified choristers? We shall go further. If we regard worship, i. e., the celebration of the liturgy, as the action of the family of God in a given place, and if we expect that every member of the family be present to take his rightful place in the service of God, then what sort of attitude are we building in the minds of Christian people as we require that they submit to musical offerings we'd shut out if they poured from our TV sets? What, in brief, does such activity, though it be packaged with what we piously call "worship," have to do with *grace* and man's awareness of the consuming presence of God in his midst?

Asking such questions recalls the dilemma that faced the 4th-century Bishop of Hippo. Says St. Augustine in his *Confessions:*

> Sometimes, indeed, I seem to grant them [i. e., musical selections] more respect than is fitting, when I perceive that our minds are moved more religiously and ardently toward the flame of piety by these holy words, when they are sung in this way, than if they are not sung . . .
>
> Sometimes, on the other hand . . . I err on the side of excessive severity. At times, in fact, I could eagerly desire that all the sweet

melody of the chants . . . were banished from my ears and from the whole church.

Yet when I recall the tears which I shed over the hymns in church at the early period of the recovery of my faith, and now today when I am affected not by the singing but by the words which are sung . . . I again recognize the great usefulness of this practice.

So I waver between the danger of sensual enjoyment and the experience of healthful employment . . . I am more inclined to approve the custom of singing in church . . . Nevertheless, when it happens that I am more moved by the song than the thing which is sung, I confess that I sin in a manner deserving of punishment, and then I should rather not hear the singing.[3]

Augustine's criterion of judgment may serve as a guidepost for present-day considerations, but would any 20th-century Christian really take seriously the saint's self-accusation that "when it happens that I am more moved by the song than the thing which is sung, . . . I *sin* in a manner deserving of punishment" (emphasis added)? Whether the music is so glorious that it transports the worshiper to joyous exultation or be it so perverted that it arouses latent hostilities, few if any modern Christians would think that in not cutting through to the text borne by the music they are committing a sin! Music may exhilarate or it may sadden; it may annoy or distract, but music in the service of the church must always let in the light of the Gospel. And if man's consciousness of this rightful role of music doesn't contribute to this end, then Augustine is right.

A century after Augustine fretted over the role of music in the church, Pope Gregory the Great suppressed the solo Gradual because this practice "led deacons to think more of their voices than weightier things." Just what Gregory meant by "weightier things" is not accurately defined, but the inference doesn't require great imagination. Etiquette had become more important than sustenance, method overrode content. Music, if Gregory's stricture is any indication, had broken loose from her moorings.

The problem, which is still with us, is twofold: on the one hand is the very nature of the music itself. What kind of music should be permitted and so encouraged in the church? And secondly, what training must be given to those performing the music so that their efforts do not attract to the performer but to that which he or she proclaims?

I shall have to forgo any comment on purely instrumental music. Others more familiar with this vast subject will deal with this far more adequately than I shall ever be able to. I would only say in passing that instrumental musicians must remember that emotions are tricky things. A Bach fugue on the organ may rouse the noblest of sentiments, evoke the most pious emotion, but so can the wail of the bagpipes!

When we consider music set to words, however, words that express the timeless truths of the Gospel, greater caution must be exercised. The church, which is the people of God, exists for the purpose of mutual conversation and interaction between God and men. The church is corporate, and so the church's speech must be intelligible to all. This is not to say that every word spoken or sung must be so carefully defined as to make it prosaic and dull. Words, like music, can be beautiful, and the language of devotion should be beautiful. But the words are the chief thing. No amount of the most glorious music to touch the ears and heart of man will ever direct a man's feet into the path of Calvary without those ears and that heart having first heard the message. The church lives to serve God, whom it knows through the Word, and words are the vehicle of the Word.

That is why music must not obscure the Word but magnify it and adorn it.

Nor should it be forgotten that when the people gather to converse with God and share with Him in a mutual exchange of themselves, it is primarily the people, and not just a few of them, who are active. Worship, in spite of what it may have become in some times and places, is not and never can be a spectator sport. All have tongues to sing and actions to perform, and the efforts of the people dare not be thwarted, no matter how grand the musical selections.

Perhaps all this sounds as if I'm saying — to go back to Reston's satire which began this essay — that service on the railroads is so bad that the trains should be permitted to go the way of the covered wagon. No one would seriously suggest such a fate for church music, although there may have been times when some of us have been sorely tempted. What is needed in the church is a standard, a criterion by which church music can be and will be judged. Are we in our American congregations so impregnated with what we inaccurately label "the democratic system" that we are forever captive to any wellmeaning fellow who wants to parade his wares before us in the name of worship? Is there no redress from bad music other than to stay away from church?

I am sure that thoughtful people will agree that a standard can, no, must be found. But what shall it be? Vatican II, speaking to the larger area of liturgical reform, also spoke to the practice of church music: ". . . sacred music is to be considered the more holy in proportion as it is more closely connected with the liturgical action, whether it adds delight to prayer, fosters unity of minds, or confers greater solemnity upon the sacred rites." [4]

The notes that march across the lines in our service books and hymnals are there to serve grace. Now grace must first come from the Word, and the Word speaks to us in words. Music therefore must serve the words, not sentimentalizing them or dominating them, not sucking away their power and drawing attention to themselves, but lifting up the words and making them sing. Let music do this and man — even the "postmodern man" of these days — may yet learn to sing the *New Song!*

NOTES FOR CHAPTER 2

1. Perrin, Noel, "Golden-Voiced on the Lobby Floor," *The New Yorker* (June 13, 1959), pp. 109 ff.
2. *Minutes,* The United Lutheran Church in America (1930), p. 437.
3. *Confessions of St. Augustine,* X, 33.
4. "Constitution on Sacred Liturgy," VI, 112, *The New York Times,* Dec. 5, 1963, p. 19.

3

TWENTIETH-CENTURY CHURCH MUSIC — AMERICAN STYLE

V. Earle Copes

As one tries to portray an accurate objective picture of American Protestant church music in mid-twentieth century, he finds much more to write about than space permits. Indeed, there is perhaps more serious activity in the field among the various denominations now than at any other time in our nation's history. This activity stems from a general growth spurt in the culture of a dynamic but still immature nation that has outgrown its childhood and is developing rapidly in its appreciation for and participation in the arts.

PERSONS

Protestant churches are just beginning to recognize and realize a bit of their potential in appropriate utilization of the arts, architecture and music getting foremost attention at the present time. The present surge of enthusiasm owes its immediate debt quite obviously to pioneer personalities whose vision and genius pointed the way for ever-increasing numbers of eager disciples. Several persons of the 20th century who deserve special mention for their tremendous leadership must be named and their contributions noted. They fall into two broad classifications: educators and composers, neither being mutually exclusive, and both including men who were also practitioners.

Dickinson, Clarence: Founder and for many years director, School of Sacred Music, New York; hymnal editor (Presbyterian, 1935); concert organist; prolific composer, teacher of many prominent church musicians.

Williamson, John Finley: Founder and for many years director,

Westminster Choir College, Princeton, New Jersey; conductor of world renowned Westminster Choir; outstanding educator of choral directors and church musicians.

Christianson, F. Melius: Noted choral conductor, music educator, composer and arranger whose influence was especially strong in the Midwest and in Lutheran churches.

Sowerby, Leo: One of the most gifted composers to write extensively for the church, his works have won many awards and been performed widely throughout the world. Dr. Sowerby now heads a college for church musicians at the National Cathedral in Washington, D. C.

Countless others of the same generation as these mentioned have played significant roles in colleges, universities, and seminaries to challenge, inform, and inspire a host of able and aggressive church music leaders throughout the country. At this writing members of the "second generation" have already assumed key positions as directors of educational programs in church music in our leading institutions. Many of this second generation have augmented their American training with European study. They are a highly qualified group, unsurpassed in ability by any similar group in any other single nation. The products of their labors already can be seen in the countless still younger persons who are taking positions of leadership in thousands of churches throughout the country.

American churches can look forward to an overwhelming abundance of skilled, dedicated musical leaders in the years ahead. But they must ready themselves to accept and follow such leadership as it becomes available. The effectiveness of the best possible qualified church musician can be cancelled by a congregation whose ultraconservative tastes bind them to proverbial ruts and blind them to the vision of dynamic if not prophetic leadership.

PRODUCT

It is lamentable in our time that the church rarely challenges our greatest contemporary composers to create for its services. The fault lies ultimately with the timidity of local church musicians who are far more concerned with providing "what the congregation wants" than with what it "ought to have." The forthright witness of our most prophetic ministerial voices must be emulated if music in our churches is to assume its rightful role. As someone said, "Church music should not only comfort the afflicted but it should also afflict the comforted."

Its role in worship, Christian nurture, and re-creation needs to be more thoroughly understood not alone by leaders but by all who would follow. When congregations will listen with open minds to the musical voices of prophecy, our most sensitive creative spirits will then interpret God's Word for mankind in our time.

Thus far the musical "Word" as proclaimed by the most gifted has been stronger than congregations can bear. Consequently, most of our very greatest composers have directed their attention to the concert hall, where their "message" is more readily heard, and church music composition has been left largely to an increasing number of capable, devoted composers who recognize the need to communicate with those they would lead into paths of righteousness, often diluting the "Word" to accomplish this end.

Commercial interests have exerted tremendous influence on the "product." Although most publishers maintain a fair degree of integrity, there is much evidence on every hand of a prostituted art. Although there is an understandable necessity to publish material that will sell, the temptation to publish *only* that which has ready popular appeal seems to control the policies of some firms in the industry.

But ultimately control rests with the consumer. As he grows in his understanding of the purpose of church music, his enlightened taste will demand a superior product from publishers, and in turn from composers. Musicologists have served church musicians, and especially organists, extremely well in our time. Through their efforts and those of editors and publishers, a wealth of early music of great worth is now readily available. No longer need the young student organist play themes with strong secular associations in worship services; nor must he resort to transcriptions of operatic arias. Rather he may choose from an endless supply of excellent material conceived specifically for church use by composers dating from the 16th century to the present. Although a large percentage of the suitable literature is made up of preludes and fantasies on chorales or hymn tunes, there is also a healthy trickle of "absolute" music being written for church use.

Much of the contemporary literature by better composers is contrapuntally conceived, utilizing the stylistic characteristics of the Baroque era. Harmonies range from mild to extremely dissonant, with a healthy renewal of interest in modal rather than major or minor tonalities.

Eighteenth- and early nineteenth-century American religious folk

tunes are receiving belated consideration by many composers as basic
ingredients for both choral and instrumental literature for the church.

Jazz and other "secular" idioms are being used experimentally as
vehicles for religious expression, although their acceptance in the
church thus far has been limited. In due time such experimentation
probably will leave its mark on the church music of our era.

An important part of the "product" picture is the development of
the classic American organ and the increased use of other instruments
in Protestant churches. Especially since World War II activity in pipe
organ manufacture in this country has increased greatly. Following
the leadership of such persons as the late G. Donald Harrison and
Walter Holtkamp, all major builders and numerous smaller firms now
design and install instruments that are far superior in tonal design to
any heretofore produced in this country. Far closer adherence to the
tonal concepts established in Germany and Holland during the 17th
and 18th centuries is now practiced, so that the pipe organ has regained its integrity as the "king of instruments."

Parallel to this renaissance in pipe organ construction is a significant activity in electronic organ construction. Although commercial
factors have led to a flooding of the market with so-called "organs"
that are no more than musical toys, intensive and continuing research
is bearing fruit. Today's electronic industry boasts sizeable instruments with very respectable specifications and surprisingly accurate
imitation of pipe organ tone, even including the "chiff" of unnicked
pipes. Another 25 years may see the perfection of such instruments.

Orchestral instruments are used increasingly to accompany cantatas and oratorios in churches, and both in solo and ensemble with
organ for anthem accompaniments and instrumental voluntaries.
A number of churches have developed choirs of handbell players,
and high quality handbells are now manufactured in the United
States. Such activity with instruments other than the organ indicates
a broadening of taste and a more ready acceptance of various ways
by which man may offer praise to his Creator.

PROGRAM

Mid-twentieth-century American Protestantism has all but seen
the last of the "solo quartet" as leaders of music in corporate worship.
For a quarter of a century or more the growth of large volunteer
choirs and highly organized programs for children's and youth choirs
have mushroomed in practically every major denomination. Full-time

staff members in large churches, part-time employees in middle-sized churches, and volunteer leadership in small churches have taken on the task of organizing and directing choirs of children and youth. Millions of boys and girls find such musical experiences ideal opportunities for self-realization and worthy of their best efforts. Ideally such choirs cooperate closely with the ongoing programs of Christian education in the various denominations.

In some communities church and school musical experiences complement each other handsomely. In others, where there is little or no music in the public school curriculum, the church plays a vital role in the cultural as well as spiritual nurture of the child.

Although most local congregations are free to develop music programs according to their own needs and desires, denominations have officially encouraged such efforts in many ways.

Some denominations employ staff personnel at the national level to organize and administrate training institutes and workshops to provide improvement opportunities for local music leaders. (The Southern Baptists, Methodists, and Presbyterian [U. S.] have taken notable strides in this way.) The Southern Baptists in addition to a large national staff, employ full-time state directors of church music.

Publishing ventures by denominational houses have produced books, recordings, music for choirs and organists, and other materials to help raise standards. Three Lutheran branches, through Fortress Press, Augsburg, and Concordia, have published a wealth of excellent material; Westminster Press (United Presbyterian); Broadman Press (Southern Baptist); and Abingdon Press (Methodist) have similar successful publishing programs.

Three denominations produce educational periodicals for leaders in church music: Southern Baptist: *The Church Musician;* Methodist: *Music Ministry;* Lutheran: *Journal of Church Music* and *Response.* Each magazine in its own way renders a distinctive service to its respective constituency, and all cross denominational lines with their subscription lists.

Several denominations have nationwide organizations: Methodists (National Fellowship of Methodist Musicians, organized 1956); Disciples of Christ (organized 1961); Lutherans (Lutheran Society for Worship, Music, and the Arts, organized 1958); and Southern Baptists. These groups have active programs of leadership education, which in time will surely bring significant influence to bear on their respective denominations.

Within the past 25 years every major denomination has revised its official hymnal. (The newly revised Methodist Hymnal became available in 1966.) Generally the materials contained in the books are superior to those of their predecessors in musical quality and theological content, so that future generations will have a far richer repertoire of hymnic material than did their forefathers. "Ditties for the kiddies" in curriculum materials used in Christian education are being replaced by more solid hymnody at earlier ages. Denomination-wide programs in hymn education are encouraging more meaningful congregational singing and the broadening of hymn repertoire. Increasing use of audio-visual resources in the music education programs of American Protestantism will help accelerate the Herculean task that lies ahead. Several denominations now produce recordings, filmstrips, and films to serve as teaching aids in the area of church music.

Protestant church music in mid-twentieth-century America is on the threshold of a new day when every professing Christian will find it significant to "Sing unto the Lord a new song," and following the admonition of St. Paul to sing "not only with the spirit but with understanding."

4

THE DILEMMA OF CHURCH
MUSIC TODAY

Helen E. Pfatteicher

Church music has many different meanings. What it means to an individual depends to a large degree on what he hears from his childhood on, and in his adult life his willingness to concentrate upon and think about what he hears. The subconscious mind tucks away sounds from our early life which we were scarcely conscious of hearing. These influence our taste and surprise us by coming to the surface many years later.

When I was a child, my musician uncle had a cottage next to ours in Vermont, where we spent our vacations. I played out of doors between the cottages while my uncle practiced Bach's organ works on his upright piano with pedal board attached. This went on year after year, as my uncle taught music in a boys' school and gave weekly organ concerts. I scarcely noticed the music, except when I heard some grownups wonder why he wanted to spend his vacation in such an odd fashion. But today the music of Bach speaks to my inner being as nothing else can. We can grow in our musical tastes, but basically the foundations are laid for us and are not something of our own doing at all.

Music of all kinds can be heard in almost all homes today with the turn of a dial. There is, however, little good church music going out over the air waves in comparison with all of the other kinds of music which can be heard daily. On Sunday there is more music which passes for church music than on any other day of the week. Most of this music is the kind which satisfies some and nauseates others. The so-called gospel songs seem to be the most sincere vehicles of worship for some people. To others they seem very close to blasphemy.

To some there is no music so fitting for worship as Gregorian chant. To others there is none as fine as the Baroque. To still others this music may be meaningless, but the music of the romantic composers carries a message more clearly than any other. Others find this music shallow and unworthy. Some people find great satisfaction in the explorations of contemporary composers and think that no music speaks to our present day as truly and clearly as this. To others modern music is meaningless or offensive.

Churches are made up of people with all of these varying views and many in between. With music playing so large a part in our services of worship, what are we to do? Can a piece of music be at the same time a vehicle of God and a vehicle of the devil? Can it be good for one person and bad for another?

In our church music programs we are similar to the woman whose manner of dressing was described as being somewhat scattered. We have one kind of music in our church schools, another in our services of worship for congregational singing, and still another for our choirs. We have a beautiful and meaningful liturgy too often interrupted at various points by misplaced anthems and inappropriate hymns. Ours is indeed a dilemma.

We all need to grow, but our growing edges are at such different places. With several hundred different growing edges in a congregation, what is the director of music to do? Act as if everyone else had his growing edge or as if he had none, but had already reached the ultimate?

Is it possible for some to stoop in order to raise others and still to be able to worship? Is it possible for others to stretch in listening to music which is beyond them and at the same time to worship sincerely? If this is not possible, must there be many in every service who cannot worship because the music stands in the way?

Some of our music is in the hands of well-trained musicians with excellent resources and equipment. Many people in charge of the music programs in our churches have had little or no training and must work with very limited instruments and resources.

The professional musician knows of a wealth of music of wide variety which he can play with ease and teach his choir to sing. He insists that his choir is not professional, and if they can sing difficult anthems, anybody can. He cannot at this point realize that while his choir started out by being an ordinary choir, it is now far from ordinary, because it is taught by an extraordinary teacher.

The choir director who has taken over the job because there was nobody else to do it says, "Good music is too hard for our choir. They can't read music and can't sing classical or modern music. Besides we don't have enough to sing four parts."

These two viewpoints are poles apart and represent part of the dilemma of present-day church music. On the one hand we have excellent church musicians who do a fine job in their own churches and who are capable of giving aid to the untrained church organist and choir director, but who cannot see their problem because they themselves have been beyond it for so long.

On the other hand there are the choir directors with little training who think that there should be anthems they can look at and immediately understand and teach their choirs in one or two rehearsals.

The matter of the choice of anthems is many-sided. Some churches have sufficiently large music budgets to add new anthems regularly. Many churches do not allot any money at all for new music, and the choir director has to get along as best he can with what is already in the music library. Such limited resources make it difficult if not impossible to carry on an adequate church music program.

Good anthems that fit into the theme of the service and are sung well have a place. Poor anthems, even though sung well and fitting the propers for the day, do not. Good anthems that do not fit the service have no place even if they are sung well. Good anthems fitting the propers for the day have no place if they are sung poorly. All three ingredients are necessary, yet they seem to be too much to expect in most churches.

Most of the time at choir rehearsals is spent in learning anthems. Even if we grant that they are good anthems, fitting the service, and within the capabilities of the choir, why must so much time be spent on them, when the liturgy and hymns are of primary importance? How can choir directors and choirs be convinced that things they do regularly need rehearsal so that they both understand and sing them better? If we are not continually conscious of the need for improvement, we soon go backwards.

If hymns are not sung with careful attention to words and music, they soon are treated as if each stanza were the same and had no particular meaning. On the other hand, hymns should not be sung or played with so many changes in expression and accompaniment that attention is drawn away from the meaning of the hymn to the mechanics of its presentation.

It is just as essential for a well-trained organist to rehearse the liturgy as it is for the organist of the little church in Blankville. Sometimes there is need for much more than rehearsing. One of the saddest experiences in visiting a large church with a well-known and competent organist is to hear the service played as if it were an organ recital.

One very real part of the dilemma is the tendency, as the quality of music in a church improves, for fewer of the congregation to enter into the singing of the liturgy and hymns. They say they cannot sing — their voices are too bad. Has someone told them this, or are their ears that keen? What does the choir director do to keep this from happening? If the music of the church improves only if the rank and file of the congregation keep their mouths shut, the cost is too great. It is better to have full participation and lower quality of sound than to deprive the congregation of what rightfully belongs to it.

Polls of favorite hymns always turn up such hymns as: "Jesus, Lover of My Soul," "The Old Rugged Cross," and "What a Friend We Have in Jesus." What is it that is so appealing to people in these hymns? Is it the emotional response which such hymns engender in them? Do people really hear the voice of the Lord more clearly in these hymns? Or is it the music which holds them — the same music which repels others?

Where are the people who like such hymns as: "Come, Holy Ghost, Our Souls Inspire" (*Veni, Creator Spiritus*), "Deck Thyself with Joy and Gladness" (*Schmücke dich*), "Jesus, Priceless Treasure" (*Jesu, meine Freude*), "In the Bleak Mid-Winter" (*Cranham*), and "Ride On, Ride On in Majesty" (*King's Majesty*)? Are people who like hymns such as these so few, or are their opinions never asked?

The dilemma of church music today is many-sided. For every city or town having good musical resources there are hundreds of small towns with no musical resources at all and thousands with very limited resources. Help is needed desperately. How much help can be given by outsiders? Not as much as anyone would hope for, but certainly something can be done. Opportunities must be given for choir directors and organists to get out of their own communities and meet with other choir directors and organists. The printed word must get through to them, and it must begin where they are. It cannot stay there, but that is where it must begin. This must become a two-way street in which the church musician who is isolated physically and mentally can ask for help where he needs it and receive an answer given in love and understanding by our finest musicians.

Good church music has a remarkable impact on those who know how to listen, but learning how to listen requires time and thought, and guidance too, with a guide who remembers what it was like when he was just beginning in the field of music and needed the help of those more experienced than he.

5

THE STRUGGLE FOR BETTER HYMNODY

Armin Haeussler

Cultural struggles never have been of short duration. The development of music has been no exception. Western music owes its development primarily to the church. The evolutionary process has sometimes been rapid, at other times almost stationary. It was servants of the church who invented the system of musical notation; formulated the laws of musical grammar; transformed the primitive organ of Ctesibius (200 B. C.) and the hydraulus of Carthage into that noble-sounding, highly responsive instrument of today.

Out of early Christian psalmody came, one by one, the Gregorian chant, counterpoint, multiple metrics, harmony, the oratorio, the lyrical drama, and the choreographic musical narrative. Through Beethoven music became a major art. He was the first of the classical symphonists. The three centuries following the Renaissance saw the emergence of the so-called Baroque, Classical, and Romantic eras. Forgotten by many is the fact that there was a time when there was no dichotomy between sacred and secular music. The art of music was then one and indivisible; there was not one idiom for weekday madrigals, operas, and symphonies and another for Sunday Masses and Vespers.

In the 19th century there was a rapid transformation of musical techniques and expression through such composers as Wagner, Berlioz, Verdi, Franck, Brahms, Debussy, and Moussorgsky. Frequently they got rather far away from the classical tradition, although all maintained they had not actually departed from the normative patterns established by Beethoven. Indeed, both Wagner and Brahms sought to inherit Beethoven's prestige.

Music, whether sacred or secular, has three basic elements: rhythm, melody, and harmony, which came into being in that order. How is the emotional nature of man affected by the three? If *melody* is dominant, it expresses itself in *song;* if *rhythm* prevails, it calls for the *dance;* if the total impression is *harmonic,* the composition is an *expanded form of melody,* represented by chords instead of single notes.

In recent decades, composers like Stravinsky have made rhythm the major element in their works, a throwback to the time when musical language was still in its infancy. Others, like Schoenberg, have glorified chromaticism and confounded tonality by outlandish, crashing, loud productions, in the process of which musical sound is thoroughly pulverized into something supposedly of the utmost delicacy. European proponents of integrated serialism and "invigorating metrical asymmetries," composers like Karl Heinz Stockhausen, Pierre Boulez, and Luigi Nono, and their American counterparts, Henry Cowell, Edgar Varèse, and John Cage, think their productions are "still a dialect of Bach."

Since Bach's works were deeply religious, it is somewhat difficult to find a really fundamental relationship between them and the creations of these integrating serialists. Bach's cantatas were an elaboration of hymns and through them, his Passion oratorios, and his *Mass in B Minor,* he became a preacher of the Gospel. The late "Quintus Quiz" (Edward Shillito) put it this way in an article on "Bach" in the *Christian Century,* October 10, 1940:

> There is something in this interpreter which goes to the heart of every man. On the wings of his music, it may be, the Lord Himself steps out of the Book and is once more in the midst of us. . . . Why do we not use more seriously this great evangelist?

On the other hand, Karl Barth has said: "Whether the angels play only Bach in praising God — I am not quite sure!" Oskar Söhngen says in his blunt way that "Bach cantatas do not speak the language of our day." He takes issue with those who say that music as a language will not be evolving much more. He will not agree with those who believe that our musical language is complete, that the gamut of church music has been entirely explored, and that all we need to do now is to codify the works of the past. In the case of hymnody, the hymnals of the past in England and Germany have not included the authors of texts and composers still living at the time of publication.

The frontispiece of such hymnals might well have shown a picture of Lot's wife after she had faced backward and had been turned into a column of sodium chloride. This is a pertinent remark by Thomas Tiplady, one of England's present-day hymn writers, a number of whose hymns are to be found in American hymnals.

Some years ago the American Music Conference conducted a survey to ascertain the types of music preferred by Americans. The result revealed an interesting sequence: church music and hymns, first; then followed popular dance music, folk tunes, semiclassical and opera, cowboy and hillbilly, classical music, and in the last place — boogie woogie. The preference for church music, particularly hymns, is subject to a number of interpretations. Polls conducted by magazines listing hymns according to degree of popularity differ widely in their results. Periodicals published by denominations belonging to the "third force" category or by most church bodies dominated by strong fundamentalism invariably report that their subscribers give the top spots in their voting to such songs as "In the Garden," "The Old Rugged Cross," "Count Your Many Blessings," and "When They Ring the Golden Bells," while such classics as "Our God, Our Help in Ages Past" and "A Mighty Fortress Is Our God" either are way down on the list or do not make the list at all. If Lutheran denominational organs would conduct such a poll, it is a foregone conclusion that the great texts and tunes which have stood the wear and tear of the centuries would be found in the uppermost part of the listing. A poll undertaken by such periodicals as the *Christian Century* or the *United Church Herald* would undoubtedly have much the same results.

However, shouldn't Christians of all persuasions try to create something *new* in hymnody? Was the psalmist's exhortation, "Sing unto the Lord a *new* song," meant only for his contemporaries? Didn't Heinrich Schuetz produce "new music" in his time, and wasn't Bach highly "modern" in his time? Is genuine church music confined to Hassler chorales, *Lutherlieder,* and Schuetz motets? Isn't Söhngen right when he says: "Die ausschliessliche Pflege alter und ältester Kirchenmusik hat etwas vom ästhetischen Feinschmeckertum an sich"? And must we not concur with him when he declares: "Jede Kirchenmusik, die nicht dem Heute und Hier ihr Recht gibt, bedeutet darum eine Flucht vor ihrer eigentlichen Aufgabe"?

As far as hymnody is concerned, it is generally agreed that it is exceedingly difficult to write a great hymn. The extreme difficulty of truly creative writing and composing in this field should, therefore, constitute a real challenge to our contemporaries to produce something that will be something of superior worth. It will have to be genuine *Gebrauchsmusik* but at the same time superbly lovely. Can anyone out-Bach Bach in producing tonal structures outranking his masterful creations? And can authors of new texts put Martin Luther, Isaac Watts, and Charles Wesley in the shade? Have there been any concerted efforts to promote such literary and musical activity?

The International Fellowship for Research in Hymnody, organized in 1959 at Lüdenscheid, Germany, by outstanding authorities in church music representing 13 nations, including Walter E. Buszin, is confining itself to research and is not active in exploring the possibility of creating a newer type of hymnody in the linguistic and musical idiom of our century. However, they are aware of the necessity of discarding certain hymns such as those with obsolete concepts about the Creator and present-day society. In a new age in which the cultures of the nations are gradually being homogenized and the amorphous in the varied aesthetic endeavors is being assiduously cultivated, there is room for much-needed positive expressions of the Christian faith in the language of our time. Max Reger was convinced that only a believing person can create true music. This naturally and inexorably should be the case in hymnody. What is happening, for example, in English-speaking countries?

In an address delivered before the United Church of Christ Ministerium of Chicago on Nov. 4, 1963, Roger Pilkington, widely known English scientist, said that man is being forced to rethink his image of God, a God who today is primarily concerned with the universe, and not just with the earth, and an earth in which matter has essential lifeness and ability to respond, something that writers and artists are portraying in unique ways. Strangely enough, some of them are of the beatnik type, and at London coffee bars they are introducing new forms of hymn singing to the accompaniment of guitars. The texts are anything but stereotype, and they do express a real faith. The churches of Britain attract only a handful of worshipers and have lost a large part of their membership; however, the young people are like most young people elsewhere in the civilized world — they are wondering what kind of future they have in the new atomic age. Hymns which are current in an age with feudal overtones will not fit into one in which democracy holds sway. A good example is the third verse of "All Things Bright and Beautiful":

> The rich man in his castle,
> The poor man at his gate.
> God made them, high and lowly,
> And ordered their estate.

It is quite likely that hymns by contemporary authors will finally be included in the newer hymnals of Britain and Germany.

In the United States, where freedom of expression is one of our prized liberties, our people have sometimes been forced to put up with freakish developments. We are referring to a hymnody that is a caricature and travesty of the real thing. One finds it especially entrenched in the South, where the lovers of true hymnody are greatly outnumbered.

In the year 1936 in Dallas, Texas, one V. O. Stamps began to broadcast purported "hymns" over Station KRLD. He is the most notorious of a group in the South who have jazzed up gospel songs, "drooly rock 'n' roll," resorting to tricks of vocalization, or of the melody, *portamento,* when it leaps more than a third, zooming up to the next note like an express elevator. His stock in trade is various combinations of chromaticism, which feminize a hymn, also varied loudnesses, high and low pitches, pauses, durations, something making one wonder whether he and his fellow perpetrators of sacred "music" are trying to transfer the loudnesses of the integrating serialists to the religious field.

Many Texans, back there in 1936, "just ate it up," so much so that the owners of this radio station decided to step up its power from 10,000 watts to 50,000 watts, the Federal Communications Commission slowly relenting and consenting. The Stamps-Baxter Music Company was organized, and 53 singing groups were sent out to sing and to sell on the side a "hymnal" entitled *Pearly Gates.* Stamps wrote a bouncy theme song, "Give the World a Smile," and while there are smiles that make us happy, this song gave the lovers of good hymnody the blues. In the course of time every gospel quartet had to use it in order to "rate." Those quartets at times plan all-night programs, actually lasting from 8:00 p. m. to 2:00 a. m., with as many as 10 of these quartets participating. The customers pay an admission price of $1.00. Wally Fowler, one of these singing gospelers, admitted in 1956: "Since 1948 my contribution to gospel singing at the gate would be better than $6,000,000." This is a rather strange use of the word "contribution."

Said a church columnist in one of Birmingham's newspapers: "They've simply jazzed up religious songs to bebop rhythms for a fast buck." He was referring to independent quartets as well as those in the Stamps-Baxter organization. The Chuck Wagon Gang, which records on Columbia Records, has sold far more than a million disks. When last heard of, the Statesmen were riding around in a luxurious, air-conditioned limousine with beds and individual radiophones. Some of these quartets that go by such names as the Revelaires, the Foggy River Boys, the Blackwoods, the Rebels, the Oak Ridge (not atomic) Quartet, and the Sunshine Boys have paid more than $100,000 income tax in a single year (1956). Al Richman of the Sunshine Boys, one of the veterans of the business, is entirely unabashed in speaking about the commercial motive of these groups:

> Let's face it, we believe that anybody who has paid his buck should be entertained. They like this kind of music, and we give it to them. Some people say we deal in "corn." Maybe we do, but we know what our audience wants.

Suppose a physician viewed his professional duties in such a cynical way, or for that matter, the pastor of a church. Since these quartets conduct a sort of "Spike" Jones hymnic depreciation hour, they are not interested in promoting worship but in mere entertainment. It is not surprising that they have run full-page advertisements in *Billboard* and *Variety*, the top magazines in the show business.

How the cause of hymnody would be helped if such great crowds of people at these all-night programs — attended by as many as 10,018 in a single night (at Winston-Salem, N. C.) — were taught the great hymns of the church, the kind that will continue to be sung long after the saccharine concoctions and dizzy chromaticizations of Stamps have been forgotten!

The South, on the other hand, has contributed something unique to the field of hymnody — the spirituals, mostly Negro, but some of them White. They constitute a sacred folk music, which in the case of the Negro spirituals is born out of the pains, frustrations, humiliations, and heartaches, as well as the fleeting joys of existence. As one Negro writer, Wayman B. McLaughlin, has put it: "The soul-life of a people is here woven into a testament of mystery and holiness." He goes on to say: "Spirituals represent the personal mysticism of the

Christian tradition. . . . They personalize in the concrete the individual's 'I-Thou' encounter with God." Since some of them are dialogs between God and man, their words qualify them in that respect as hymns. Some of the catchiest ones are spiritual songs (in which the direction is man to man), but because of their symbolical and mystical insights and their interplay of the Eternal Spirit with the soul of the worshiper, they are finding their way into standard denominational hymnals.

There is, for instance, this touching declaration as an old slave stands in spirit at the foot of the Cross (not included in any hymnal):

> They crucified my Lord, and He never said a mumblin' word,
> Not a word, not a word,
> The blood came twinklin' down, but He never said a mumblin' word,
> Not a word, not a word.

Obviously "twinklin" is an arresting semantic substitution for "trickling," but "twinklin" is a true image of the sparkling, bejeweled blood of Jesus trickling down the Cross. Thus it reflects something of the poetic essence of these adoring, lowly souls.

The search for new texts and tunes in our country has been conducted on a nationwide basis by the Hymn Society of America. This organization has held contests in order to secure new hymns expressive of the faith and hope of Christians living in this day and age. Thus such categories as Christian education, social welfare, Christian patriotism, stewardship, Christian unity, and others have been enriched by new texts and tunes of enduring worth. The English language is in need of some outstanding hymns on the Christian home. Also needed are more hymns on the true significance of the Passion of our Lord, of which there are far more in the German language than in the English.

One of the most striking hymns to find its way into the newer hymnals of the United States is an ecumenical hymn by Georgia Harkness, the well-known woman theologian and writer. It was chosen by the Hymn Society of America from nearly 500 new texts submitted in recognition of the Assembly of the World Council of Churches held at Evanston, Ill., in 1954. Ten other texts also won high recognition, all eleven being issued in pamphlet form by the Society under the heading "Eleven Ecumenical Hymns." The hymn by Dr. Harkness, set to the tune *Donne Secours*, first appearing in the *Genevan Psalter*, 1551, is herewith submitted together with the French and German translations:

1. Hope of the world, Thou Christ of great com - pas - sion,
1. Christ, notre es - poir, aie com - pas - sion du mon - de,
1. Hoff - nung der Welt, Du heil - and voll Er - barm - en,

Speak to our fear - ful hearts by con - flict rent.
Ban - nis le peur qui fait glac - er nos coeurs,
Schenk uns in Angst und Not Dein gött - lich Gnad'!

Save us, Thy peo - ple, from con - sum - ing pas - sion,
Sau - ve les tiens de la ter - reur im - mon - de
Ret - te Dein Volk, das sich trotz Dein - em Warn - en

Who by our own false hopes and aims are spent. A - men.
Des faux es - poirs et des dou - tes trom - peurs.
In Sünd' und selbst - be - trug ver - lor - en hat.

2. Hope of the world, God's gift from highest heaven,
   Bringing to hungry souls the bread of life.
   Still let Thy spirit unto us. be given
   To heal earth's wounds and end her bitter strife.

3. Hope of the world, afoot on dusty highways,
   Showing to wandering souls the path of light;
   Walk thou beside us lest the tempting byways
   Lure us away from Thee to endless night.

4. Hope of the world, who by Thy cross didst save us
   From death and dark despair, from sin and guilt;
   We render back the love Thy mercy gave us;
   Take thou our lives and use them as Thou wilt.

5. Hope of the world, O Christ, o'er death victorious,
   Who by this sign didst conquer grief and pain.
   We would be faithful to Thy gospel glorious:
   Thou art our Lord! Thou dost forever reign!

.2. Christ, notre espoir, répands des lieux célestes
    Le pain divin de la terre et du ciel.
    Guéris les tiens des gangrènes funestes
    Et leurs pensées d'amertume et de fiel.

3. Christ, notre espoir, sur la route poudreuse
   Maintiens nos pas loin des sentiers pervers
   Où l'on finit perdu dans la nuit creuse
   N'ayant plus rien que fatigue at revers.

4. Christ, notre espoir, qui de la croix rayonne,
   Et qui détruit autour de nous la nuit,
   Reconnaissant à l'amour qui pardonne
   Chacun de nous, ravi, t'aime et te suit.

5. Christ, notre espoir, à toi soit la victoire.
   Tu as vaincu la mort, la vanité.
   A toi l'honneur, la puissance et la gloire
   Dès maintenant et dans l'éternité.

Tr. John A. Maynard, 1954

2. Hoffnung der Welt. Geschenk von Gottes Gnade,
   Füll' unsre Herzen jetzt und alle Zeit
   Mit Deines Geistes wundertät' ger Gabe;
   Heil' unsre Wunden, ende allen Streit.

3. Hoffnung der Welt, Du suchst auf allen Pfaden
   Irrende Seelen, weisest sie zum Licht;
   Bleibe bei uns, schütz' uns vor ew'gem Schaden;
   Denn ohne Dich wird uns das Heil doch nicht.

4. Hoffnung der Welt, Dein Kreuz hat überwunden
   Tod, Sünde, Schuld und alle bittre Not;
   Dein' grosse Lieb' hat Wiederhall gefunden;
   Dein lass uns sein und bleiben bis zum Tod.

5. Hoffnung der Welt, O Christus, Held im Streite,
   Du hast den Tod und alle Pein besiegt.
   Zu treuem Dienste unser Herz bereite,
   Dass wir Dich rühmen, der uns so geliebt.

Tr. Leopold W. Bernhard, 1954

Involved in the struggle for better hymnody is not only the securing of texts and tunes of the highest quality but also the educational techniques needed to teach them to young and old. Hymn singing has played a great role in certain periods of church history. There have been eras of hymn singing by large masses of people. Arius made headway with his heterodox Christology by writing hymns about it, hymns that caught on but that were themselves counteracted successfully by the same method by the staunch defender of Athanasius, St. Ambrose. When the Roman Church cut off the lay worshipers from singing hymns, men appeared from time to time to lead them in singing outside the church, among them St. Francis of Assisi, whose *laude spirituali* in the Italian vernacular were patterned after the singing of the French and Provençal troubadours. The Reformation movement gained strong momentum after Luther adopted the practice of hymnodizing its basic principles and beliefs. During Calvin's brief exile in Strasbourg he was so deeply impressed with the chorale singing of Lutheran congregations there that he vowed to have something just as powerful eventually in Geneva. The Geneva congregation had many exiled Englishmen who upon their return to England introduced not only congregational singing but mass singing in the streets of London in which many thousands participated. Hymns have at times been sung on the occasion of great athletic spectacles in England, such as the Football Association's Cup Final of 1927, which involved a crowd of more than 100,000 persons. They sang "Abide with Me," which the average Englishman knows from memory.

When America entered World War I in 1917, Secretary of War Newton D. Baker and Harry Emerson Fosdick's brother Raymond decided to use the community chorus idea in the armed forces to strengthen the morale of the men in the service and to promote a healthy liaison between army camps and nearby towns. Marshall Bartholomew, conductor of the Yale Glee Club, and Robert Lawrence Wier were put in charge of training directors and singers for this special work. They turned out 123 men with gratifying results. There was company singing, full regimental singing, singing while marching, singing in the barracks, sometimes after lights were out and the all-quiet order was supposed to be obeyed. The men loved it. When General Pershing reached France, he requested Newton D. Baker to send him the best song leader available. Thus Stanley Hawkins, a professional tenor and song leader, was commissioned to teach a final total of four million men the joys of singing. When the boys came home, music had many new friends in the schools, the newly developed service clubs, and the churches; however, one thing was quite noticeable — not so many in the churches. It was most unfortunate that the church did not take full advantage of the opportunity of using these returned men by capitalizing on their enthusiasm for mass singing.

The trouble was that most of the men were taught very few hymns. They preferred secular numbers, such as "Over There," "Let Me Call You Sweetheart," "There's a Long, Long Trail Awinding," "Just a Baby's Prayer at Twilight," "It's a Long Way to Tipperary," and others composed at that time, plus Stephen Foster's imperishable folk songs "My Old Kentucky Home," "Jeanie with the Light-Brown Hair," "Come Where My Love Lies Dreaming," "Old Folks at Home," "Beautiful Dreamer," etc. Their repertoire was composed almost entirely of songs of sentiment. Hymn singing was confined primarily to carols like "Silent Night" and to the Christmas hymn "O Come, All Ye Faithful," now sung in at least 38 languages.

When the men came back, those who went to church discovered in many instances that the hymns in the hymnbook of their home churches were pitched too high. Consequently some of them resorted to the device of singing "dog bass," that is, one octave below the melody. Many of America's hymnals have tunes in the same keys as those found in the hymnbooks of England. The Dykes-Barnby school of English composers and other writers of tunes before and after them used keys best suited for boys' or children's choirs, which sang regularly in many English churches. Furthermore, some authorities tell us that the average voice in England is higher than in the United States. When, for example, the "Star Spangled Banner" was sung to "Anacreon in Heaven," an old English song, it was written with two sharps, the key of D. Then it was lowered to C, later to B flat, and now it is often sung in A flat. With this in mind the compilers of some of the newer hymnals, such as the Episcopal *Hymnal 1940*, 1943, decided to have the key of each hymn low enough so that male voices would have no trouble taking part in the congregational singing.

In speaking on this subject I am well aware of the fact that nothing in the service of public worship can be more controversial than this matter of congregational singing. Likes and dislikes are often violent. There have been cases where dissensions over hymnody have even led to arrests and court procedures. In 1615 a case came up in England in the Essex Court of the Archdeaconry in which a defendant was tried on a charge worded as follows:

> For he . . . singeth the Psalms in the church with such a jesticulour tone and allitonant voice, viz., squeaking like a pig, which doth not only interrupt other voices, but is altogether dissonant and disagreeable unto any musical harmony, and he hath been requested by the minister to leave it, but he doth obstinately persist and continue therein.

The defendant obviously was not just trying to counteract some singing that was "an anemic warble," but was deliberately trying to draw attention to himself and thus disrupt the service. There have always been those who can sing but refuse to sing, and others of whom the late Cleland McAfee said: "They think they can sing, when they really cannot sing, and perhaps should think it over at Sing Sing."

The Church of England has had authorized psalters, but it never has had any authorized hymnbooks. With the rise of hymnody a number of clergymen brought out their own publications in this field. One of them, the Rev. T. Cotterill, was prosecuted by the Consistory of the Court of York for issuing in the year 1818 a collection of psalms and hymns for use in his own church. The trial was held on July 6, 1820, before the chancellor of the archbishop's court, who found the case so complicated that he refused to render judgment or to assess the costs, but registered only an opinion. The case, Holy and Ward vs. Cotterill, was then referred to the archbishop, who settled it by compiling a hymnal himself for Mr. Cotterill's church, and since the rector of that perish had already incurred a financial loss by publishing his own hymnal, the archbishop took it upon himself to defray all the costs for producing the new hymnbook. Thus peace and harmony prevailed. Fortunately the precedent set by him in the financing of such an undertaking has been disregarded since then by bishops and synodical presidents of all and sundry persuasions without loss of prestige or popularity.

Another type of controversy in England was settled much earlier. It arose among the followers of John Smyth, the founder of the General Baptists. In extreme reaction against forms, he advocated singing "by the gift of the spirit," which meant, at least in theory, that a member of the congregation had the right to stand up in the midst of the service and create a hymn right then and there impromptu. Since no enduring literature nor music has ever been fashioned "right off the cuff," such a procedure was never carried out. But the subject smoldered for a long time, and one congregation, that of the Independent Church at Arnheim, gathered by T. Goodwin and Philip Nye, argued for some time as to whether only one person in the congregation should sing or whether it should be "conjoined." In a rather facetious mood Roland Bainton once said to me: "Have you heard of the ultra-Congregationalist? He is the one who will sing at any time in the church service, whenever it suits him best!"

All worship should be an aesthetic experience. Too often the parts of a service of public worship do not hang together. On one occasion I attended a service in a church designed by Ralph Adams Cram, a veritable piece of frozen poetry in stone similar to the magnificent chapel he designed for Mercersburg Academy. Outwardly everything could make the worshipers amenable to the promptings of God's Spirit. The minister had a moving pastoral prayer and delivered a good sermon. The organist played a prelude and a postlude by Bach, and the choir sang two well-selected anthems. A capable soprano soloist performed most acceptably Crist's setting of the well-known prayer of St. Francis of Assisi. But the hymns of the service were poorly selected both as to text and tune; they were really not hymns at all, but gospel songs in the bantam-weight category, which badly marred the aesthetic unity of that hour of worship. The use of such congregational song must have had a centrifugal effect on many of the worshipers, causing them to leave the church with confused emotions. Later inquiry revealed that the gospel songs were chosen to please the old-timers in the congregation who were brought up on that kind of congregational song and who felt that they were enduring a kind of martyrdom when the organist or the choir presented something new. Two such distinct types of music in the same service make one think of something that might happen sometime in Washington: an ambassador going to a brilliant diplomatic function wearing "tails," silk hat, gloves, and a pair of white tennis shoes! That church service reminded me of something very incongruous I had seen one day at the airport in Houston, Texas — the fancy "get-up" of an Episcopal bishop who wore clericals, a big cross on his chest, a tan, ten-gallon hat, and cowboy boots — his fleshly tabernacle thus decked out with high church and low accouterments.

All parts of the service must be subordinated to its totality. In accordance with the principles of dramaturgy, every element of the service must be coordinated organically with the other parts; otherwise, as one writer has put it, it will not be "valid aesthetically, sound psychologically, or effective spiritually." For this reason it will always be difficult, if not impossible, to "have something for everybody." The liturgy is there to take care of the needs of the *entire* congregation, those shared in common, and not every individual need. The last-named may have to be ministered to in one or more counseling sessions with the pastor. Ministers are pressured to look upon the congregation as but a segment of the culture of the local community and to treat its membership in the worldwide fellowship in Christ as an incidental thing. When we come to God in worship with fellow members of the local congregation, we are uniting with *all other* worshipers throughout the nation and the world. Public worship is a "corporate celebration of our spiritual unity" with all of every clime and race whose lives are pledged to Christ and committed to His service.

From time immemorial Christian worship has been composed of four elements: praise, confession, illumination, and dedication. The hymns at the beginning of the service should naturally center in the praise of God and never be of a subjective nature. In other words: they do not begin with the perpendicular pronoun. The prayer of confession is something that Christians of all the ages have always included in the early part of the service and subscribed to with the *Kyrie* of the apostolic age. The hymn before the sermon has the purpose not only of continuing the mood of worship, but also, at least in a general way, of leading up to the message of the day. Whether the service ends or not with a recessional, a hymn of dedication is always in order followed by a postlude that makes one feel that the Church Militant will most assuredly become the Church Triumphant.

Years ago Edward MacDowell wrote in his *Critical and Historical Essays:* "Music . . . is a language, but a language of the intangible, a kind of soul language." If that be true, then the church has much at stake and consequently should devote much of her time and talent to educating children, youth, and adults in the field of sacred music. All of which points up the very important role of the organist and choir director, or of the minister of music in the larger churches.

Just as a college may have a beautiful campus, fine buildings, and excellent equipment but a faculty that is weak in several departments, so a church may have a high-grade and well-installed organ, but a second-rate organist. He may, indeed, be a good perfomer, but inadequately schooled in *church* music. At times churches are forced to accept teachers of high school bands and orchestras as choir directors, persons who often are the friendliest of extroverts and well qualified for their own specialty, but who simply do not have the training required for work with church choirs and for teaching appreciation of the better kind of hymnody. A minister serving in such a situation can never tell what such choir directors might uncork next; a bandmaster turned choir director once offered a bizarre arrangement of "Jingle Bells" for a Christmas service while another with similar training thought that "I'm Dreaming of a White Christmas" would do for that festival occasion. If it is necessary for a minister to have conferences with his organist and choir director, it becomes doubly necessary whenever he is faced with that kind of problem.

It is the minister's primary responsibility to bring the Word of God and its interpretation in the service of worship. It is the responsibility of those in charge of the music, both instrumental and choral, to set the mood of the worshipers, so that their meditations will be lifted above the routine of their workaday lives. Strangely enough, one finds organists who do not regard hymns as worthy of any preparation. No Protestant service will serve its purpose unless the hymns are played and sung effectively. "Hymns don't sing themselves. Someone has to teach them." The organist has little sense of proportion if he devotes all of his time to getting the instrumental numbers and anthems ready but does not prepare at all for the playing of the hymns. Hymn playing is an art in itself. Choirmasters who give hymns just a perfunctory run-through on rehearsal night also underestimate their great importance. Both organist and choir director should know thoroughly the text and tune of all hymns to be used in the following Sunday's service. Some organists give little or no attention to registration for the hymns and play each stanza in the same wooden, unvaried way. Why have every stanza in the same key? Congregational singing is livened up by changing keys in one of the hymns of the service and by using descants or free accompaniments for one of the other hymns. Thus "Fairest Lord Jesus" may be begun in the key of E flat, and continued in the second stanza in F major, or it may be sung in the last stanza in F sharp. When it comes to descants and free accompaniments, the following publications can be of valuable help:

> Descant Hymn Tune Book, Books I and II, by Geoffrey Shaw
> A Book of Descants, organ edition and voice edition, by Alan Gray
> Eighteen Descants on Well-Known Hymn Tunes, by Henry Frey
> Free Accompaniments to 100 Well-Known Hymn Tunes,
>   by T. Tertius Noble

The descants and free accompaniments should not be used unless first rehearsed together by the organist and choir; furthermore, the congregation should have advance notice in the church bulletin of any new version of the tune. It should also be borne in mind that it is not desirable to have too many singers on the descants.

There are other ways of introducing variety into organ accompaniments. Alexander McCurdy suggests that the organist "play the bass part on either the upper or lower part of the pedal board, the soprano, alto, and tenor parts on the manuals." The harmony can be enriched by adding stops to the chords, particularly when the pedal notes are in the lower octave. How much registration should be provided? If too much, it is as bad as too little. The people want to hear themselves sing and don't care to be overpowered by the organ; on the other hand, they won't sing if the registration is too weak. My preference is for a registration that is definitely on the plus side. The tempo is very important; follow it as indicated in the hymnal and by the spirit of the words.

If a hymn is played as if it were nothing but a straight *Strophenlied*, each stanza identical with the others, it leads to monotony and boredom. If some churchgoers get wearied and languid in a service, it is usually attributed to a tiring sermon, but it may be due to other factors, such as hymn singing that is stereotype and without the tiniest spark of enthusiasm. Being bored in church can have sad results; since church decorum will not permit "Bronx cheers," just as it conversely does not allow encores, the only way of registering disapproval is by staying away. Enthusiasm engendered by great hymn singing and inspired playing of hymns has much to do with drawing large congregations.

How are new hymns to be introduced? Some churches have
a weekly "Hymn Study Night," usually conducted by the minister of
music or the pastor of the church. In some communities there is an
annual "Hymn Festival," in which new hymns are often featured. In
Evansville the new Evangelical and Reformed *Hymnal* was introduced to members of other church bodies as well as the E. and R. folk
by such a hymn festival sponsored by the Evansville Organists' and
Choir Directors' Guild. It was a truly ecumenical affair, for it was
held in St. Paul's Episcopal Church, and the person in charge was
a Presbyterian, Dr. Reginald McAll. For 45 years he was the organist
and choirmaster of the Church of the Covenant in New York and also
served as the executive secretary of the Hymn Society of America.
The event had been promoted for more than a month with gratifying
results. All of the pews of that beautiful stone church were filled, and
more than 100 persons were forced to stand in the aisles throughout
the evening. Dr. McAll singled out for special consideration several
of the brand-new hymns not published before, among them that great
new gem for Good Friday, "Now All Is Still," with words by G. J. Neumann, now dean of Wartburg College, Waverly, Iowa, and musical
setting by Karl P. Harrington, for many years faculty member at
Wesleyan University.

While hymn study groups in local parishes and hymn festivals
are most valuable, unfortunately they do not reach the majority of
the church's members. Therefore other procedures must be set in
motion. One is to have the congregation practice before or after the
service. When I attended the 11-o'clock service at the Cathedral of
St. John the Divine in New York on Sunday, July 28, 1957, a member
of the cathedral staff stepped into the pulpit at 10:45 and announced
that the congregation would immediately rehearse the hymns to be
sung in the following service, adding that such a practice period had
become a custom there. One of the tunes, *Ora Labora,* an unusual
setting by T. Tertius Noble for Jane Borthwick's hymn, "Come, Labor
On," was entirely new to the majority of those present, but everybody
cooperated goodnaturedly, and it went surprisingly well with glorious
organ accompaniment in the regular service following.

A good way to kill any chance of acceptance of a fine new hymn
is to throw it suddenly at the heads of the congregation during the
Sunday morning service. Let the introduction be gradual; have the
organist play it one Sunday as an offertory number, repeating it with
improvisations; the next Sunday have it sung by one of the choirs as

an anthem number; on the third Sunday let the congregation finally sing it, supported by the adult choir in the chancel and by a children's choir at the other end of the church. With strong support coming from both ends of the house of worship, the worshipers will have no hesitation about joining in, assured that there will be no danger of being left suddenly adrift amidst the efforts of a few individual voices. Many churchgoers have a strange fear complex when it comes to such singing; they will gather courage quickly, however, when they notice how many seem to know the new hymn.

Another good place to introduce a new hymn is at a congregational dinner. There are glorious stories connected with many hymns and a good place to tell them is when the families of the parish are gathered together in relaxed manner and there is a spirit of happy camaraderie. I think it ill-advised to have all singing on such an occasion in a lighter vein, the "Killy-killy-wash-wash" kind. Years of experimentation prove that at such dinners the parishioners, both young and old, like to sing the great hymns of the church.

The most strategic place in the church to teach hymn singing is in the Sunday church school. This is where many children often have their first contact with music. Teachers in our church schools today are more fortunate in many respects than those of a generation ago. In most churches then the pianos were hardly ever in tune, and it was a rare thing to have pianists who could really play. Worst of all, the song books were often very inferior, with plenty of waltz tunes and words that weren't worth memorizing. Children like to sing stories according to a rhythmic pattern; furthermore, they sing out of understanding, not out of experience. Therefore a sweet little boy or girl is singing a falsehood if either is asked to sing, "I was sinking deep in sin, far from the peaceful shore." How can we expect children to sing such untrue confessions? In sound pedagogy we go from the known to the unknown, and a child certainly has not gone through such experiences as living the life of a wayward son or daughter who has to be pulled out of the gutter and saved.

Children's hymns should lift up a loving Christ who at the same time is strong and manly. Imagery is always in place provided it has been explained beforehand. The poetry should be simple and easily understood because clearly expressed. There is no reason why children's hymnals should be trivial and devoid of literary merit. As far as the tunes are concerned, they can be vigorous for some texts, but should have none of the "um-pah-pahs" of the German waltzes.

The most effective work among children is done through the medium of children's choirs. The smallest tots are taught the texts and tunes by rote. There are Sunday church schools in which the first 15 minutes in the Primary department are devoted to the singing of hymns. Thus all children in the department, whether or not members of the church choir drawn from the department, learn good hymns. As they grow older, the boys prefer hymns recounting deeds, while the girls show a preference for those dealing with home and friends. It should be borne in mind that by the time they are Juniors, they have in most cases learned to read music in the public school. In many churches the regular church hymnal is now in use in all departments of the church school from the Intermediates up; in some cases the Junior department also uses it. This makes good sense to an educator. The time when one should begin learning the great hymns of the church is in his childhood years. This does not mean that there is no place for such songs as "Jesus Loves Me, This I Know," but that from the Primary department on we can begin teaching the hymns which are the great classics of hymnody. The idea that children should be taught jingles primarily is fast becoming obsolete. Where there is any doubt as to the meaning of certain words and phrases, these should be explained, sometimes with the help of pictures. A child's intelligence too frequently is underestimated.

A unique experiment has been conducted for some years in a French Reformed church at La Roche, Switzerland, by Andre Bourquin, organist of the congregation. All children of the parish ranging in age from 9 to 15 are members of one of the children's choirs he has called into being. He has the advantage of having the children of an orphanage, the "Choeur des Billodes," within the confines of the parish. In England such groups from the so-called "charity schools" have long played an important role in the development of congregational hymn singing. Mr. Bourquin uses a book called the *Psautier de Jeunesse,* comprised of 22 psalms and 72 hymns with chorale settings, and divided according to the age of the singers into three categories of difficulty: 6–8 years; 8–10 years; 11–16 years. By the time the children have taken the seven years of training involved, each one will have learned 90 hymns from memory. No Sunday school songs are used, because Mr. Bourquin holds them to be of inferior quality, having little or no value for the future. He believes that children should know by heart the great hymns which go with them through life and support them as they meet its strains and tensions.

Children's choirs are worthy of the best direction they can get. The hymnbook is one of the best sources of good material. You do not need to have them sing in parts. Good unison singing on the part of children is lovely, and that is all they need to do. A man who is placed in charge of a church's music must know psychology as well as music and must sometimes use a bit of holy guile in order to get the better things accepted. Howard Kelsey sometimes came into difficult situations where it was hard to wean a congregation away from certain substandard musical numbers; proceeding cautiously, he would at first throw in what he called a "gumdrop" now and then, but this invariably would be discussed in an educational follow-up at the next congregational dinner, at which time he would point out the weaknesses of the requested number. The result was that it was never asked for again.

A hymn serves a double purpose; it is not only an expression of beauty but also an act of worship. That is why it is such a wonderful thing to have children in church services in the early years of their life. Let us beware, however, of such remarks as "Aren't they cute!" Children do not like to be on exhibit in church any more than they do at home when there is company and dad and mom want them to show off their particular talents. Neither should we play up the idea that the existence of a multiple choir system necessarily makes the church look more active. And heaven forbid that any in the pews should ever get the notion that the contribution of children's choirs to a service is in the realm of entertainment. Our main concern is to have the children feel that the church cares tremendously about them and for that reason has them just as much in mind as the carpets, utilities, improvements, and other items when the annual budget is prepared and adopted. Whatever we reserve in the budget for their athletic and musical activities is very well spent.

The late Dr. Nevin C. Harner wrote in his book, *The Educational Work of the Church,* page 96: "A church can give the Christian religion to its children only if it gives itself as well." Children don't become religious by donning choir robes, or by appearing periodically in the sanctuary, or just by listening to able teachers. They must feel that we really love them and that their presence and participation in public worship means as much to the grown-ups as to them. As much as their sponsors in Holy Baptism, the congregation has some real obligations to meet if Christianity is to bring children the wealth of its hymnody. Failure to meet that may preclude or materially impair the next generation's appreciation not only of hymnody, but of the Christian philosophy and way of life as well.

The struggle for better hymnody is seemingly one that will not end. You will always have difficulties with those who hold that there is no such thing as objectively good or bad music. They may even quote music critic Paul Hume: "One man's Stravinsky is another man's strychnine, and anyone has the right to love or to loathe any piece of music he chooses." But we shall have to remind them that Hume goes on to say: "A trained musician can look at a piece of paper and tell you whether the music is good, bad, or indifferent, or merely impossible." In the church field we have frankly had too much of the "merely impossible." As in all reform movements, there are no permanent victories of what is best. It reminds us of the words of Charles Parkhurst, spoken many years ago but still, alas, too true: "The difficulty is that the good people get tired of being good before the bad people get tired of being bad." The corrupters of church music, those who use musical comedy and opera numbers and sentimental ballads at church weddings, or popular songs at funeral services, and third-rate hymns in services of public worship, present a problem which becomes compounded gravely if ministers, organists, and choir directors do not care what kind of music is used in their places of worship. It calls for an intensive educational campaign that must begin right in our theological seminaries. Concordia Theological Seminary, Saint Louis, has long recognized this responsibility and acted accordingly. Not only the members of The Lutheran Church — Missouri Synod but countless devotees of church music in many other church bodies feel indebted to Dr. Buszin for new insights gained from his many articles in various publications and his lectures. Although we first met in 1945, I became much better acquainted with him in September 1959, when we were the two representatives of the United States at the First International Conference for Research in Hymnody held at Lüdenscheid, West Germany. He is a contributor to the *Jahrbuch für Liturgik und Hymnologie*, published annually since 1955, the only publication of its kind in the Protestant world. Not all seminaries are as fortunate as Concordia; there are indeed many whose curricula offer very little if anything in this highly important field of church music and liturgics, including a special course in hymnody.

This universe is built on the principle of growth. We are not the preservers of a changeless past but as Christians committed to the constant improvement of life in all its phases. Paul's worst congregation was at Corinth, yet he saw potential saints among its members. In a letter to that congregation he said that they were "called to be saints." To him a saint was not a person who had arrived in terms of perfect character, but one who was moving ever and always in the right direction. That is what we must bear in mind as we think of church music in general and hymnody in particular. Although it is a most difficult thing to achieve perfection, we must press ever forward toward that goal without lowering our standards.

6

CHURCH MUSIC INSTRUCTION IN THE CHURCH MUSIC SCHOOLS OF GERMANY

Karl Ferdinand Müller

The Evangelical church music schools of today are an establishment of the 20th century. In the present form as independent institutions of the church, these did not exist before. They owe their origin to both an external and internal necessity.

The first external impulses were given by very important changes in the preparation of grade-school teachers in connection with the establishment of pedagogical academies after World War I. The new curricula and professional goals of these academies were based on pedagogical needs and on a newly arranged relationship between school and church. The new goals led to a considerable deterioration in the preparation of church musicians in these institutes. Thus the elimination of the position of teacher-organist as the 19th century had created it in its teachers seminaries was in sight. To be sure, a limited number of younger people still came from the organ classes of the music academies and conservatories. But these young people either had majored in school music to teach in the high schools and had received only incidental training in church music, or they were free-lancing artists with or without an organist's or choir director's state certificate. Before 1933 there was no established church music profession that provided lists of available openings through a central office and regulated salaries of church musicians according to fixed and unified scales. Then, of course, under National Socialism every type of state-sponsored instruction in church music gradually ceased. Church music was just barely tolerated at the academies or suppressed until it disappeared entirely, with exception of the purely artistic performance of organ music. Obviously the instruction in church music at the state institutions did not stop suddenly on a given day. But basically, from 1933 on, the switch was left open in such a way that the decisive, vital track for instruction in church music was narrowed and cut down to such a degree that the end of the professional church musician was in sight, unless the church itself took the initiative.[1]

But alongside this external development, the singing movement, the organ movement, and the new church music had led from within to a new departure in church music that could not be erased even by National Socialism. Because of all these developments, the church felt obliged to initiate a constructive program also in the field of church music. This began with the "Church Musician Ordinance of March 1, 1933" in Hannover and the "Principles for Training and Employing Church Musicians" of the Old Prussian Union, July 15, 1935. Other churches followed.[2]

During this time the first church music schools as church-owned, independent institutes were established. The first establishments were the church music schools in Heidelberg (1931), Spandau near Berlin (1934), Hamburg (1938), Stettin (1939), and Halle/Saale (1941). After 1945 additional church music schools were opened in Hannover (1945), Esslingen near Stuttgart (1945), Schlüchtern (1947), Görlitz (1947), Bayreuth (1948), Herford (1948), Düsseldorf (1949), Dresden (1949), Eisenach (1950), Frankfort on the Main (1955).

Besides these church schools, the state music academies again organized church music departments, but in their training program these concentrated on purely artistic subjects. The state music academies in Berlin, Cologne, Freiburg, Frankfort on the Main, Munich, Hamburg, and Lübeck added such departments. Up to 90 percent of the entire output of church musicians since 1945 have come from the church music schools.

To give the instruction a unified thrust, the directors of the German Evangelical church music schools and of the church music departments of the state academies held their first meeting in Schlüchtern April 25–27, 1949. The discussions dealt with problems not only of church music in general and of methodology but also of the reorganization of the profession of the church musician. This conference of directors addressed to the leadership of all the churches a resolution that considered the problems mentioned and so laid the foundation for future unified action. This resolution reads:

> The directors of the German Evangelical church music schools and of church music departments at state academies were gathered

for a conference in Schlüchtern April 25–27, 1949. In addition to problems of methodology, questions relating to the general state of church music and to its future were discussed. The responsibility of the church to provide future generations of church musicians became forcibly evident. The conference proposes that the church leadership of the EKiD (Evangelical Church in Germany) weigh the following considerations and declare its position over against them:

1) Since the Age of Enlightenment the position of the church musician has fallen prey to an ever-increasing process of secularization. The conference observes that a clearly traceable change is taking place in this matter; the church musician has again come to realize that he is placed into the service of the congregation through the Word of God.

2) This opens up the possibility of assigning to the work of the church musician a permanent place among the services rendered within the congregation. We are reminded that the office of the cantor was a ministerial office in the Reformation era.

3) It is of decisive importance for the life of the worship service and of the congregations of our Evangelical church that this realization come into general favor. The Bible requires music as a means of proclamation and adoration, and for that reason it cannot be surrendered. This imposes on the church the obligation to recognize the indispensability of the office of the church musician and to guarantee the incumbents a living wage such as it takes for granted in the case of the pastorate.

4) In carrying out this ideal, efforts should be made to grant to the regional church an influential voice in filling church music positions and in determining salaries.

5) The conference does not overlook the fact that the possibilities for creating full-time *musical* positions in the church are limited. Therefore the participants of the conference suggest that the instruction of church musicians, especially on the C and B level, be amplified with catechetical training. The combination of the church musician's work with that of a catechist, or that of a youth worker too, is justifiable on concrete theological, historical, and practical grounds.

6) The legitimacy of these endeavors is proved by the "Church Musician Ordinance of March 1, 1933," in Hannover; the "Principles for Training and Employing Church Musicians" of the Old Prussian Union, July 15, 1935; and the "Regulations Governing Employment Conditions of Church Musicians in Hamburg, 1939."

Schlüchtern, April 27, 1949

The names of the signers follow:

Wolfgang Auler	Gerhard Bremsteller	Kurt Fiebig
Walter Blankenburg	Johannes Brennecke	Martin Flämig
Friedrich Blume	Wilhelm Ehmann	Hans Klotz

Walter Kraft	Hermann Poppen	Karl-Wolfgang Schäfer
Gustav Lamprecht	Siegfried Reda	Ferdinand Schmidt
Hans Arnold Metzger	Philipp Reich	Gerhard Schwarz
Friedrich Meyer	Walter Reindell	Helmut Walcha
Friedrich Micheelsen	Ernest Karl Rössler	Eberhard Wenzel [3]
Karl Ferdinand Müller		

This conference became a standing institution and to this day comes together for an annual meeting. Very early it began work on extensive studies and plans for examinations, and these were accepted and legally put into practice by all synods. A necessary concomitant development was a new legal definition of the status of the church musician by the church authorities and synods. This entire development was achieved basically between 1949 and 1955. This is not accidental, for it was, in time and intent, a development parallel to the introduction of the Evangelical church hymnal and to the church's revision of the Agenda.[4]

In general, the Evangelical church music schools in Germany present a unified appearance. This does not prevent their individual features from being shaped in different ways according to the history, constitution, and confession of the individual state churches and according to the makeup and individual features of the faculties. The basic structures and the life rhythm flowing through the course of studies and the common plans for examinations are the same everywhere, and yet each church music school is different from the next. But the basic type is uniform, since the tasks and the goal of the instruction are the same. This assimilation to one another and the development of one particular fixed type has been made possible in such a short time because the Evangelical church music schools have had a precisely defined ideal from the very beginning: to prepare for the office of the church musician, with the cantor and organist as the musician of the congregation, who is committed to the forms of the worship service and the expressions of the life of the church.

The Evangelical church music school is a team, a fellowship of studies and a fellowship for life. As a rule it consists of 30 to 40 students with 12 to 15 instructors, depending on how many instructors are teaching on a full-time or part-time basis. One should not forget that a number of teachers give only two to four lessons per week. All institutes have their own buildings today. Most of them have boarding schools and dormitories.

The rhythm of work and forms of life are decisively determined by the artistic instruction of the individual, by group and seminar lessons, and by lectures. Essential factors are a conversational method and an entirely personal adaptation of the studies to the needs of the individual student. A subject is always kept in contact with the other subjects. The study plan follows in an organic fashion and takes into consideration the talent of the individual, but overall it forms a unit. Specific attention is given to the artistic side of the instruction. The best intentions are useless unless the necessary technical capacity is present. This instruction embraces all skills necessary, first, for the work of a cantor and, secondly, for the duties of an organist. A third unit is formed by the music theory subjects, and a fourth by the theological and liturgical subjects. But all four instructional units are adapted to one another and have contact with one another; they have their own principles and yet a secret center — singing. In the last analysis, all music and all music making receives its life from singing and its performance. Instrumental music making and composing spring from singing as well. One who has no relationship to singing can never become a good musician.

But this purely artistic and professional training is, from the very beginning of the course, also directed toward life. It always takes into consideration the world around us, the world around the work of art as well as its place in life. While every work of art is a world perfect in itself, a world which carries its worth in itself and accordingly is able to communicate this worth, this work of art, church music, as a rule possesses a specific function in addition. Of all arts, church music has least use for the slogan "art for art's sake." But as in everything else, relevance here, too, is necessary for comprehension of the inner life of church music. In other words, church music training in a church music school, regardless of subject, cannot take place without a continuous relationship to the world around us and to life, and, to be sure, not only to the life of the church but also to that of the world. Thus the training in church music actually proceeds with open doors and windows much more than any other musical training; and it is — quite apart from the breadth of its fundamental studies — always open for the world and turned toward the world. All artistic, theoretical, and musicological skills and accomplishments are governed by this signature. The student must therefore have well-timed opportunity to come into contact with practical situations without harm to his studies. This is provided by assigning him regularly to certain projects as a singer, choir director, organist, and instrumentalist. This can take place in the services of the institute or, if the student is able to do so, in the parish. In the same way the public presentations of the church music school, their performances, choir tours, and study trips are an essential part of the training.

In addition to the artistic education of the individual and its functional relationship to life, the life rhythm of a church music school is shaped by the worship life within the school building and within the congregation of the area in which the church music school is located, or in which the student has a substitute job. The church music school looks upon itself as a congregation in the home and at the same time reaches out into the parishes.

All the more, a certain pulse beat of spiritual life belongs to the life of the church music school. The bond which continually keeps and binds everyone and everything together is prayer. A church music school will not solve its own inner problems unless a spiritual pulse of life is present. Thus at least morning prayer belongs to its rhythm of life. The church music school must know that, in addition to many other duties, it has also a spiritual commission – to practice the praise of God and to pray. The broader, the nearer to life, and the more natural this is, the better. Naturally studying, practicing, and learning are always prime concerns. But a church music school cannot organize its life as if God and the church did not exist.

The church music school, too, has had to get its experience in the course of the years, and it has paid its apprentice's fee too. One of the greatest dangers, which it has to encounter again and again, is that of cutting up or expanding the subject matter too much. The class schedule cannot be overloaded if enough time for practicing on the instrument, for composing, and for reading should remain available. Another point of crisis is the right balance between the practical musical work, including ear training and the theoretic-intellectual occupations; that is, the right balance between the handling of the instrument and musical literature. While the C training must provide mainly for the technical foundations and skills, the B training cannot omit intellectual penetration and comprehension of the historical connections, but the A training demands much greater independence of study and cultivates and exploits the creative impulses. Obviously the limits are flexible and are again determined by the talents and interests of the student. The class schedule should never be handled according to a pattern, but it must be so flexible that there is always room for advancing the individual. Again and again in this context the ques-

tion must arise whether this or that course can be dropped or combined with something else and whether this or that material must be
condensed or exchanged for something else. This can be decided only
from case to case. Therefore a new coordination of the subjects and
of the contents of the courses must take place every semester. But
this is only possible if the instructors form a real working team. The
responsibility for the right arrangement and execution of the studies
is one of the most important tasks of the director.

The course is subdivided into cantoral, instrumental, theoretical,
and church-related subjects. The whole is like a chain in which one
member is linked to the other. It is of importance that each subject
always keep the total picture of the course in view.

The cantoral subjects:	Voice (singing and speech)
	Choral voice training
	Chorale singing and congregational singing
	Conducting (chorus, orchestra)
	Kantorei and performance practice
The instrumental subjects:	Organ playing for the worship service (liturgical organ playing)
	Playing of organ literature (artistic organ playing)
	Piano and harpsichord
	One melody instrument: trumpet, trombone, recorder, or a string instrument
The theoretical subjects:	Composition
	Ear training and dictation
	Score reading and figured-bass playing
	Music history
	The organ and other instruments
The church-related subjects:	Bible, doctrine, and church history
	Liturgics
	Hymnology

This plan is similar in all church music schools. The subjects are
the same everywhere. Only the distribution of the contents, the number of hours, and the methods of instruction used are different here
and there. Thus the church music school in Hannover, for instance,

has had very good results in the C training with a concentrated basic training directed purely toward the practical needs. Subjects are combined, and special areas of concentration are set up, for instance, in organ playing, composition, and practical liturgics, while a definite isolation of subjects takes place only in the B training for purposes of penetrating deeper into the material.

Instruction takes place in the form of private instruction, seminar sessions in smaller or larger groups, and lectures. With 35 students, the weekly number of lessons is about 180 instructional hours, which fall mainly on the days from Tuesday to Friday. This often creates very difficult problems in scheduling space and time.

However, we should not forget that each student must practice at least two hours every day on the organ and one hour on the piano. Then there is still the work to be done for composition and theory subjects. There should also be time for ensemble playing, ear-training practice, concert and theater attendance, and for general presentations of the school. The study of church music is incomparably gratifying but also very difficult.

The following beautiful motto of bishop Guardius of Marseilles (d. 492), could be taken as the watchword for the church music course for cantors:

> *Psalmista, id est cantor, potest absque scientia episcopi, sola iussione presbyteri, officium suscipere cantandi, dicente sibi presbytero:*
> *Vide ut quod ore cantas corde credas et quod corde credis operibus probes.*

[The psalm singer, that is, the cantor, can receive the office of singer even without the knowledge of the bishop, only on the recommendation of the elder, when the elder says to him:

Watch out that you believe with your heart what you sing with your mouth, and that you prove through works what you believe with your heart.]

NOTES FOR CHAPTER 6

1. Cf. O. Söhngen: *Kämpfende Kirchenmusik* (1956), pp. 57 ff.
2. For further information, see O. Söhngen, *Das Kirchenmusikalische Amt* (1950), pp. 15 ff.
3. Cf. *Musik und Kirche*, XIX (1949), 76 ff.
4. Cf. K. F. Müller, "Schlüchtern, 1949," *Musik und Kirche*, XIX (1949), 67 to 77.

CHANGES IN CHORAL SINGING IN EUROPE TODAY

Wilhelm Ehmann

Like its society, the musical life of Europe throughout the centuries since the Middle Ages was organized according to social ranks. This organization according to ranks was dissolved by the French Revolution at the end of the 18th century. The "third estate," the middle class, took over the leadership. Cultural responsibility also was shared by the basic strata of the middle class. For this the middle class was not prepared. For choral singing, for example, it had to develop new and characteristic forms on its own initiative. The middle-class club became a way of life for this middle-class society. It was the vogue also in the field of choral singing. Models of singing societies were developed above all in Switzerland (Hans Georg Nägeli), and in Germany (Karl Friedrich Zelter). Members of middle-class society who liked to sing gathered in "music societies" and "music academies." They formed "mixed choirs," in which men and women sang together as musical amateurs without a technical musical education. The full, soft, and warm sound of the mixed choir replaced the thin and cool sound of the boys' *Kantoreien* of the preceding Baroque period. The men who sang in the *Liederkränze* and *Liedertafeln* were dilettantes too. Frequently, these men's choirs originated as musical divisions of professional organizations (artisans, academicians). Appropriate literature had to be created for these men's choirs. It leaned on the folksong which then experienced a new Romantic rediscovery. The political idea of freedom also played a role in the literature of these men's choirs. The great mixed choirs soared into musical ecstasy in the performances of the oratories Haydn and Mendelssohn were writing for this kind of organization and in the Romantic revivals of the oratorios of Handel and Bach. The origin of these choral societies occurred simultaneously with the rediscovery of the folksong and the works of Handel and Bach. In the oratorios of Haydn the virtue of this middle-class society is celebrated, just as in Beethoven's *Ninth Symphony* the thought of humanity and fraternity amid the revolutions of the late 18th century is celebrated in song. Education, cultivation of religious sentiments, sociability, and fellowship belong to the purposes of such singing. To the present day, Haydn's *Creation* and Handel's *Messiah* form the highpoints of a year's work of these choirs. Frequently the "brave dilettantes" (Spohr) are directed by professional conductors. The choral forms of this period have become known all over the world.

The feeling of security of this middle-class society and its forms of life have been shattered in Europe in the revolutions of the 20th century, the world wars, which took place above all on European soil, the great migrations of people, the torrents of refugees, the concentration camps and places of extermination, and the total industrialization of the population. Thus its choral societies likewise have lost their claim to absolute sovereignty. At the same time new choral forms originated in the European musical life of the last decades. This took place partly through the ideal means and possibilities of the Romantic era, whence the middle-class choral groups originally came. Choral singing has therefore attempted to realize a movement of self-renewal based on its own store of ideas and sounds. Europe's choral music has produced clearly recognizable new forms of performance and invented new sounds that cannot be ignored. It is significant that these new forms at first attach themselves to choir styles that existed in Europe before the French Revolution, survived, even if only in faint traces, through the middle-class era to the present, and remain recognizable.

THE BOYS CHOIR

The term "boys choir" has a specific meaning — a choir which uses boys for the upper parts and young men for the lower parts. Such are the oldest choirs of Europe's musical culture. Their best-known representatives are the choirs of the Sistine Chapel in Rome and of Notre Dame in Paris, the St. Thomas Choir in Leipzig and the choir of the *Kreuzkirche* in Dresden. The latter two trace their existence in an unbroken line from the Middle Ages. In earlier times such a choir was known as a *Kantorei*. Already in the restoration time of the 19th century these boys choirs were greeted with renewed interest. In our time this interest has grown to an astonishing degree. New social groups connected with the care of refugees and orphans and the influence of the church on the school system in the democratic state have contributed to the revival of such boys choirs in our time. Many such boys choirs have been connected with various school systems and boarding schools. We have to add here that modern performance practice makes the light, neutral, and transparent sound of a boys choir appear desirable. There are in Europe today newly formed boys choirs that belong to the best choral organizations of the country: for instance, the Windsbach Boys Choir of Nuremberg, which was originally established with orphans from refugee families.

THE SCHOOL CHOIR

Undoubtedly, students in schools have always sung. But modern progressive pedagogy, which counts the artistic do-it-yourself method one of its basic principles, and which not only considers a school a purveyor of knowledge but also aims to bring to realization values of the mind and character in the student body, must therefore cultivate choral singing in the school particularly. Such schools developed their own particular kind of routine especially in the reformatory rural foster homes established between the two world wars. They did not engage in concert work like that of the boys choirs but usually limited their activity to the community life of the individual schools themselves. There are schools in Europe today in which a school choir (all students included) and a boys choir (a selected number of students) exist side by side. This work is done above all in the high schools.

CHOIRS FOR MUSIC MAJORS

A further development of the efforts just described, but on a professional artistic level, we find in the choirs of the professional music schools, the music academies, music conservatories, church music schools, etc. It is a fairly recent innovation that all students at these professional music institutes have to participate in choral singing as a required subject, even the orchestra students of these schools must take choral singing. Since all members of such choirs intend to become professional musicians, the musical background is generally quite good, even though only the voice students have properly trained voices. By this means choral singing, as the most natural musical expression, is to be of benefit to the instrumental training as well. Some choirs of such professional institutions in Europe today are of highest professional quality. This is true for secular and church institutions alike.

THE PROFESSIONAL CHOIR

In association with the opera, the professional mixed choir originated and flourished in Europe in the 17th century. In conjunction with the opera, this professional mixed choir also has maintained itself through the period of the middle-class amateur choirs to the present day. Special demands of radio work give the professional choir in our time opportunities and assignments that never existed before. This is true especially for state-owned radio companies and stations of the network systems that have their own radio choirs. In general, the members of these choirs must pass an entrance examination; they are in the position of employees and, like an orchestra, must rehearse daily. Understandably, their artistic work is very high. There are radio companies that subdivide their choir into various groups, assigning them special tasks (sacred music and oratorios, operas, light music). Through concert tours these professional radio choirs achieve great fame also outside their radio work. They have become pioneers of new music, since only professional singers are capable of singing some of the very difficult technical parts written into the choral scores (Schönberg, Krenek). The best European radio choirs of this kind are resident in Stockholm and Hilversum.

THE COLLEGIUM MUSICUM

This type of music making can form a bridge between the old and the new models of choral activities. Telemann and Bach had already established and directed a *collegium musicum* at the University of Leipzig. It was available for social and artistic occasions, for example, for serenades and cantatas. This form of music making, however, became extinct again at the end of the 18th century. Only in our century did Hugo Riemann again organize a *collegium musicum* with the old title at the same University of Leipzig. But now it achieved a new significance. Its director was not a cantor or a municipal *director musices,* but the music historian of a university. One must remember that in the German, and most European, universities the subject of musicology belongs to the philosophical division, and the musico-practical education takes place separately in professional music schools. At the universities of our time the *collegium musicum* is therefore associated with musicology, but it recruits its audience from all divisions. Therefore the program of such establishments is not so much a matter of presenting public recitals, a function which other choirs and orchestras also perform, but rather, the *collegium musicum* serves primarily for academic-scientific investigation. Since modern musicology appears in the form of music historical studies, this investigation is directed above all toward history. The emphasis on historical studies in music coincides with a renewal of historical music in the second third of our century. The old music from the Middle Ages to the Baroque period, on which the music historian made his scientific research, found its practical performance test in the *collegium musicum*. Such a circle of student musicians perhaps has the significance of a "musical laboratory," a "field for artistic experiments." It serves knowledge. But since in more recent times numerous choir directors, school musicians, church musicians, hymnologists, and orchestral conductors in Europe also attend the university and its musicological courses, the *collegium musicum* has acquired an extraordinary sphere of influence. The so-called old music, which reached the musical life of Europe through various channels, would never have obtained this creative significance without the *collegia musica* of the universities. All further choral models to be mentioned here utilize in their way of music making, in their performance practice, and in their literature some form of this central sphere of influence. Today such a *collegium musicum* exists at every German university. The performances are vocal and instrumental. Its greatest significance lies in the discoveries in music history made between the two World Wars.

THE SINGING CIRCLE AND SINGING FELLOWSHIP

Already at the time of the Romantic era the law professor Thibaut had organized a "singing circle" with his students at the University of Heidelberg. With this group he performed old music exclusively, singing it in the Romantic a cappella style. The performance was educational and a factor in creating fellowship. No listeners were present. Without knowledge of these proceedings, a new departure in youthful music making has taken place in Germany among the educated youth of the last 30 years. We refer to the German "singing movement." Music making was enjoyed as a basic expression of life, and it appeared to be a youthful form of living that was consciously in revolt against all forms of music that represented organized efforts of clubs and societies. The point was, above all, to embrace musical activity as the outstanding means for developing a young person in "truth and self-respect." Thus it was not important to present "recitals"; indeed, the recital was rejected as "bourgeois." Music making remained basically a purpose in itself. All that mattered was to make music with others. The folk song, old choral music, and music to be played by small ensembles chosen ad libitum formed the fundamental repertory. In youthful enthusiasm and isolationism frequently one composer, selected from the great European history of music as a guiding model, was followed in a kind of enthusiastic discipleship. This gave rise to Bach-, Schütz-, Monteverdi-, Gabrieli-, Lassus-, Lechner-, Praetorius-groups, and many others. Everywhere an idea of reform was at work, and this did not stop solely with music but strove toward a renewal of life as well. This singing movement, which originated in Germany, has certainly passed its prime, but there is scarcely any vigorous choral activity today that has not been influenced by the singing movement and its numerous variants. Non-German countries in Europe today are adopting the results of this singing movement and are exploiting them in their own way. This is true particularly in German-speaking countries and those that border Germany. In these youth circles the new music, too, is naturally accepted more and more. In more recent times the *jeunesse musicale,* which comes from Belgium, promulgated its fresh ideas of music performance without the ideological burden of the German singing movement.

THE KANTOREI

The term *Kantorei* likewise originated in European history. Polyphonic music from the Gothic to the Baroque era was performed by the *Kantorei.* In our day the idea of the *Kantorei* has been taken up mainly by church choirs. In the 19th century the church choirs were sacred choral societies. The *Kantoreien* in our time aim toward a renewal of singing in the church. The youthful element also plays an important role in them. While the musical societies of the 19th century filled amateurs with a strong feeling of ethos, the young *Kantoreien* of today consciously bridge over toward the professional musician. The *Kantoreien* of the European history formerly also consisted of professional singers. Often the soloists of today are the section leaders of these choirs. Instruments also belong to a *Kantorei.* When a young church musician begins his work in a congregation today, he makes an effort to liquidate the church choir, which perhaps is organized like a society, and tries to establish a *Kantorei* with young people participating. While the choirs of the 19th century were organized in local areas and were thought of as agencies for keeping the local citizenry together, *Kantoreien* of today consist of the musical elite of an entire province, and thus we have the *Hessische Kantorei*, the *Fränkische Kantorei*, the *Westfälische Kantorei*, etc. The idea that unites them is the work of art and its interpretation based on musicological research and understanding of church music. Obviously there are many in-between forms among these choirs too.

SOCIAL CHOIRS

Social choirs are concerned with the musical culture of the social strata of the modern industrial society. The attempt is made to keep alive the humanistic idea of making a man's education well rounded through music as a natural counterthrust in the technical world and the world of labor. Industry has become the center of large working and housing communities. In the Middle Ages the monastery represented such a center. The industrial enterprise is its successor today in many ways. The management of a factory cannot avoid taking care of, and carrying the responsibility for, the culture of its employees. Through the shortened working hours and the extended time for leisure, certain problems and possibilities become especially acute and urgent. Old work songs, songs of the professions, miner's choirs, and miner's bands suggest a beginning. National Socialism took advantage of this situation, creating a certain myth around work by artistic means. A similar thing is taking place today under Communism in the East Zone. Today the lack of know-how in this area is great. But the task will become increasingly urgent, as man struggles to preserve and educate himself in this machine-age world. In the ever-expanding leisure time of industrial society, the decision is left to man himself. These efforts reach even to the choral singing among soldiers and prisoners.

The singing societies of the middle-class period of Europe are still in existence. They have joined together to form large and powerful associations, and they receive public support. Naturally the younger choral forms which I have described briefly do not have as great an organizational power as those choral groups had, and they are rarely included in the budget of the authorities. However, the younger choral groups not only have rejuvenated and enriched choral singing, raised questions of performance practice and music making procedures, but they have also given choral singing in Europe today its proper position. At the same time their stimuli exert a great deal of influence on the older choral practice.

8

WHAT IS THE POSITION OF CHURCH MUSIC IN GERMANY TODAY?

Oskar Söhngen

In one of Gottfried Benn's last poems, the five-part *Epilog*, of which the first part concludes with the couplet:

> *Leben ist Brückenschlagen*
> *über Ströme, die vergehen,*

this warning and appeal to every man rings out curt and clear:

> *Die Himmel wechseln ihre Sterne — geh!*
> *Die Himmel wechseln ihre Sterne — geh!*

Of late I have often asked myself whether this expression, which without pathos — though with a secret wistfulness — an inexorable conclusion from a calm observation, is not applicable also to church music. Indeed, hasn't the constellation of the stars changed, first to an unnoticeable, but today to an unmistakable degree, so that the inevitable conclusion is: The fateful hour of church music has passed? The rebirth of church music, full of wonder and joy, which we experienced 35 years ago, was it only an episode to which we must now say farewell?

Do not misunderstand me! Whatever the outcome of our estimate of the position of church music today may be, there can never be any thought of saying that from now on church music should keep silence in our services. Even though its song sound ever so wretched in the ears of the world, the Alleluia of church music will have to remain, until the end of the days, the *vox perpetua ecclesiae*, "the never-ending voice of the church," as Martin Luther expressed it. Regardless of whether church music possesses artistic rating or not, it will always be a characteristic of the church of Jesus Christ, since it is a witness of the Word of God and a praise-offering by the congregation. "Wherever you see and hear the Lord's Prayer being prayed and taught, wherever psalms and sacred songs according to the Word of God and to the true faith are sung, there, be assured, lives a holy and Christian people of God" (Luther). When this is understood, however, still another point must be made at once — that the full strength and power of expression of music, also that of worship music, rests decisively in its *artistic* power, its *vis*, as both Luther and Calvin agreed. Therefore it is always short-circuited thinking and short-sighted acting when a church accords less respect and care to the artistic side of church music than to that which seems more immediate, the ecclesiastical-liturgical side. It is by no means true that the decline of church music would mean only a loss of artistic substance and that church music would appear poor and destitute before its "secular" sister — this it should be able to bear; but rather, the sacred and the artistic substance come from the same root, and church music that is artistically poor can only insufficiently do justice also to its liturgical duties. The governing principle is that mysterious paradox to which I used to refer with untiring devotion during those blessed years when the new church music was beginning to flourish, a principle that loses none of its validity if we should today perchance have to enter it on the debit side of the ledger: Only music that is more than strictly functional service music, namely, an artistically valid expression of the music of its time, can be church music in the ultimate and profoundest sense.

After this necessary prefatory note, let us return to our initial inquiry.

I

Die Himmel wechseln ihre Sterne ("The heavens are changing their stars"). Before we speak of the new constellation, we shall do well to look back at the old once more. The revival or decline of church music involves not only a musical change but a complex process in which different kinds of forces and evolutionary tendencies play a role. Theological, liturgical, sociological, and musical factors stand in the foreground, and not in a specific order according to rank but in the totality of their presence. Not one of these elements may be absent if a favorable constellation, a new kairos of church music is to begin; the omission even of one single factor may bring about a decline. How did the constellation stand around the year 1925?

In *theology* the Luther-renaissance and Karl Barth's dialectic theology had created a completely new situation: a new earnest occupation with the Word of God as the only foundation of the church replaced the theology of the religious experience. Not only theological dignity was regained for music, but to church music was assigned again its original task to "bring in motion" the Word of God. Whereas hitherto church music was to awaken devout feelings and sentiments, now the preaching of the Gospel and praise of God became the two poles of its activity.

The *liturgical movement* rediscovered the worship service as the heart and core of the life of the church. The liturgical order of the worship service was joyfully accepted and put into practice: not only as the proper form for presentation of that great *Opus Dei* with which God serves His congregation in Word and Sacrament, not only because the organization in fixed sacred forms is wholesome for everybody in the sense of the old rule: *Serva ordinem, et ordo te servabit* ("Preserve order, and order will preserve you"), but also because the liturgical act of standing and praying in the presence of God placed the individual on equal footing with the congregation. All individual and self-centered personal thoughts and feelings disappeared before the presence of the holy God, and there remained only the collective basic experiences of the congregation, which with *one* mouth, like a great We, praised the deeds of God.

For church music this meant the regaining of its original soil and of an area for growth. Church music was no longer merely a piece of ornament and decoration for spiritual edification, but it again formed an integral part of the theological-musical makeup of the worship service. At the same time, the new encounter of music with the worship service proved to be a wellspring of overflowing productivity. The first presentations of numerous important works of the new church music before a larger public took place during the "festival of German church music" in Berlin in 1937. It became one of the most important cultural events of that otherwise politically and culturally troubled time.[1]

This brings us to the *sociological conditions* of the rebirth of church music. As long as church music was a refuge for musicians who were not good enough for the concert stage and opera house, as reported by the composer Arnold Mendelssohn during his youth (b. 1855), as long as the position of a church musician was, as a rule, only on a part-time basis, there was no hope that church music could again occupy a respectable place in the framework of German musical

life.[2] We are indebted to Max Reger (d. 1916), who was the first to
again challenge organists with formidable artistic demands, and to
his friend Karl Straube (d. 1950), who, as a "new German organist-
maker" in his key position as director of the Church Music Institute
in Leipzig, applied the most exacting standards to the education of
the young generation of church musicians, so that the new church
musician, musically too, stood at the highest level of the demands of
his time. And in the same way, the social position of the church musician had experienced a basic uprating within the church, when he
was advanced from "lower church servant" of the general common
law to legitimate incumbent of a liturgical position.

Not less decisive were the changes in the *musical domain*. That
radical breakthrough, which Ernst Pepping called "Stylistic change of
music," [3] began already in the last years before World War I, starting in 1911. It involved a determined detachment from the late Romantic art of the end of the century, a new elaboration of all musical
means from the rudiments, a break with functional harmony and
tonality, a rediscovery of the primary forces of music, the emancipation, indeed, the freeing, of rhythm, but also the return to the genuine melody, melody which does not depend functionally on harmony
and the eight-measure period, the introduction of the serial and
ostinato principle, instead of the Classic-Romantic developmental
technique. It consisted, furthermore, of the will to find the way back
from the ivory tower of the *l'art pour l'art* concept to art rooted in
life, from the egocentric expression of feeling to the feeling of being
bound in fellowship, and, finally, to an ideal of music making in which
the composer receded entirely behind his task. With this stylistic
change music had completed a process of withdrawing radically from
romanticization, individualization, and refinement. Music had found
its way home to the basic elements of music. Above all, the works of
Igor Stravinsky, Bela Bartok, and early Paul Hindemith were like the
signal beacon of a new departure for an entire generation. What is
decisive in our discussion is the fact that the basis for a new awakening of liturgical music, of church music proper, was given at the same
time by this stylistic change. New music and new church music came
from the same root.

Once again after more than one and a half centuries a period had
begun which was characterized by stylistic equality in sacred and
secular music. The composer did not have to change pens if he wanted
to write a secular work today, a sacred one tomorrow. Simultaneously

church music was blessed with composers who would be considered true masters and who began to work actively on the freshly plowed fields. They were led by a team of three: Ernst Pepping (b. 1901), Hugo Distler (1918–1942), and Joh. Nepomuk David (b. 1895). An essay by Werner Oehlmann, written in 1948, "New Sounds of Preaching of the Gospel" (*Der Tagesspiegel,* Dec. 27, 1948), describes impressively how much people were aware of a new beginning: "Between the Christian world and our own there was the century of the emancipation of man, the century of the humane and materialistic philosophies, of the exact sciences and the world-dominating technology, of Classic-Greek oriented poetry, and of Romantic music. . . . One has to keep the entire scope of this apostasy in mind, one must experience the faithlessness of the mind in its entire radical dimensions, in order to comprehend the renewal of the Christian element in a grossly profaned music as the miracle of a new proclamation of the Gospel.[4]

II

For some 25 years, until about 1950, church music could unrestrictedly indulge in the enthusiasm of its new mission and its tasks. From then on the first shadows fell, and an ever-growing discomfort spread out gradually. This had to do, above all, with the fact that the effects of the reencounter with international secular music, above all, the music of Arnold Schönberg and of his school, from which Hitler's Germany had been sealed off hermetically, made itself felt. Other factors were added to this, not least the circumstance that the enthusiasm for the movement of a new departure of church music had necessarily run dry after a quarter of a century, and that the first symptoms of an institutionalization of church music appeared.

I would like to quote some symptomatic remarks of discomfort and of criticism of the new church music as I have encountered them in the last 12 to 15 years before I discuss the new constellation of church music in the third part of this essay.

The first blaring fanfare of attack was made in 1949 in a book by Theodor W. Adorno, *Philosophie der neuen Musik.*[5] This attack was aimed not directly at church music, to which Adorno has no relationship, but nevertheless at that new music which had descended from the same root as the new church music — the music of Stravinsky, Bartok, and Hindemith. It was condemned as restorative by Adorno, for he maintained that musical progress is to be found only in Arnold Schönberg and his followers Alban Berg and Anton Webern. This thesis by Adorno powerfully fascinated, above all, wide circles of the musical youth because it appeared in the form of a sociologically based historical prophecy. Music, too, it stated, must fulfill the law of socio-historical development in its function as a kind of ideological superstructure; this development, however, is irresistibly advancing in the direction of a continuing technification, of greater individualization, of differentiation and refinement, of emancipation from everything that is traditional, and of bold and abstract new construction. Therefore the only type of music that is legitimate is that which in this manner proceeds consistently toward autonomy — avant-garde music. This music proceeds toward an ever-increasing autonomy of the tone material, toward an ever-increasing radical separation from anything that is seemingly a gift of nature — even tonality with its interrelations of tones and its consonances is by no means given in nature, toward the setting up of new laws and conventions, toward an ever more conscious independence of the individual as opposed to the inactivity of the masses. The cultivation of old music is "reactionary," and a triad is, as Adorno says literally, "simply wrong today," in the same way as a sacred work of art at a secular time like ours is basically impossible.

A thorough discussion of Adorno's concepts would require a separate essay; therefore permit me for the present to dismiss the subject by referring to the essay "What is New Music?" which the Heidelberger composer Heinz Werner Zimmermann wrote for the Festschrift *Gestalt und Glaube,* commemorating my 60th birthday.[6] Zimmermann objects, above all, to Adorno's misunderstanding of art as science. He says that the original problem about the artistic effect of a work is bypassed, and the secondary question about its historico-evolutionary significance, that is, about the means used, is asked instead. The "newness" of the material is considered more important than its artistic formulation.

In the same year, 1949, an essay by Albert v. Reck, "Concerning the Position of Church Music," appeared in the *Süddeutsche Zeitung,*[7] in which the thesis was presented that modern music had sprung from the same source as the new church music, but that in the meantime it had developed past the level of the church music. Secular music had adopted only certain principles of specific historical models, while the new church music took over not only the principles but the historical language as well. To be sure, it did not imitate the historical language like an epigone, but it transformed it in the sense of creative metamorphosis and development. But there still remains a discrepancy between the language of church music, which adjusted itself to the style of the 16th and 17th centuries, and the expanded need for expression of modern man: "Even the most modern restoration cannot reproduce the lost unity of church and life, for here life sounds forth only as if kept behind closed windows."

This objection that the works of the thirties and forties are actually not new church music has been raised in the most manifold variations again and again. Against this I would like to state emphatically that none of the really important works of the new church music, beginning with Distler's partita *Nun komm, der Heiden Heiland,* through Pepping's *Passionsbericht des Matthäus* and Ahrens' *Cantiones gregorianae,* all the way to David's last Gospel motets and Bornefeld's *Te Deum,* speak the language of the Reformation or the Baroque era; they are all authentic works of our time: only doctrinaire prejudice can doubt this.[8] That there is at the same time a great deal of music that is new only in name and publication date is not a score for the real "new departures."

The implied problem of historicism still creates so much confusion that it seems necessary to say at least a few words about it. Under the term historicism, one understands mainly the condition of being in love with phenomena of the historical past that one attempts to revive. Historicism is therefore found to be identical with a "craving for history"[9] or a penchant for restoration. But this overlooks the fact that genuine renaissance periods do not at will control the entire output of accessioned history; this may possibly be done by custodians of historical monuments and by archivists, or perhaps by publishers who hope to profit from business by promoting old art, and by aesthetic snobs, for whom the patina of old age is the same as the work of art itself. Genuine movements of renewal will always realize a characteristic selection and adhere only to the historical phenomena to which they feel themselves mysteriously related and in a profound sense of the word "con-temporaneous." Not the passive act of receiving is at the beginning but the spontaneous act of selecting. The latter seeks to understand itself with instinctive consciousness of purpose by means of an encounter with related historical periods. It attempts to find itself by using a historical detour. History is not a one-way process that moves on a level of continuous progress from the past directly into the future, but it is similar to a system of concentric circles whose determinative, selective, and organizing center is any given present time. From the standpoint of here and now, the present period appropriates the different epochs with circles which are closer or more distant according to the degree of their actual significance. It gathers in the innermost circle all those historical phenomena which are situated closest to it not in a temporal but in a structural sense. But this process of finding oneself in specific, analogous periods will always have to be not only a spontaneous but also a creative occurrence: on a higher level something new, self-supporting, and continuous will arise. Thus, for instance, the organ movement would have denied the logic of its origin, had it stood still at the rediscovery of the old principles of organ construction and registration, if it had not pressed forward to organ types that do justice to the changed, present-day sense of sound. In his essay "Kritik des Musikanten," [10] Theodor W. Adorno attempted to defame the movements of renewal as such: "They despise the modern way and yet want to be up-to-date; the formula for this is renewal." The provocative character of this thesis is not matched by truthful content, for even Adorno will not be able to deny that various Renaissance movements of Western civilization, to name only the Carolingian Renaissance, Humanism, and the Reformation, advanced historical development in a concentrated fashion and led to always new historical phases.

From 1957 on, Helmut Bornefeld and the group of followers around Siegfried Reda contributed greatly to the discussion of new church music. In the program notes of the 88th Heidenheim motet of Nov. 17, 1957, Bornefeld announces a church music "of the left wing, which is really concerned with the essence of the matter and not only with bourgeois and ecclesiastical enjoyment." It adheres to "practical music" for the worship service — in conscious contrast to Adorno — yet without "betraying the essence of the subjectively autonomous art work." In a circular letter of April 1958, the statement concerning new church music becomes even more aggressive: "The regard for the popular and officially acceptable norm, the exploitation of the historical element at the expense of genuine actuality have taken on frightening proportions with almost collectivistic features. . . . I believe that the new church music will become more and more an affair of a small minority of intellectually independent persons." In 1959 Reger's organ music, the very music that Helmut Walcha had expelled from the halls of church music scarcely a decade before,[11] is declared a shibboleth. It is stated that a wave of new organ compositions has been inspired by the type of instruments brought to life again through the organ movement and that these "will further develop and, we hope, lead to victory Reger's idea of an autonomous organ art" (in other words, one no longer regimented by liturgical and bourgeois considerations). In a letter of the same year, Reda's student Wolfgang Hufschmidt complained to me about the "conformist bustle of church music": "Even the history of church music cannot free itself from Hegel's dialectics. As important and full of merit as it once was to preach the law of a theological and liturgical reorientation to those who were engaged in the virtuoso's superficial bustle in church music, so important and full of merit it would be today for you, because of your authority as a church musician, to open the valves of the church music apparatus of our time, now hopelessly under the domination of theological and liturgical considerations, and to let in the fresh air that it urgently needs."

To conclude this part, I shall mention two additional characteristic attacks: first, Wolfgang Fortner's significant lecture at the Schütz festival in Düsseldorf, 1956, "Sacred Music Today." [12] For Fortner composing in the twelve-tone style is simply *the* modern music. There is no structural bridge from it to the liturgical music that is marked by the chorale. Church music proper must consequently remain outside the struggle for new forms of musical language. If the modern composer wants to express Christian thoughts, he can do it only in the form of nonservice "sacred music."

Friedrich Blume's intelligent essay "The Problem of Church Music in Our Time" [13] follows suit. In it Blume makes an impressive plea for "sacred" music. He maintains that Beethoven's *Missa Solemnis*, Bruckner's masses, and Brahms' *German Requiem* are definitely works of Gospel proclamation and that there is hardly in the entire history of music another exposition of the Word of the Bible that possesses the same ardent depth as the *Four Serious Songs* by Johannes Brahms. More recent Protestant church music, he says, has grown from the assimilation of old church music and from the conscious or subconscious appropriation of the confessional character that "sacred" music of the 19th century displayed.

III

In the following brief outline of the new constellation in which I believe church music must be viewed, the reader should not conclude from my rejection of many a wrong doctrine and thesis in the previous section that the total picture will turn out more pleasant; on the contrary, I shall follow the same outline as before, considering theological, liturgical, sociological, and musical factors.

In *theology*, the last 25 years have witnessed the transition from Karl Barth's neoorthodoxy [14] to the kerygma-theology of Rudolf Bultmann and his followers, with their program of demythologization.[15] Much of what the simple Bible reader up to now had accepted as the message and teaching of Jesus Christ Himself is now presented to him as the product of a later parish theology. The so-called facts of faith have largely slipped into a twilight that even the most daring dialectic procedures, like, for instance, the thesis that Jesus Christ rose from the dead into the kerygma, cannot always clear away. Please understand me correctly: I am not arguing with these theologians; I have far too much respect for their serious regard for the truth. I am only indicating the change. Certainly we must list it as an asset that with the theology of Barth the attitude of critical aloofness toward culture has receded into the background. Paul Tillich's theology of symbolism even opens up new perspectives for a theological appreciation of art.

At the same time the idea of a "secular" theology could be proclaimed. This was referred to in Dietrich Bonhoeffer's improvisations on the "world which came of age" and the "nonreligious interpretation of Biblical concepts." [16] Not only is Jesus Christ designated to be the end of any sacral art, but the process of secularization itself now obtains a favorable signature. The result of (a): The absolute indispensability of the Word of the Bible as the foundation for creative work in church music is no longer above doubt. Along these lines Friedrich Blume, in the essay already mentioned above, declares the restriction of church music to Biblical text and chorale untenable and demands that a place be given to the interpreting word of poetry. The result of (b): There are already today enough theologians for whom any art that is consciously ecclesiastical is an offence.

The *liturgy*, too, has not been left untouched by this change. To be sure, the liturgical movement still has its effect: New Agendas are still created and introduced, new liturgical choir books are offered, but one cannot overlook (or fail to hear) that this process has passed its zenith. The slogan of "healthy secularity" of churchly thinking and activity has achieved it that the consciousness about the main spiritual center of this world, the worshiping congregation of Jesus Christ, has in many places been put into the background. The "daily worship service," the achievement of the individual Christian in society and profession appears to be more important than the Sunday service in the congregation. Typical, too, is the increasing criticism of the *Evangelical Hymnbook*; evidently it is impossible in many circles to rise to an appreciation of the fact that this hymnbook is intended for the worship assembly of people who want to be Christians in earnest. Thus this hymnbook constitutes a test of their spiritual maturity. But we must speak of another danger, which comes from the camp of the friends of the liturgical movement: The demand for perfect, "chemically pure" worship services goes hand in hand with the rejection of the large forms of church music, from organ playing to motet and cantata performances. But the amusia that camouflages itself liturgically is as much the object of suspicion and defense as every other type.

In the *sociological* field it was possible to extend further the position of the church musician within and outside the church; one should, however, be fully aware that changes in theology and in the evaluation of the congregational service may one day have their effect on the evaluation of the church musician's position.

The *musical* heaven, too, has changed its stars. A "second modern era," under the sign of Schönberg and his followers, has replaced the first era. Decisive as Schönberg's contributions were from the beginning in the destruction of the tonal material used up to then and in the elaboration of new systems of coordinating tones within musical thinking and creation, still his music, because of its expressive, romantic, and emotional foundation, has always held a special place in the new music. It always remained a highly sensitive, sophisticated, and individualistic art of expression, whereas overcoming the individual and blending him into the musical or liturgical fellowship were the ideals of the other composers during those revolutionary years. The thoroughly romantic-individualistic attitude remained even after Schönberg realized that, in order to avoid a complete abandoning of musical form after having dissolved tonality, the counteracting force of a new method of musical structure was needed — the "method of composing with twelve tones," discovered in 1922. We cannot here describe the further development of twelve-tone music through Anton Webern's "serial music," in which dynamics, agogics, time duration, and timbre of the individual tones are brought into a fixed order. One should not consider it a tragedy that the problems of further technical treatment of the tone material all the way to electronic music and the problems of the compositional craft led many young composers for 10—15 years into the esoteric world of an ivory tower; musical *ex-*

pression and music as a means of communication, not the secrets of the guild, were important for their masters, Schönberg, Webern, and Berg.[17] Today this has been called to mind again.

IV

I now draw the conclusion. Do we again find ourselves exactly in the same place where the new church music had its beginning? I do not think so. To support my contention, let me present a resumé of the positive and negative sides of our discussion concerning the position of church music in a series of concrete statements and challenges.

1. As is well known, nothing is more durable than change. It can be only of benefit to church music when the storm for a moment blows in its face and thus rouses it from its comfortable position. Like the church, church music, too, needs continuous and incorruptible self-examination. We should be grateful that it is thrust toward it by outer and inner forces.

2. In my opinion, it is a good sign that many young church musicians today are so seriously aware of their artistic responsibility also as church musicians, that they are not willing to make compromises and in a possible conflict between musical needs and liturgical order give priority to music. Thus they express in an exemplary way the dynamic quality which will always be characteristic of Protestant church music — to flood the fixed forms of the liturgy with music carried by the current of faith. Schütz and Bach would never have become what they are for church music if they had not acted in the same way. What the church needs for its worship services is not the complaisant service of a mediocre practical church music but the genuine partnership of great church music. It would be good if this were recognized also by the theologians.

3. It is necessary to remember that Luther's praise of music refers to *all* good music, above all, when it is connected with the Word of God. In contrast to Calvin, there is not a single place in Luther where a word is put in for the preference of *worship service* music. If Wolfgang Fortner's prognosis should be correct that the development of new music would bestow on us Christian declarations only in the form of "sacred music," and no more in the form of church music, we should have no reason to lament over this. "Sacred music," too, falls under the royal motto of Protestant freedom, "Everything is yours"

(1 Cor. 3:22). Thus, we want to rejoice with all our hearts about any great work of music that professes a spiritual confession *in partibus infidelium,* that is, over against the world. We want to be openly grateful for it, be it for the sacred music of the 19th century, to which we certainly have not always done justice in the zeal of the revolution in church music, or be it Schönberg's deeply moving *Moses und Aaron,* Dallapiccola's *Job,* Fortner's *The Creation,* or, let us hope, for a great many works of the future.

4. But precisely when we have explained and clarified this beforehand, we must insist all the more resolutely that church music, in its form as music for the worship service, cannot resign itself to a minimum of an *objective* musical language and a *congregational* style — in other words, to that minimum which for the sake of honesty is indispensable if church music is to be the speech and expression of the great "We" of the congregation. Here we are not dealing with an external law, imposed like a yoke on composers, much less with a Procrustean bed into which composers are to squeeze their compositions, but with what our forefathers used to call *consentire de ecclesia,* the ability of "being a part of the circuit of the congregation." Now I have already indicated the tension which one has to bear and which is inherent in the name "church music" — to give the church what belongs to the church, but to do so without failing to give music its due. Only truly great music will be genuine liturgical music. Likewise, only a master can write really simple music that does not sound *pauvre.* In other words, this means: No music is fit to be used in the liturgical service if it is not confessional music at the same time ("I believe, therefore I speak" — Ps. 116:10). And equally indispensable is the other consideration: that it is really a "new song" (Psalm 98) which resounds in the worship services of the congregation of Jesus Christ, and that the liturgical music is always new and current because it speaks the language of Here and Now. Purely imitative art is nowhere less in place than in worship. This does not mean, however, that at any given time only the works just created and just published should be performed (works that often are not "new" in the present sense). They could also be works of old music that are "contemporary" with us, for the church lives from the depth dimensions of history too. In any case, these works must possess the magnetic and enthusiastic vitality, which is the secret of any real actuality.

What I have pointed out so far on the purpose of church music does not differ from what I have advocated for the last 30 years. But if I want to address myself to the concrete situation of today, I must nevertheless modify two points I have always stressed.

First, concerning the problem of *objectivity* I have often stressed that truly artistic music will personalize and vitalize the liturgical order and make it flexible thereby. But I believe that today's trend away from "the new practicality" to "the new cordiality" not only urges but also allows us to make more room for the emotional, "romantic," element in liturgical music. In the same manner the interpretation of Bach's music has found its way back from the machine-and-motor method of performance to an organically animated one. Martin Luther saw precisely in the emotional content of the musical language that particular element which it was to contribute to enliven the Biblical text.[18] We, too, should apply the emotional contents as a criterion in the defense against all so-called liturgical music that confounds objectivity with boredom.

And a second remark concerns the topic of *congregational style*. This does not constitute a fixed quantity, but it can positively be changed and developed. The introduction of the Evangelical Hymnbook and of the new Agendas has shown that one can expect something from congregations. The pastor's conception of what is a proper congregational style and what is not does not always agree with the conception of the congregation itself. From this we should draw the proper conclusion.

5. What is the situation in creative church music? By no means would I like to belittle what I have pointed out just now, but, to begin with, it is after all only a theory that new music is to be found exclusively among the twelve-tone and serial-technique composers. It is always hazardous to assume the role of the prophet as far as music is concerned. Furthermore, a great work of art is not only an expression of its own time, but it also creates its own time and is thus always new. This is valid also for church music. Thank God that a number of the true masters who were molded by the spirit of those years of "new departure" in the third decade of our century are still with us and still present us with valid works of church music. That the powers of those times of awakening have still not been exhausted is proved by the meteoric rise of a composer like Heinz Werner Zimmermann, whose creative impulses ought to be thought of as related to Igor Stravinsky's writing rather than to jazz. His last works confirm the hope that a real master of church music is growing up here. A further indication along the same lines, it seems to me, is that the young Munich composer

Wilhelm Killmayer in our own day still managed to adapt successfully Orff's musical language for liturgical music in his *Missa brevis*.[19]

What conclusions can we draw from this? The reminder to all organists and choir masters: Honor the masters of church music! Do not only praise them but also perform them! We simply cannot allow an important composer like Joseph Ahrens to remain almost unknown among Protestant church musicians. How rarely one hears the masterful, indeed, often marvelous works of Pepping! And do not most organists and choir masters still make a detour around the compositions of Bornefeld and Reda? Of course this music often is not easy to perform, but the level of our choral work today is such that many more choirs could perform them. I must say it once more: the most effective means to overcome certain phenomena of crisis is the decisive affirmation of one's obligation to church music as a great art.

6. But now we must once more discuss the relationship of the new music to Schönberg's "second modern era." The generation that was shaped by the youth and singing movement has died out in the meantime, or it is about to do so. Doubtless the feeling for life, the spirit of the age of our time, is different from that of the year 1925. The message of a truly current musical composition will express this change, and it will do so the more distinctly, the more sensitive the antenna of the composer is. Schönberg once said, "art is the cry of distress of those who experience the destiny of humanity." Twelve-tone music certainly can contribute to the expansion and increase of the expressive possibilities of music. Therefore it is no coincidence that a number of church music composers, beginning with Joh. Nepomuk David, came to grips with serial music and from it derived new stimulation for their creative work. Others, like Wolfgang Fortner and Siegfried Reda, even held to its rules strictly and consistently. And some young church musicians, such as Rudolf Kelterborn, Klaus Huber, and Michael Beyer, used twelve-tone music as their very starting point. But is not the desire to unite twelve-tone music with church music an undertaking condemned to failure from the very start? If one considered the Kranichstein experiments a legitimate accomplishment, and Adorno the authentic interpreter of the goals of twelve-tone music, this would indeed be inevitable. But for Schönberg and for Webern as well, not the tonal and formal constructions as such were important but what emerged from them — the contents and the expression. Schönberg pointed this out once by saying: "The rules [of the method of twelve-tone composition] are merely restrictive and not

creative. You must in spite of it be able to produce music." Schönberg likewise frequently pointed to the dualism that exists between the brain and the heart, which causes periods of highly intellectualized art comprehension to be relieved by those of a free relaxation of the imagination.

Proceeding from this assumption, three things seem to become important: First, the observation that one can very well employ the serial technique without denying one's personal style of writing. This became clear to me, above all, in Stravinsky's *Canticum sacrum* and in his ballet *Agon,* which are at the same time tributes to Anton Webern and masterworks among Stravinsky's compositions. Secondly, one can conclude from this: it cannot be taken for granted that the message of serial music must necessarily and permanently remain a romantically individualistic, sublime, and sophisticated nature just because Schönberg, Webern, and Berg came from the Late Romantic school of writing. If I understand it correctly, there is an opposite tendency at work already today to consolidate the musical language in the direction of progressive abstraction and constructive intellectualization. Joseph Ahrens' new organ works seem to be as characteristic for this development as Joh. Nepomuk David's last organ compositions. In the third place, we observe that the rediscovery of the vocal melody was a providential turning point in the renewal of church music in the twenties. But twelve-tone music depends on absolute, purely abstract tone rows, which have developed neither from vocal principles nor from the performance practice of musical instruments. Therefore one cannot count on lay choirs such as our *Kantoreien* and church choirs to be able to master pure twelve-tone music.

7. Finally, in all the things that we have discussed together it is not the internal concern of the church and of its music but the fate of modern man that is in the last analysis at stake. "Before whom are we to kneel now?" This question of Gottfried Benn's, whether we wish to admit it or not, is the perplexed, often desperate question of modern man. We owe him the testimony that human existence is decided lastly and only in the dimension of worship: "Take Thou me and give Thyself to me!" But where do our worship services actually ask men to make a decision? And how much does church music contribute to the character of decision in the worship service? I have made inquiries diligently to discover what kind of music is being performed, in general, by our church choirs and *Kantoreien* in the worship services, above all, during the festival services at Christmas,

Good Friday, and Easter, when hundreds of thousands come to church who otherwise are not to be seen there. I do not want to do injustice to anyone, but what I met with always were "little songs," nice, harmless choral settings that could have been omitted altogether. I know of course that among these song settings there are also compositions from which the spiritual impact of great works of art emanates, for instance, Praetorius' setting of "Lo, How a Rose E'er Blooming," or many chorale arrangements in Pepping's *Spandauer Chorbuch*. The *viva vox* of church music must aim at the actual, present situation of man here and now and must be resolved to bring about decisions that have to do with his life experience. The deepest meaning of its liturgical commitment is that an unsurpassable boundary line be erected against all attempts to perform church music with the music lover's or the music fancier's lack of responsibility evident in our public sings or public concerts. God has destined that great works of music are permitted to aid in leading to ultimate decisions. Therefore we should take seriously our responsibility toward the worship service and the man of today, above all, in that we do not withhold from him *that* church music in which and through which something actually *comes to pass.*

NOTES FOR CHAPTER 8

1. Compare especially Oskar Söhngen, "Die Stunde der Kirchenmusik," *Die Wiedergeburt der Kirchenmusik. Wandlungen und Entscheidungen* (Kassel: Bärenreiter-Verlag, 1952), pp. 69—76.

2. See Oskar Söhngen, *Das kirchenmusikalische Amt in der Evangelischen Kirche der Union. Die wichtigsten geltenden Verordnungen und Erlasse auf dem Gebiet der Kirchenmusik* (Berlin: Edition Merseburger, 1949), esp. pp. 33 to 116.

3. Ernst Pepping, *Stilwende der Musik* (Mainz: Verlag B. Schotts Söhne, 1934).

4. *Der Tagesspiegel* is a West Berlin newspaper.

5. Theodor W. Adorno, *Philosophie der Neuen Musik* (Tübingen: L. C. B. Mohr, 1949). Of later works by Adorno, also see in this connection *Dissonanzen. Musik in der veralteten Welt* (Göttingen: Vandenhoeck & Ruprecht, 1956), especially "Kritik des Musikanten," pp. 62 ff.

6. Heinz Werner Zimmermann, "Was ist neue Musik? Zur Kritik der Kriterien," *Gestalt und Glaube. Festschrift für Oskar Söhngen zum 60. Geburtstag* (Witten: Luther Verlag, and Berlin: Verlag Merseburger), 1960, pp. 197 ff.

7. Compare the discussion with Albert v. Reck: "Ueber die Lage der Kirchenmusik," in Oskar Söhngen, *Die Wiedergeburt der Kirchenmusik,* pp. 97 ff.

8. The cited works of Hugo Distler, Ernst Pepping, and Helmut Bornefeld appeared in the Bärenreiter-Verlag, the *Cantiones gregorianae* (3 vol.) of Joseph Ahrens in the B. Schotts Söhne edition and the *Sechs Evangelien-Motetten* (1958) of Joh. Nepomuk David in the Verlag Breitkopf und Härtel in Wiesbaden.

9. Walter Kiefner: *Geschichtssüchtigkeit.*

10. Adorno, *Dissonanzen*, pp. 62 ff.

11. Helmuth Walcha, "Regers Orgelschaffen kritisch betrachtet," *Musik und Kirche*, XXII (1952), Part 1, pp. 2 ff.

12. Wolfgang Fortner, "Geistliche Musik heute," *Musik und Kirche*, XXVII (1957), Part I, pp. 9 ff.

13. "Das Problem der Kirchenmusik in unserer Zeit," *Musik und Kirche*, XXX (1960), 129.

14. *Die kirchliche Dogmatik*, 4 vols. (Zurich: Evangelischer Verlag, 1932—1959).

15. Hans Werner Bartsch, ed., *Kerygma und Mythos: ein theologisches Gespräch.* Mit Beiträgen von Rudolf Bultmann et al. (Hamburg: Reich & Heidrich, 1948—1954).

16. Dietrich Bonhoeffer, *Schöpfung und Fall: theologische Auslegung von Genesis 1—3*, 2d ed. (Munich: Chr. Kaiser Verlag, 1937).

17. Impressive evidence for this is found in Schönberg's letters. Cf. *Arnold Schönberg, Briefe*, sel. and ed. Erwin Stein (Mainz: B. Schotts Söhne, 1958).

18. Cf. Oskar Söhngen, "Theologische Grundlagen der Kirchenmusik," *Leiturgia, Handbuch des evangelischen Gottesdienstes*, IV (Kassel: Johannes Stauda-Verlag, 1961), 185 f.

19. In 1954, Killmayer (born Aug. 21, 1927) received the prize from Fromm's Music Foundation in Chicago for the a cappella *Missa brevis* and for his *Lorca-Romanzen* (Soprano, piano, and percussion).

BIBLIOGRAPHY

Compiled by Johannes Riedel

LIST OF ABBREVIATIONS

BV   Bärenreiter-Verlag, Kassel and Basel.

CH   Christian Hymnody. The Lutheran Brotherhood Insurance Society, Minneapolis, Minn.

CPH   Concordia Publishing House, St. Louis, Mo.

CTM   Concordia Theological Monthly. Concordia Publishing House, Saint Louis, Mo.

D   The Diapason. Chicago, Ill.

H   The Hymn. New York.

JAMS   Journal of the American Musicological Society. William Byrd Press, Richmond, Va.

JCM   Journal of Church Music. Fortress Press, Philadelphia, Pa.

JLH   Jahrbuch für Liturgik und Hymnologie. Johannes Stauda-Verlag, Kassel.

L   Der Lutheraner. Concordia Publishing House, St. Louis, Mo.

LE   Lutheran Education. Concordia Publishing House, St. Louis, Mo.

LS   The Lutheran Scholar. St. Louis, Mo.

LW   The Lutheran Witness. Concordia Publishing House, St. Louis, Mo.

MHC   The Musical Heritage of the Church. The Valparaiso Church Music Series. Concordia Publishing House, St. Louis, Mo.

MQ   The Musical Quarterly. G. Schirmer, New York.

N   Notes. School of Music, University of Michigan, Ann Arbor, Mich.

P   C. F. Peters Corporation, New York, London, Frankfurt.

R   Response in Worship — Music — The Arts. St. Paul, Minn.

SHM   Schmitt, Hall & McCreary, Minneapolis, Minn.

UCH   United Church Herald. New York, St. Louis.

WMC   The Willis Music Company, Cincinnati, Ohio.

I. ESSAYS

Dietrich Buxtehude (1637—1707): On the Tercentenary of His Birth. MQ, Vol. XXIII, No. 4 (October 1937), 465—490.

The Import and Content of Luther's Exegetical Lectures on the Epistle to the Hebrews. CTM, Vol. IX, No. 2 (February 1938), 100—114.

Benefits Derived from a More Scholarly Approach to the Rich Musical and Liturgical Heritage of the Lutheran Church. MHC. I, No. 1 (1945), 8—127.

Problems Connected with Editing Lutheran Church Music. MHC, I, No. 1 (1945), 31—41.

Luther on Music. MQ, Vol. XXXII, No. 1 (January 1946), 80—97.

The Doctrine of the Universal Priesthood and Its Influence upon the Liturgies and Music of the Lutheran Church. MHC, II (1946), 96—126.

Johann Walther: Composer, Pioneer, and Luther's Musical Consultant. MHC, III (1947), 78—110.

Making Church Music Attain Ideal Status; Some Suggestions. D, August 1, 1948, Vol. 39, 6—7.

The Integration of the Lutheran Service of Worship. CTM, Vol. XIX, No. 9 (September 1948), 653—663.

Ein Wort über das Benehmen beim Gottesdienst. L, April 26, 1949.

The Genius of Lutheran Corporate Worship. CTM, Vol. XXI, No. 4 (April 1950), 260—275.

Organ Music for the Liturgical Service. *The Second Institute of Liturgical Studies.* Valparaiso University, Valparaiso. June 1950, 28—56.

Lutheran Theology as Reflected in the Life and Works of J. S. Bach. CTM, Vol. XXI, No. 12 (December 1950), 896—923.

Liturgical Developments in Europe. CTM, Vol. XXII, No. 12 (December 1951), 949—954.

Music for the Church Wedding. LW, Vol. LXXI, No. 12 (June 10, 1952), pp. 4, 13.

The New St. Louis Seminary Organ. LW, Vol. LXXII, No. 11 (May 26, 1953), 177.

Leiturgia — An Opus Magnum in the Making. CTM, Vol. XXIV, No. 6 (June 1953), 404—417.

The Chorale — Through Four Hundred Years by Edwin Liemohn, publ. in Philadelphia, 1953. A brief study. CTM, Vol. XXIV, No. 10 (October 1953), 749—757.

Johann Gottfried Walther. MHC, IV (1954), 12—30.

Cultural Values of Liturgical Worship and Ecclesiastical Music. MHC, IV (1954), 64—76.

Die Heiligung. L, two installments: Nov. 30 and Dec. 14, 1954.

Die Kraft des Wortes Gottes. L, May 3, 1955.

A Singer of Christian Faith and Joy. LW, LXXVI (1957), March 26, p. 8.

Das heilige Abendmahl — Allerlei Gebräuche. L, two installments: April 16 and 30, 1957.

The Liturgies and Music of the Lutheran Church. Publ. in the *Proceedings of the Fourteenth Convention of the Iowa District East of The Lutheran Church — Missouri Synod.* Assembled at Blairstown, Iowa, August 12—15, 1957. Three essays.

Johann Rist zum Gedächtnis, L, Dec. 10, 1957.

Der Christenstand ein Ehrenstand. L, four installments: Sept. 2 and 16, Dec. 9 and 23, 1958.

The Life and Work of Samuel Scheidt. MHC, V (1959), 43—67.

Johann Pachelbel's Contribution to Pre-Bach Organ Literature. MHC, V (1959), 140—155.

Our Lutheran Worship. LW, Vols. LXXVII and LXXVIII, Jan. 14, 1958 to Dec. 15, 1959 (27 installments).

Aussprüche Luthers über die Musik. L, Jan. 20, 1959.

Joint Musicological Enterprise Among German and American Lutherans Today. LS, Andrew J. Buehner, editor, St. Louis, Vol. XVII, No. 3 (July 1960), 836—841; No. 4 (October 1960), 847 f.

A Tribute (to Prof. Christhard Mahrenholz). R, Vol. II (1960), No. 1, 21—23.

The Role of the People in the Lutheran Liturgy. R, Vol. II (1960), No. 2, 19—24.

Theology and Church Music as Bearers and Interpreters of the *Verbum Dei*. CTM, Vol. XXXII, No. 1 (January 1961), 15—27. Also MHC, VI (1963), 17—31.

Hymn Tunes in the Service of the Gospel. LE, Vol. 96, No. 5, (January 1961), 245—253.

Music in the Life of the Church. JCM, Vol. 3, No. 6 (June 1961), 2—5.

The Rhythmic Chorale in America. H, Vol. 13, No. 3 (July 1962), 71—85.

Johann Crüger: On the Tercentenary of His Death. R, Vol. IV (1962), No. 2, 89—97.

Lutheran Church Music in the Age of Classic Lutheran Theology. Publ. by The Symposium on Seventeenth Century Lutheranism. Edited by A. C. Piepkorn, Robert Preus, Erwin Lueker. Vol. I (St. Louis, 1962), 62—76.

The Dynamic Power of Christian Hymnody. MHC, VI (1963), 38—54.

Johann Crüger. L, 119 (1963), 10—11; 43—44.

The Old and the New in Church Music. UCH, Nov. 15, 1963.

Church Music in the Lutheran Churches of the U. S. A. R, Vol. V (1963), No. 2, 57—66.

Foreword, *Sixtus Dietrich, Antiphons*. Ed. by Walter E. Buszin (Kassel: Bärenreiter Verlag), 1964.

The Hymn in the Mass. R, Vol. V, No. 4 (Easter, 1964), 187—192.

The Beauty of the Lord. R, Vol. VI, No. 1 (Pentecost, 1964), 17—19.

The Christian Hymn in the Battles of the Church for Scriptual Truth. CH, n. d.

Bach and Hausmusik. Chapter VI of *The Little Bach Book*. Edited by Theodore Hoelty-Nickel. Valparaiso University Press, 1950.

Many biographical articles on musicians of the past and of the present associated with the Lutheran Church and numerous musicological articles on topics related to the church in Julius Bodensieck, ed., *The Encyclopedia of the Lutheran Church*. 3 vols. Minneapolis; Augsburg Publ. House, 1965.

II. REVIEWS
(L)

1948

The Lutheran Liturgy (of the Ev. Luth. Synodical Conference of North America). St. Louis. Feb. 17.

Liturgical Motet Book. Matthew N. Lundquist. New York. March 16.

Christmas, Its Carols and Legends. Ruth Heller. Chicago. Oct. 26.

Chorale Collection. Elvera Wonderlich. New York. Dec. 7.

1949

The Lutheran Agenda. (Synodical Conference). St. Louis. Jan. 18.

The Lutheran Lectionary (Synodical Conference). St. Louis. March 15.

Das Stundengebet. Evangel. Michaelisbruderschaft. Kassel. March 29.

Christliche Weihnachtsfreude (1946). Simon Dach. Kassel. March 29.

Generalbass — Choräle. Christhard Mahrenholz. Kassel. Oct. 25.

1950

Symphoniae Sacrae, I. Heinrich Schütz. Kassel. Jan. 31.

Kleine Geistliche Konzerte. Schütz. Kassel. Jan. 31.

Cantiones Sacrae: Motetten XVII/XVIII. Schütz. Kassel. Jan. 31.

Ausgewählte Orgelwerke and Sieben Choralpartiten. Johann Pachelbel. Ed. by Karl Matthäi. Kassel. Jan. 31.

Von Wesen der zeitgenössischen Kirchenmusik. Hans Hoffmann. Kassel. Jan. 31.

Die Musik in Geschichte und Gegenwart. Edited by Friedrich Blume. Various authors. Appears in installments. Kassel. Jan. 31ff.

1951

Das Quempas-Heft. Wilhelm Thomas and Konrad Ameln. Kassel. March 13.

Die Orgel-Disposition. Walter Supper. Kassel. July 3.

1952

Luthers Lieder und Gedichte. Wilhelm Stapel. Stuttgart. Jan. 1.

Orgelchoräle des 17. und 18. Jahrhunderts. Ed. by the Organistenverband of Berne. Kassel. Jan. 15.

Harmonische Seelenlust. Georg Friedrich Kauffmann. Ed. by Pierre Pidoux. Kassel. Jan. 15.

The Lutheran Order of Service. Paul H. D. Lang. St. Louis. March 25.

The Seven Words of Christ on the Cross. Heinrich Schütz. Ed. by Richard T. Gore. St. Louis, March 25.

Geistliches Chorlied, I & II. Gottfried Grote. Berlin. June 3.

Musik und Kirche. Edited by Mahrenholz, Ramin, Reimann. Walter Blankenburg, editor-in-chief. A bimonthly. Kassel. June 3.

62 Choräle mit beziffertem Bass für Orgel. Georg F. Kauffmann. Ed. by Pierre Pidoux. Kassel. June 3.

Lesebuch für Orgelleute. Walter Supper. Kassel. June 3.

Musikalische Exequien. Heinrich Schütz. Ed. by Friedrich Schöneich. Kassel. June 3.

Johann Sebastian Bach in unserem Leben. Wilhelm Ehmann. Wolfenbüttel. Dec. 30.

Johann Sebastian Bach — Geistige Welt. Fred Hamel. Göttingen. Dec. 30.

Bach in Köthen. Friedrich Smend. Berlin. Dec. 30.

1953

The Order of Service. Theo. Dierks. Milwaukee. March 10.

The Parish Organist, Vols. 1—4. Heinrich Fleischer. St. Louis. Aug. 11.

1954

Böhmisches Orgelbuch, I. Ernst Pepping. Kassel. March 9.

Zwölf Choralvorspiele für Orgel. Reinhard Schwarz-Schilling. Kassel. March 9.

Allein Gott in der Höh' sei Ehr. 20 Choralvariationen der deutschen Sweelinck Schule. Ed. by Hans Joachim Moser. Kassel. March 9.

Orgelmeister des 17. und 18. Jahrhunderts. Kassel. March 9.

Das Graduallied, I: Advent — Pfingsten. Siegfried Reda. Kassel. March 9.

1955

General Rubrics for the Conduct of Divine Worship in the Lutheran Church. St. Louis. Feb. 8.

Johann Sebastian Bach — Neue Ausgabe Sämtlicher Werke. Prepared for publication by the Joh. Seb. Bach Institut of Göttingen and by the Bach-Archiv of Leipzig. Kassel. March 8 and various subsequent issues.

Organum. Ed. by Max Seiffert and Hans Albrecht. Lippstadt. June 28.

Kleine Orgelstücke. Siegfried Reda. Kassel. July 26.

The Childhood of Jesus. Johann Christoph Bach. Ed. by Lowell Beveridge. New York. Sept. 6.

Deutsche Kantionalsätze des 17. Jahrhunderts. Hans Burkhardt and Walther Lipphardt. Kassel. Sept. 20.

Einstimmige Choräle mit Basso Continuo und einem Instrument und Continuo. J. S. Bach. Ed. by Walther Reinhart. Kassel. Sept. 20.

Fünf Kleine Festmotetten. Karl Marx. Kassel. Sept. 20.

13 Fantasien. Paul Siefert. Ed. by Max Seiffert. Lippstadt. Dec. 27.

14 Präludien, Fugen und Toccaten. Matthias Weckmann. Ed. by Max Seiffert. Lippstadt. Dec. 27.

1956

15 Praeludien und Fugen. Heinrich Scheidemann. Ed. by Max Seiffert. Lippstadt. Jan. 24.

Psalmbearbeitungen für Orgel. Anthoni Van Noordt. Ed. by Pierre Pidoux. Kassel. Jan. 24.

Orgelbuch zum evangelischen Gesangbuch. Otto Brodde. Kassel. Jan. 24.

Quellen zur Geschichte des christlichen Gottesdienstes. Joachim Beckmann, ed. Gütersloh. June 26.

Musika (Kalender). Ed. by Karl Vötterle. Kassel. Nov. 27.

Liturgische Orgelsätze. Prepared by Rudolf Utermöhlen. Kassel. Dec. 11.

1957

Kantorei-Sätze, I—IV. Helmut Bornefeld. Kassel. April 30.

Hamburger Motettenbuch für zwei- bis fünfstimmigen Chor, I—III. Hans Friedrich Micheelsen. Kassel. April 30.

Sechs geistliche Lieder. Kurt Hessenberg. Kassel. April 30.

Choralbearbeitungen. Jan Pieters Sweelinck. Edited by H. J. Moser. Kassel. May 28.

Liturgische Sätze über altevangelische Kyrie- und Gloriaweisen. Hugo Distler. Kassel. May 28.

Evangeliensprüche zum Kirchenjahr. Johannes Driessler. Kassel. July 9.

Pachelbel: Ausgewählte Werke. Ed. by Helmut Schultz. New York. July 9.

English Organ Music of the 18th Century. Ed. by Vernon Butcher. London. July 9.

Choralbearbeitungen für Orgel. Fritz Münger. Kassel. Aug. 6.

Johann Pachelbel: Ausgewählte Orgelwerke, III. Ed. by Karl Matthäi. Kassel. Aug. 6.

Orgelmeister des 17. und 18. Jahrhunderts. Compiled and edited by Karl Matthäi. Kassel. Aug. 6.

Acht Toccaten und Fugen. Joseph Seeger. Edited by Max Schneider. Lippstadt. Sept. 17.

XX kleine Fugen. G. P. Telemann. Kassel. Sept. 17.

Orgelsonaten durch das Kirchenjahr. Johannes Driessler. Kassel. Sept. 17.

Orgelchoräle. Bernard Reichel. Kassel. Sept. 17.

1958

The Sermon and the Propers. Vol. I & II. Fred. H. Lindemann. St. Louis. April 29.

Leonhard Lechner Werke, I: Motectae sacrae. Ed. by Ludwig Finscher. Kassel. July 8.

Kanons in den Kirchentönen für zwei und drei gleiche Blas- oder Streichinstrumente. Johann Walter. Ed. by Wilhelm Ehmann. Kassel. July 8.

Sechs Choralkonzerte für zwei gleiche Stimmen und Generalbass and *Drei Choralkonzerte für zwei Soprane, Tenor und Generalbass.* Johann Hermann Schein. Ed. by Ludwig Doormann. Kassel. July 8.

Zwölf geistliche Lieder Paul Gerhardts. Johann Georg Ebeling. Edited by Christhard Mahrenholz. Kassel. July 8.

Neun geistliche Lieder. Johann Crüger. Edited by Christhard Mahrenholz. Kassel. July 8.

(R)

The New Bach Edition. Editor: Hans Albrecht. Kassel. 12 vols. Vol. I (1959), No. 1, 38.

The Organ in Church Design. Joseph Edwin Blanton. Albany, Texas, 1957. Vol. I (1959), No. 1, 39.

Jahrbuch für Liturgik und Hymnologie. Vol. III, Ameln-Mahrenholz-Müller. Kassel, 1958. Vol. I (1959), No. 1, 40.

The New College Encyclopedia of Music. J. A. Westrup and F. L. Harrison. New York, 1960. Vol. II (1960), No. 2, 35 f.

The New Oxford History of Music. Vol. III. Edited by Dom Anselm Hughes and Gerald Abraham. New York, 1960. Vol. II (1960), No. 2, 36 f.

A Pictorial History of Music. Paul Henry Lang and Otto Bettmann. New York, 1960. Vol. II (1960), No. 2, 37.

The New Bach Edition. Editor: Hans Albrecht. Kassel. 4 vols. Vol. II (1960), No. 2, 39.

The New Bach Edition. Editor: Hans Albrecht. Kassel. 4 vols. Vol. III (1961), No. 1, 39.

The Art of Music: A Short History of Musical Styles and Ideas. Cannon-Johnson-Waite. New York, 1960. Vol. III (1961), No. 1, 40 f.

A History of Western Music. Donald Jay Grout. New York, 1960. Vol. III (1961), No. 1, 44 f.

Musicologica et Liturgica. Gesammelte Aufsätze von Christhard Mahrenholz. Editor: Karl Ferdinand Müller. Kassel, 1960. Vol. III (1961), No. 2, 40.

A History of Song. Editor: Denis Stevens. New York, 1961. Vol. III (1961), No. 2, 40.

Leiturgia — Handbuch des evangelischen Gottesdienstes. Editors: Müller-Blankenburg. Vol. IV: *Die Musik des evangelischen Gottesdienstes.* Kassel, 1961. Vol. III (1961), No. 2, 40 f.

Introduction to Contemporary Music. Joseph Machlis. New York, 1961. Vol. IV (1962), No. 1, 51.

Christian Church Art Through the Ages. Katharine Morrison McClinton. New York, 1962. Vol. IV (1962), No. 1, 51 f.

The Autobiography of Thomas Whythorne. Edited by James M. Osborn. New York, 1961. Vol. IV (1962), 102 f.

Church Music in History and Practice. Winfred Douglas. Revised by Leonard Ellinwood. New York, 1962. Vol. IV (1962), No. 2, 104.

The English Hymn. Louis F. Benson. Richmond, Va., 1962 (reprint). Vol. IV (1962), No. 2, 106.

The Songs of Hugo Wolf. Eric Sams. New York, 1962. Vol. V, No. 1 (Pentecost, 1963), 43.

Paperbacks, Vol. V, No. 1 (Pentecost, 1963), 43—45:
  Alte Musik in der neuen Welt. Wilhelm Ehmann. Darmstadt, 1961.
  Hymns and Worship. G. F. S. Gray. London, 1961.
  Johann Sebastian Bach: The Master and His Work. Wilibald Gurlitt. Trans. Oliver C. Rupprecht. St. Louis, 1957.
  Vom Wesen der zeitgenössischen Kirchenmusik. Hans Hofmann. Kassel, 1949.
  Liturgie am Scheideweg. Helmuth Kirchmeyer. Regensburg, 1962.
  Worship in Word and Sacrament. Ernest B. Koenker. St. Louis, 1959.
  The Choir School. Linden J. Lundstrom. Minneapolis, 1957.
  They Wrote Our Hymns. Hugh Martin. London, 1961.
  Johann Sebastian Bach: An Introduction to His Life and Works. Russel H. Miles. Englewood Cliffs, 1962.
  Igor Stravinsky: An Autobiography. New York, 1962.
  Copland on Music. Aaron Copland. 1963.
  Essays on Music. Alfred Einstein. 1962.
  Vivaldi: Genius of the Baroque. Marc Pincherle. Trans. Christopher Hatch. 1962.
  Stravinsky: A New Appraisal of His Work. Ed. by Paul H. Lang. 1963.
  Rossini: A Study in Tragi-Comedy. Francis Toye. 1963.

The Organ as Musical Medium. John Festerman. New York, 1962. Vol. V, No. 1 (Pentecost, 1963), 46.

Man and His Music: The Story of Musical Experience in the West. Alec Harman and Wilfred Mellers. New York, 1962. Vol. V, No. 2 (Advent, 1963), 93.

Listening to Music. Douglas Moore. New York, 1963, revised ed. Vol. V, No. 2 (Advent, 1963), 95.

Das Heilige Amt. Paul Kramer. Bern, Switzerland, 1960. Vol. V, No. 2 (Advent, 1963), 95.

The Choral Tradition. Percy M. Young. New York, 1962. Vol. V, No. 4 (Easter, 1964), 199.

The World of the Virtuoso. Marc Pincherle. Trans. Lucile H. Brockway. New York, 1963. Vol. V, No. 4 (Easter, 1964), 199 f.

The New Bach Edition. Editor: Hans Albrecht. Kassel. Series I, 14; IV, 9; V, 5. Vol. V, No. 4 (Easter, 1964), 200.

Dixit Dominus (Psalm 109). Georg F. Händel. Ed. by Händel Gesellschaft. Kassel, 1962. Vol. V, No. 4 (Easter, 1964), 201.

The Creative World of Mozart. Edited by Paul Henry Lang. New York, 1963. Vol. V, No. 4 (Easter, 1964), 201 f.

Justus Jonas — Loyal Reformer. Martin Lehmann. Minneapolis, 1963. Vol. VI, No. 1 (Pentecost, 1964), 36.

Music in America: An Anthology from the Landing of the Pilgrims to the Close of the Civil War. W. Thomas Marrocco and Harold Gleason. New York, 1964. Vol. VI, No. 1 (Pentecost, 1964), 36.

Negro Folk Music U. S. A. Harold Courlander. New York, 1963. Vol. VI, No. 1 (Pentecost, 1964), 36 f.

The Royal Priesthood of the Faithful: An Investigation of the Doctrine from Biblical Times to the Reformation. Cyril Eastwood. Minneapolis, 1963. Vol. VI, No. 3 (Epiphany, 1965), 137.

A Prelude to the Purchase of a Church Organ. The Commission on Worship. Philadelphia, 1964. Vol. VI, No. 3 (Epiphany, 1965), 137.

What an Altar Guild Should Know. Paul H. D. Lang. St. Louis, 1964. Vol. VI, No. 3 (Epiphany, 1965), 137.

Der Kantor: Sein Amt und seine Dienste. Karl Ferdinand Müller. Gütersloh, 1964. Vol. VI, No. 3 (Epiphany, 1965), 137 f.

Kleine Geschichte der deutschen evangelischen Kirchenmusik: Liturgik und Hymnologie. Georg Eberhard Jahn. Berlin, 1962. Vol. VI, No. 3 (Epiphany, 1965), 138.

The Great Operas of Mozart. Nathan Broder. New York, 1964. Vol. VI, No. 3 (Epiphany, 1965), 138.

The Recorder and Its Music. Edgar Hunt. New York, 1963. Vol. VI, No. 3 (Epiphany, 1965), 138.

Wyeth's Repository of Sacred Music. Part Second. New York, Vol. VI, No. 3 (Epiphany, 1965), 138.

Music and Musicians in Early America. Irving Lowens. New York, 1964. Vol. VI, No. 4 (Easter, 1965), 188.

New Edition of the Complete Works of J. S. Bach. Vol. VI, No. 4 (Easter, 1965), 188 f.

　　Vol. I/35: *Festmusiken für die Fürstenhäuser von Weimar, Weissenfels und Köthen.* Ed. by Alfred Dürr, 1963.

　　Vol. I/36: *Festmusiken für das kurfürstlich-sächsische Haus I.* Ed. by Werner Neumann, 1963.

　　Vol. VI/3: *Werke für Flöte.* Ed. by Hans-Peter Schmitz.

Protestant Church Music. Charles L. Etherington. New York, 1962. Vol. VI, No. 4 (Easter, 1965), 189 f.

(JLH)

Vol. I (1955)

Hymnologische Notizen aus Nordamerika. Pp. 132 f.

The History of American Church Music. Leonard Ellinwood. New York, 1953. P. 232.

Spiritual Folk-Songs of Early America. G. P. Jackson. New York, 1953 (2d ed.). P. 233.

The Medieval Latin Hymn. Ruth E. Messenger. Washington, D. C., 1953. P. 233.

The Pius X Hymnal. Faculty of Pius X School of Liturgical Music. New York, 1953. P. 233.

Hymns and Human Life. Erik Routley. New York, 1953. P. 233.

Patterns of Protestant Church Music. Durham, N. C., 1953. Pp. 233 f.

Vol. II (1956)

Hymnologische Notizen aus Nordamerika. Pp. 150 f.

Hymnody in the American Indian Missions. J. Vincent Higginson. (Pamphlet). New York, 1954. Pp. 257.

Eleven Ecumenical Hymns. Ed. by P. S. Watters and E. E. Harper. New York, 1954. Pp. 257 f.

Our Songs of Praise. E. W. Klammer. St. Louis, 1954. P. 258.

Vol. III (1957)

Hymnologische Notizen. P. 146.

The Papers of the Hymn Society. Various authors. New York, 1949 ff. Pp. 232 f.

The Hymnbook. Publ. by the Presbyterian Church in the U. S. and the Reformed Church in America. Richmond, Va., 1955. P. 233.

The Children's Hymnal. Ed. by Harry Bernthal, Allan Jahsmann, Edward Klammer, Arnold Mueller. St. Louis, 1955. P. 233.

Tudor Church Music. Denis Stevens. New York, 1955. P. 233.

Bach — The Conflict Between the Sacred and the Secular. Leo Schrade. New York, n. d. P. 233.

The Practice of Sacred Music. Carl Halter. St. Louis, 1955. Pp. 233 f.

The Bach Family — Seven Generations. Karl Geiringer. New York, 1954. P. 234.

Music of the Bach Family. Karl Geiringer. Cambridge, Mass., 1955. P. 234.

Dietrich Buxtehude — The Man, His Music, His Era. Farley K. Hutchins. Paterson, N. J., 1955. P. 234.

Vol. IV (1958/59)

Hymnologische Notizen. P. 159.

The Bay Psalm Book (2 vols.). Zoltan Haraszti. Chicago, 1956. P. 263.

The Hymnody of the Christian Church (Reprint). Louis F. Benson. Richmond, Va., 1956. P. 263.

The Organ in Church Design. Joseph Edwin Blanton. Albany, Tex., 1956. P. 263.

Essays on Music in Honor of Archibald Thompson Davison. By his associates. Cambridge, Mass., 1957. P. 263.

Johann Sebastian Bach, the Master and His Work. Wilibald Gurlitt. Trans. Oliver C. Rupprecht. St. Louis, 1957. P. 263.

Concordance to The Lutheran Hymnal. E. V. Haserodt. St. Louis, 1957. P. 263.

A Dictionary of Hymnology (Reprint). 2 vols. John Julian. New York, 1957. P. 263.

The Choir School. Linden Lundstrom. Minneapolis, 1957. P. 263.

The Divine Quest in Music. R. W. S. Mendl. New York, 1957. Pp. 263 f.

Hymn Tune Names — Their Sources and Significance. Robert Guy McCutchan. New York, 1957. P. 264.

Ideals in Church Music. Leo Sowerby. Greenwich, Conn., 1957. P. 264.

Five Publications of the Moravian Music Foundation. Ed. by Donald M. Mc-Corkle 1956—1959. P. 264.

Vol. VI (1961)

Hymnologische Notizen aus Nordamerika. P. 157.

Gregorian Chant. Willi Apel. Bloomington, Ind., 1958. P. 251.

The Church Music of William Billings. J. Murray Barbour. East Lansing, Mich., 1960. P. 251.

The Art of Music — A Short History of Musical Styles and Ideas. Cannon-Johnson-Waite. New York, 1960. P. 251.

Music in the Medieval and Renaissance Universities. Nan Cooke Carpenter. Norman, Okla., 1958. Pp. 251 f.

Music as Metaphor. Donald N. Ferguson, Minneapolis, 1960. P. 252.

A History of Western Music. Donald Jay Grout. New York, 1960. P. 252.

Luther and Culture. Forell, Grimm, Hoelty-Nickel. Decorah, Iowa, 1960. P. 252.

The Solesmes Method. Dom Joseph Gajard. Collegeville, Minn., 1960. P. 252.

Music at the Court of Frederick the Great. Ernest Eugene Helm. Norman, Okla., 1960. Pp. 252 f.

Heinrich Schütz — His Life and Work. Hans J. Moser. Trans. by Carl F. Pfatteicher. St. Louis, 1959. P. 253.

The Hymn and Congregational Singing. James Rawlings Sydnor. Richmond, Va., 1960. P. 253.

Church Music and Theology. Erik Routley. Philadelphia, 1959. P. 253.

A History of Song. Denis Stephens, ed. New York, 1960. P. 253.

The Sacred Bridge. Eric Werner, New York, 1959. Pp. 253 f.

(LW)

Vol. 66 (1947)

Messiah. George F. Handel. Ed. by J. M. Coopersmith. New York. Oct. 21, p. 351.

Elkan-Vogel Organ Series. Ed. by H. William Hawke. Pittsburgh. Nov. 18, p. 386.

Proper of the Service. Christensen-Schunemann. New York. Dec. 2, pp. 401 f.

Vol. 67 (1948)

Treasury of Early Organ Music. Ed. by E. Power Biggs. New York. Jan. 27, p. 30.

Liturgical Motet Book. Matthew N. Lundquist. 2 vols. New York. March 23, p. 97.

Ten Sacred Songs. Ed. by Hans T. David. March 23, p. 97.

Three Liturgical Preludes. George Oldroyd. New York. April 20, p. 135.

Service Music for Organ. Compiled by T. Tertius Noble. New York. May 18, p. 167.

Wilhelm Friedemann Bach — Complete Works for Organ. Ed. by E. Power Biggs. New York. June 15, p. 198.

Choral Preludes for the Organ. Compiled by Robt. L. Bedell. New York. June 15, p. 198.

Four Pieces for the Organ. Eric De Lamarter. New York. June 15, p. 198.

Early Spanish Organ Music. Ed. by Joseph Muset. New York. June 15, pp. 198 f.

Fifty Elevations for Organ on Modal Themes. Dom Paul Benoit. New York. June 15, p. 199.

The Musical Heritage of the Church, No. 3. Ed. by Theo. Hoelty-Nickel. Valparaiso, Ind. June 15, p. 199.

Three Chorals for Organ. César Franck. Ed. by Joseph Bonnet. New York. July 13, p. 229.

Fughettas. Joseph Rheinberger. Op. 123a, Books I & II; Op. 123b, Books I & II. Ed. by W. S. Lloyd Webber. Sept. 7, p. 294.

Eight Short Preludes on Gregorian Themes. Marcel Dupre. Sept. 7, p. 294.

Six Organ Preludes. J. S. Bach. Rearranged for organ by Stainton de B. Taylor. Oct. 5, p. 325.

Choral Preludes. Eric Rowley. Oct. 5, p. 325.

Laudamus Dominum Music Series. Ed. by Martin Bangert and Paul Rosel. Saint Louis. Oct. 19, pp. 341 f.

Christmas, Its Carols, Customs, and Legends. Ruth Heller. Chicago. Oct. 19, p. 342.

Vol. 68 (1949)

Eight Chorale Preludes for Unison Chorus and Organ. Johann Ludwig Krebs. Ed. by E. Power Biggs and E. Harold Geer. April 5, p. 113.

Method of Organ Playing. Harold Gleason. May 3, p. 146.

Neunzehn Vorspiele zu evangelischen Kirchenliedern. Hans Klotz. May 3, p. 146.

Fifty Free Organ Accompaniments to Well-Known Hymn Tunes. T. Tertius Noble. May 3, p. 146.

Choral-Spiel-Buch für Tasteninstrumente. Siegfried Reda. May 3, p. 146.

Seven Chorale Preludes. Richard I. Purvis. May 31, p. 186.

The First Four Centuries of Music for the Organ. Ed. and compiled by John Klein. 2 vols. June 14, p. 202.

Steps Toward a Singing Church. Donald D. Kettring. Philadelphia. June 14, p. 202.

Preludes for the Hymns of the Lutheran Hymnal. Karl Haase. June 28, pp. 217 f.

Seven Contrapuntal Preludes on XVI Century Tunes. Garth Edmundson. Nov. 29, p. 399.

Vol. 69 (1950)

Organ Music by Max Reger. March 21, p. 94.

Organ Works by J. S. Bach. Vol. IX. Ed. by Hermann Keller. April 18, p. 127.

Ausgewählte Orgelwerke, Vols. I and IV. Johann Pachelbel. Ed. by Karl Matthäi. April 18, p. 127.

The Organ Works of Johannes Brahms. 2 vols. Ed. by Gerald Alphenaar. April 18, p. 127.

Organ Masters of the Baroque Period. 3 vols. Ed. by Gerald Alphenaar. April 18, p. 127.

Die kleinen Klavierstücke. J. S. Bach. April 18, p. 127.

Das Goerlitzer Tabulaturbuch. Samuel Scheidt. Ed. by Fritz Dietrich. May 2, p. 143.

Eight Little Preludes and Fugues for the Organ. J. S. Bach. Ed. by Caspar Koch. May 2, p. 143.

Die Musik in Geschichte und Gegenwart. Ed. by Friedrich Blume. Kassel, June 27, p. 206.

Gradus ad Parnassum — Progressive Studies for Organ. Compiled and edited by Caspar Koch. July 25, p. 238.

Apparatus Musico-Organisticus. Georg Muffat. Ed. by S. de Lange. July 25, p. 238.

Vol. 70 (1951)

The Church Organist's Golden Treasury. Vol. II. Ed. by Carl F. Pfatteicher and Archibald T. Davison. Jan. 23, p. 30.

Ausgewählte Orgelwerke. Johann Jakob Froberger. Ed. by Karl Matthäi. Jan. 23, p. 30.

Sechs Fugen über den Namen BACH. Robert Schumann. Jan. 23, p. 30.

Organ Concertos, Op. 4, Nos. 1—3. George Fr. Handel. Ed. by Karl Matthäi. July 10, p. 235.

Eucharistia (Three Modern Preludes on Communion Hymns). Garth Edmundson. Oct. 16, p. 349.

Six Chorale Preludes, Set II. Healey Willan, Nov. 13, p. 382.

Vol. 71 (1952)

80 Chorale Preludes by German Masters of the 17th and 18th Centuries. Compiled by Hermann Keller. Feb. 5, p. 14.

Spielbuch für die Kleinorgel oder andere Tasteninstrumente. 2 vols. Compiled by Wolfgang Auler. Feb. 5, p. 14.

Ten Chorale Preludes for Organ, Op. 69 and Op. 70. Flor Peeters. Feb. 5, p. 14.

Johann Sebastian Bach — Orgelchoräle Manualiter. Compiled by Hermann Keller. Feb. 5, p. 14.

Choralvorspiele für den gottesdienstlichen Gebrauch. Ed. by Adolf Graf. Feb. 5, p. 14.

Harmonische Seelenlust. Georg Fr. Kaufmann. Ed. by Pierre Pidoux. Feb. 5, p. 14.

Orgelchoräle des 17. und 18. Jahrhunderts. Compiled and edited by organists of Berne, Switzerland. Feb. 5, p. 14.

Freie Orgelstücke alter Meister. Compiled and edited by Adolf Graf. Feb. 5, p. 14.

Geistliches Chorlied. Compiled by Gottfried Grote. May 13, p. 14.

Klavierübung, Part III. J. S. Bach. Ed. by Griepenkerl and Roitzsch. July 22, p. 13.

Vol. 72 (1953)

Bach, Fifteen Symphonies. Three-Part Inventions arranged as organ trios by Caspar Koch. Jan. 6, p. 14.

Vol. 73 (1954)

Complete Works of Johann Walter. Edited by Otto Schröder and Max Schneider. Kassel, 1953. May 11, p. 18.

In Every Corner Sing. Helen E. Pfatteicher. Philadelphia. Nov. 9, p. 17.

Vol. 74 (1955)

Electronic Organs. Robert L. Eby. Wheaton, Ill.

(CTM)

Vol. XVIII (1947)

The Theory of Preaching. Austin Phelps. Grand Rapids, Mich., 1947. No. 12, 951 f.

Vol. XIX (1948)

Johann Mattheson, Spectator in Music. Beekman C. Cannon. New Haven, Conn., 1947. No. 4, 319 f.
The Song of the Church. Marie Pierik. New York, 1947. No. 4, 320.
Luther and Music. Paul Nettl. Philadelphia, 1948. No. 11, 876.

Vol. XX (1949)

My Sermon Notes on Biblical Characters. Rev. William P. van Wyk. Grand Rapids, Mich., 1948. No. 3, 238.
Steps Toward a Singing Church. Donald D. Kettring. Philadelphia. No. 6, 479.
Notes on the Parables of Our Lord. Richard C. Trench. Grand Rapids, Mich. No. 9, 713 f.
A Serious Call to a Devout and Holy Life. William Law. Philadelphia. No. 9, 716 f.
Sermon Illustrations from the Bible. Keith L. Brooks. Grand Rapids, Mich. No. 9, 717.

Vol. XXI (1950)

Vine and Branches. Martin B. Hellriegel. Vol. I, St. Louis, 1948. No. 1, 78 f.
Preaching from the Propers. Harry F. Baughman. Philadelphia, 1949. No. 10, 797 f.
The Cross Is Central. Olin C. Fjelstad. Minneapolis, 1950. No. 10, 778.

Vol. XXII (1951)

Bach — The Musical Apostle of the Lutheran Church. Luther A. Schuessler. Chicago. No. 2, 156.
The Trial and Death of Jesus Christ. James Stalker. Grand Rapids, Mich. No. 2, 156 f.
The Armed Forces Prayer Book. Daniel A. Poling. New York, 1951. No. 9, 703.
The Church's Year. Charles Alexander. London, 1950. No. 9, 703 f.

Vol. XXIII (1952)

Liturgy and Spiritual Awakening. Bo Giertz. Rock Island, Ill., 1950. No. 1, 80.
The Cross for Every Day. R. R. Caemmerer and J. J. Pelikan. St. Louis, 1951. No. 2, 156 f.
Liturgie und lebendige Gemeinde. Berthold von Schenk. Kassel, 1951. No. 2, 157—159.
The Lutheran Order of Services. Paul H. D. Lang. St. Louis, 1952. No. 6, 478.
Voice of the Heart (Cardiphonia). John Newton. Chicago, 1950. No. 6, 479.
Easter — Its Story and Meaning. Alan W. Watts. New York. No. 12, 944.

Vol. XXIV (1953)

Preaching to Preachers. Norman A. Madson. Mankato, Minn. No. 2, 158 f.

Crowd Culture — An Examination of the American Way of Life. Bernard I. Bell. New York, 1952. No. 10, 781 f.

Faith of Our Fathers. Ed. by George O. Lillegard. Mankato, Minn., 1953. No. 10, 782 f.

Lutheran Church Calendar. Ed. by Arthur Carl Piepkorn. Erie, Pa. No. 12, 958 f.

St. Augustine — Sermons for Christmas and Epiphany. Trans. Thomas C. Lawler. Westminster, Md., 1952. No. 12, 959 f.

Vol. XXV (1954)

The Breviary Explained. Pius Parsch. St. Louis, 1952. No. 12, 171—173.

Great Protestant Festivals. Clarence Seidenspinner. N. Y., 1951. No. 2, 174 f.

Great Catholic Festivals. James L. Monks. N. Y., 1951. No. 3, 254 f.

Martin Luther: Ausgewählte Werke. Volume III. Ed. by H. H. Borcherdt and Georg Merz. Munich, 1950. No. 6, 483 f.

Das Neue Mariendogma im Lichte der Geschichte und im Urteil der Oekumene. Friedrich Heiler, ed. Munich/Basel, 1951. No. 6, 485 f.

The Manual of Olavus Petri (1529). Eric E. Yelverton. London, 1953. No. 7, 572.

The Student Prayer Book. John O. Nelson, ed. New York, 1953. No. 7, 573.

Our Songs of Praise. Edward W. Klammer, ed. New York, 1953. No. 7, 573.

Lehrbuch der Liturgik. Georg Rietschel. Göttingen, 1951. No. 10, 795—798.

Action in the Liturgy — Essential and Unessential. Walter Lowrie. New York, 1953. No. 12, 954—956.

Vol. XXVI (1955)

The History of American Church Music. Leonard Ellinwood. New York, 1953. No. 1, 76 f.

Hymns and Human Life. Erik Routley. New York, 1952. No. 3, 237 f.

The Liturgical Renaissance in the Roman Catholic Church. Ernest B. Koenker. Chicago, 1954. No. 4, 314 f.

A Treasury of Hymns. Maria Leiper and Henry W. Simon, eds. New York, 1953, No. 4, 315 f.

The Hymns of Charles Wesley. R. Newton Flew. London, 1953. No. 6, 472.

Patterns of Protestant Church Music. Robert M. Stevenson. Durham, 1953. No. 6, 472.

Grundriss der Liturgik des Römischen Ritus. Ludwig Eisenhofer. (Joseph Lechner, ed.). Freiburg im Breisgau, 1950. No. 9, 718.

The Practice of Sacred Music. Carl Halter. St. Louis, 1955. No. 9, 718 f.

Electronic Organs. Robert L. Eby. Wheaton, Ill., 1953. No. 10, 799.

The Christian Approach to Culture. Emile Cailliet. New York, 1953. No. 12, 953 f.

Music in Christian Education. Edith Lovell Thomas. New York, 1953. No. 12, 957.

Vol. XXVII (1956)

A Historical Approach to Evangelical Worship. Ilion T. Jones. New York, 1954. No. 1, 71 f.

Companion to Congregational Praise. K. L. Parry and Erik Routley, eds. Chicago, 1953. No. 2, 151 f.

Congregational Praise. Chicago, 1954. No. 2, 151.

The Bach Family — Seven Generations of Creative Genius. Karl Geiringer. New York, 1954. No. 2, 155 f.

Sakrament und Musik. Gerhard Kappner. Gütersloh, 1952. No. 4, 319 f.

The Folk Arts of Norway. Janice S. Stewart. Madison, Wis., 1953, No. 4, 320 f.

The Nature of Christian Worship. J. Alan Kay. New York, 1954. No. 4, 321.

Christian Worship: A Service Book. G. Edwin Osborn, ed. St. Louis, 1953. No. 4, 321.

Worship Resources for the Christian Year. Charles L. Wallis, ed. New York, 1954, No. 4, 327.

The Prayers of Peter Marshall. Catherine Marshall, ed. New York, 1954, No. 4, 329.

In Every Corner Sing. Helen Pfatteicher. Philadelphia, 1954. No. 4, 329.

At All Times and in All Places. Massey H. Shepherd. Greenwich, 1953. No. 4, 330.

Altar Guild Workbook. G. Martin Ruoss. Philadelphia, 1955. No. 8, 667.

Uncommon Prayers. Cecil Hunt, ed. Greenwich, 1955. No. 9, 750.

Der Gottesdienst im Neuen Testament. Gerhard Delling. Göttingen, 1952. No. 10, 823 f.

Christ in the Liturgy. Illtyd Trethowan. New York, 1952. No. 10, 825 f.

Vol. XXVIII (1957)

Familiar Prayers. Herbert Thurston. Westminster, 1952. No. 2, 151.

Sponsors at Baptism and Confirmation. Derrick Sherwin Bailey. London, 1952. No. 2, 153.

Music of the Bach Family. Karl Geiringer. Cambridge, 1955. No. 2, 154.

Das Graduallied. Otto Brodde and Christa Müller. Munich, 1954. No. 4, 309.

The Forms of Music. Donald Tovey. New York, 1956. No. 6, 476.

Faith's First Response: The Art of Worship. George W. Hoyer. St. Louis, 1956. No. 7, 551.

The Evolution of the Christian Year. A. Allan McArthur. Greenwich, Conn., 1953. No. 7, 558.

The Truth About the Virgin Mary. Paul E. Schuessler. St. Louis, 1956. No. 8, 615.

The Eucharistic Liturgy. New York, 1953. No. 8, 622 f.

Concordance to The Lutheran Hymnal. E. V. Haserodt. St. Louis, 1956. No. 10, 789 f.

Vol. XXIX (1958)

George Herbert — His Religion and Art. Joseph H. Summers. Cambridge, Mass., 1954. No. 1, 66 f.

Johann Sebastian Bach: The Master and His Work. Wilibald Gurlitt (trans. Oliver C. Rupprecht). St. Louis, 1957. No. 2, 144.

The Hymnody of the Christian Church. Louis F. Benson. Richmond, 1956. No. 7, 537.

Hymnal for Colleges and Schools. Ed. under the direction of E. Harold Geer. New Haven, 1956. No. 8, 618 f.

Myth and Ritual in Christianity. Alan W. Watts. London and New York, 1954. No. 8, 631.

Lebendiger Gottesdienst. Walter Lotz. Kassel, 1949. No. 8, 634 f.

Evangelischer Gottesdienst Heute. Alfred Niebergall. Kassel, 1953. No. 8, 634 f.

Die Liturgie als Lebensform der Kirche. Karl B. Ritter. Kassel, 1949. No. 8, 634 f.

Die Erneuerung des Gottesdienstes. Horst Schumann. Kassel, 1949. No. 8, 634 f.

Mit der Kirche Leben — Was ist das? Wilhelm Stählin. Kassel, 1949. No. 8, 634 f.

The Christian Year. Edward T. Horn, III. Philadelphia, 1957. No. 8, 635 f.

God My Exceeding Joy. Amos T. Lundquist. Rock Island, Ill., 1956. No. 11, 867.

Pastoral Prayers for the Church Year. Samuel J. Schmiechen. New York, 1957. No. 11, 867.

A Treasury of the Cross. Madeline S. Miller. New York, 1956. No. 11, 867.

English and Welsh Crucifixes (A. D. 670—1550). J. Erik Hunt. London, 1956. No. 11, 867.

Within the Chancel. Thomas A. Stafford. New York, 1955. No. 11, 871 f.

To Enjoy God: A Woman's Adventure in Faith. Ruth M. Berry. Philadelphia, 1956. No. 11, 872.

The Farmer Gives Thanks. Samuel R. Guard. New York, 1956. No. 11, 872.

God Was There. Roy H. Stetler. Rock Island, Ill., 1956. No. 11, 872.

The Golden Quest of Worship. Mary C. Clapp. New York, 1957. No. 11, 872 f.

Leonhard Lechner: Werke, Vol. 1. Ludwig Finscher, ed. Kassel, 1956. No. 11, 878.

Journey to Easter. Laurence N. Field. Minneapolis, 1957. No. 12, 945.

Deep River. Howard Thurman. New York, 1955. No. 12, 948.

A Dictionary of Hymnology. John Julian, ed. New York, 1957. No. 12, 948 f.

Vol. XXX (1959)

Jahrbuch für Liturgik und Hymnologie. Kassel, 1958. No. 11, 867 f.

The Organ in Church Design. Joseph E. Blanton. Albany, Tex., 1957. No. 12, 954.

Vol. XXXIV (1963)

Go with God. Jim Bishop. New York, 1958. No. 8, 509.

Music in the Medieval and Renaissance Universities. Nan Cooke Carpenter. Norman, Okla., 1958. No. 10, 631.

Geschichte der deutschen Lyrik von Luther bis zum Ausgang des zweiten Weltkriegs. Johannes Klein. 2d ed. Wiesbaden, 1960. No. 10, 631 f.

(JAMS)

Gallus Dressler. Ein Beitrag zur Geschichte des Protestantischen Schulkantorats im 16. Jahrhundert. Wilhelm Martin Luther. Vol. 3, No. 2 (Summer, 1950), 145—148.

Caspar Othmayr — Leben und Werk. Hans Albrecht. Vol. 4, No. 2 (Summer, 1951), 165—168.

Johann Sebastian Bach — Geistige Welt. Fred Hamel. Vol. 5, No. 1 (Fall, 1952), 142—146.

Patterns of Protestant Church Music. Robert M. Stevenson. Vol. 7, No. 2 (Summer, 1954), 148—150.

Sechs Choralbearbeitungen und das Quodlibet "Was wölln wir aber heben an." Johannes Brassicanus. Ed. by Othmar Wessely. Vol. 8, No. 2 (Summer, 1955), 141 f.

(MQ)

The Bach Family — Seven Generations of Creative Genius. Karl Geiringer, in collaboration with Irene Geiringer. January 1956, Vol. 42, 99—103.

Caspar Othmayr — Ausgewählte Werke. January 1958, Vol. 44, 112—116.

(N)

Handbuch der Deutschen Evangelischen Kirchenmusik. Editors: Konrad Ameln, Christhard Mahrenholz, Wilhelm Thomas, and Carl Gerhardt. *II. Band, Das gesungene Bibelwort, I. Teil: Die a-capella Werke.* Göttingen, March 1952. The same opus, *III. Band, Das Gemeindelied.* June 1953. Second Series, Vol. IX, No. 2, 320 f.; Vol. X, No. 3, 481.

Zwei Fünfstimmige Madrigale. Ed. by Max Seiffert. Lippstadt, 1953. Vol. XII, 642 f.

Weihnachtskantate: Kündlich gross ist das gottselige Geheimnis. Gottfried Heinrich Stölzel. Ed. by Hans Albrecht. Lippstadt, 1953. Vol. XII, 643.

Die Evangelische Kirchenmusik in Deutschland. Hans Joachim Moser. September 1954, Vol. XI, 568 f.

Vierstimmige Choräle aus dem Melodeyen-Gesangbuch. Hamburg. Ed. Hans Albrecht. September 1955. Vol. XII, 642.

III. TRANSLATIONS

Johann Walther — Sämtliche Werke. Ed. by Otto Schröder and Max Schneider. BV and CPH. Translation of Forewords for Vol. 1 (1953) and Vol. 3 (1955) in Vol. 3. Translation of Foreword for Vol. 5 (1961).

Georg Rhau — Musikdrucke aus den Jahren 1538 bis 1545 in praktischer Neuausgabe. Ed. by Hans Albrecht. Vol. 1: Balthasar Resinarius, *Responsoriorum Numero Octoginta;* 2 vols. Edited by Inge-Maria Schröder. BV and CPH. 1954. Translation of the Foreword. Vol. 3: Georg Rhau, *Symphoniae iucundae,* 1958. Edited by Hans Albrecht. Translation of the Foreword, 1959.

Schule der Choralimprovisation — Hermann Keller. Translation completed but not printed as yet.

IV. FOREWORDS

(For publications other than Walter Buszin's)

The Introits for the Church Year, CPH, 1942, pp. I—VIII.

The Graduals for the Church Year. CPH, 1944, pp. 3—11 (together with Erwin Kurth).

The Practice of Sacred Music. Carl Halter. CPH, 1955.

Ausgewählte Werke für Orgel und Klavier. Jan Pieter Sweelinck. Ed. by Diethard Hellmann. P, 1957.

The Service Propers Noted. Paul Bunjes. CPH, 1960.

Psalm 94 (for organ). Julius Reubke. P, 1962.

V. EDITORIALS

Editor's Foreword. R, Vol. I (1959), No. 1, 3.

Editorial Comments. R, Vol. II (1960), No. 2, 27 f.

Editorial: "Publication Standards in America." R, Vol. III, No. 1 (1961), 37 f.

Preface: "The Lutheran World Federation Convention in Helsinki (1963)." R, Vol. V, No. 1 (Pentecost, 1963), 6 f.

Editorial: "Adiaphora as Evidence of Divine Grace." R, Vol. V, No. 4 (Easter, 1964), 193—196.

VI. REPORTS AND NOTICES

Nota Bene. R, Vol. I (1959), No. 1, 34 f.

Nota Bene. R, Vol. I (1959), No. 2, 38.

An American in Europe. R, Vol. I (1959), No. 2, 38 f.

Nota Bene. R, Vol. II (1960), No. 1, 28.

Nota Bene. R, Vol. III (1961), No. 1, 34 f.

Nota Bene. R, Vol. III (1961), No. 2, 35 ff.

From the Editor's Desk. R, Vol. V, No. 1 (Pentecost, 1963), 40 f.

From the Editor's Desk. R, Vol. V, No. 3 (Epiphany, 1964), 154 f.

VII. VARIA

Johann Walter — The Father of Lutheran Church Music. 1936. M. S. M. dissertation.

Nunc Dimittis in G Major. Eight part. 1937. M. S. M. composition. Published in St. Louis.

The Golden Age of Lutheran Church Music. 1941. S. T. M. dissertation.

The History of Church Music. A syllabus. Various editions (1936—1955).

The Theology of Christian Worship. A syllabus. 1957.

The Theology of Church Music. A syllabus. 1958.

The Theology of the Sacred Choral Works of J. S. Bach. A syllabus. 1958—1959.

The Minor Services. A syllabus. 1953—1958.

The Church Year. A syllabus, 1953—1958.

Das Wechselverhaeltnis von Theologie und dem Christlichen Kultus. 1951. Read to theological conferences in Strasbourg, Berlin, and Bad Boll in 1951.

A *Bibliography on Music and the Church.* Prepared by Theo. M. Finney, Donald M. McCorkle, and Walter E. Buszin. Published in August 1958 by the National Council of the Churches of Christ in the U. S. A. Revised and expanded, 1963.

Christian Hymns (1963). A paperback hymnal prepared by Luther Noss and Walter Buszin whose publication was sponsored by the National Council of the Churches of Christ in the U. S. A.

Culto Cristiano (Spanish Hymnal, 1964). This hymnal was prepared for all Lutherans in Latin America. Dr. Buszin is the editor of the music of this hymnal, which includes also liturgical chant.

Preserving the Musical Heritage of the Church (MS), Oct. 24, 1962, 19p.

The Organ in Worship (MS), 5p.

The Church and Her Problems in Worship and Art (MS), 8p.

Protestant Church Music (MS), 24p.

Liturgy, Hymnody, and Music in Lutheran Worship (MS), 22p.

Religion and Music (MS), 17p.

VIII. CHORAL AND ORGAN MUSIC
(BV and CPH)

Johann Pachelbel: Das Vokalwerk — Choral and Organ Works. German editor: Hans Heinrich Eggebrecht. American editor: Walter E. Buszin.
Der Herr ist König — The Lord God Reigneth.
Nun danket alle Gott — Now Thank We All Our God.
Jauchzet dem Herrn — Shout to the Lord.
Christ Lag in Todesbanden — Christ Lay in Grim Death's Prison.

(CPH)

Organ Music:

The Introits for the Church Year, 1942.

The Graduals for the Church Year, 1944.

Chorale Preludes by Masters of the XVII and XVIII Centuries, 1948.

Memorial Collection of Organ Preludes and Variations by J. G. Walther, 1948.

Johann Sebastian Bach — Memorial Collection, 1950.

God's Own Sacrifice Complete. Includes, in separate publications, Samuel Scheidt's organ partita based on *Da Jesus an dem Kreuze Stund.*

Choral Music:

Christus ist des Gesetzes Ende — Jesus Christ from the Law Hath Freed Us. Motet for double-chorus by Johann Schelle (1648—1701). Edited with English text by Walter E. Buszin, 1958.

Anthology of Sacred Music — Choral Series. This series of choral octavos was begun in 1945; it is still being extended. To date about 40 octavos comprise the series. In a few cases the octavo comprises a collection, e. g., "Ten Schemelli Chorales" by J. S. Bach (BA 3). Compositions by composers of centuries 16—20.

About ten compositions of other series of choral music published by CPH have either been composed or edited by Walter E. Buszin.

(P)

Dietrich Buxtehude: Aperite mihi portas justitiae — Open to Me Gates of Justice, 1953.

Johannes Brahms: Lass dich nur Nichts nicht dauren — Let Nothing Ever Grieve Thee, 1955.

J. S. Bach: Lobet den Herrn, alle Heiden — Praise the Lord, All Ye Nations, 1957.

J. S. Bach: Jesu, Meine Freude — Jesus, My Great Pleasure, 1958.

J. S. Bach: Komm, Jesu, komm — Come, Jesus, Come, 1958.

Flor Peeters: Speculum vitae. English Text, 1958.

J. S. Bach: Singet dem Herrn ein neues Lied — Sing Ye to the Lord, 1959.

J. S. Bach: Der Geist hilft unsrer Schwachheit auf — The Spirit Also Helpeth Us, 1959.

J. S. Bach: Fürchte dich nicht — Be Not Afraid, 1959.

(SHM)

Anniversary Collection of Bach Chorales, 1935.

Select Chorales, Harmonized and Arranged by the Masters, 1935.

Praetorius Settings for a Capella Choir, 1937.

Motets and Chorales for Treble Voices, 1938.

A Second Book of Bach Chorales, 1941.

Choral Music Through the Centuries, 1948.

101 Chorales Harmonized by Johann Sebastian Bach, 1952.

In addition to the collections listed above, about 15 octavos of sacred choral music were also prepared by Walter E. Buszin and have been published by SHM.

(WMC)

Three octavos (1944):

Soul, Be Still. Johann Wolfgang Franck (born ca. 1641).

Thou, Wretched World, Deceivest Me. Johannes Brahms, Op. 110, No. 2.

In the Midst of Earth Life. Pre-Reformation melody, adapted 1524.